purpose
definition
initiation (negotion)

CONTEMPORARY CHINA INSTITUTE PUBLICATIONS

The Contemporary China Institute
School of Oriental and African Studies, University of London,
sponsors research on Twentieth-Century China and
seeks to promote such studies in the U.K.

THE POLITICS OF MARRIAGE IN CONTEMPORARY CHINA

Publications in the series are:

Party Leadership and Revolutionary Power in China (1970)
edited by John Wilson Lewis

Employment and Economic Growth in Urban China, 1949–1957
(1971) *by Christopher Howe*

Authority, Participation and Cultural Change in China (1973)
edited by Stuart R. Schram

A Bibliography of Chinese Newspapers and Periodicals in European Libraries (1975) *by the Contemporary China Institute*

Democracy and Organisation in the Chinese Industrial Enterprise, 1948–1953 (1976) *by William Brugger*

Mao Tse-tung in the Scales of History (1977) *edited by Dick Wilson*

Shanghai: Revolution and Development in an Asian Metropolis (1980) *edited by Christopher Howe*

Mao Zedong and the Political Economy of the Border Region. A Translation of Mao's *Economic and Financial Problems* (1980) *edited and translated by Andrew Watson*

THE POLITICS OF MARRIAGE IN CONTEMPORARY CHINA

ELISABETH CROLL

CAMBRIDGE UNIVERSITY PRESS

Cambridge

London   New York   New Rochelle

Melbourne   Sydney

Published by the Press Syndicate of the University of Cambridge
The Pitt Building, Trumpington Street, Cambridge CB2 1RP
32 East 57th Street, New York, NY 10022, USA
296 Beaconsfield Parade, Middle Park, Melbourne 3206, Australia

First published 1981

Printed in Great Britain at the University Press, Cambridge

British Library Cataloguing in Publication Data
Croll, Elisabeth Joan
The politics of marriage in contemporary
China. – (Contemporary China Institute.
Publications).
1. Marriage – China – History – 20th century
I. Title   II. Series
301.42'0951   HQ684   80-40586

ISBN 0 521 23345 3

CONTENTS

List of tables	*page*	vii
List of figures		viii
Preface		ix
Note on romanisation and weights and measures		xii
Glossary		xiii
1	Introduction	1
2	The initiation of negotiations	24
3	Pre-marital ritual forms	41
4	Age at marriage	60
5	Choice of marriage partner	80
6	The ceremonial of marriage	108
7	The 'modernisation' of marriage and kinship structures	127
8	Marriage and the domestic group	142
9	Marriage and primary groups	165
10	Conclusions	184
List of abbreviations		189
Bibliography		190
Index		208

TABLES

1 The range of conscious models in the People's Republic of China   *page* 25
2 The initiation of marriage negotiations   40
3 Pre-marital rituals ✓   43
4 Recommended ages of marriage in the People's Republic of ✓ China   65
5 Age of marriage in Republican China   66
6 Age of marriage: Jiang village   69
7 Age of marriage: a comparison by decade: Jiang village   69
8 Age difference of spouses: Jiang village   69
9 Age and marital status: Jiang village   70
10 Preferential marriage in Republican China   81
11 Source of wives: Jiang village   85
12 Average size of household: Guangdong 1977   146
13 Range in household size: Jiang village   148
14 Household composition: Jiang village   149
15 Ratio of wage-earners to household members: Jiang village   153
16 Occupations of men and women in the labour force: Jiang village   154
17 Urban household accounts: a sample from Guangzhou city   160

FIGURES

Fig. 1.   Choice of mate: political status gradient   *page* 93
Fig. 2.   Choice of mate: social status gradient   94
Fig. 3.   Choice of mate: political and social status gradient   106
Fig. 4.   Patterns in the negotiation of marriage: the People's
           Republic of China   128
Fig. 5.   Ideal and real lines of social change for the negotiation of
           marriage   130
Fig. 6.   Household plan: Jiang village   147
Fig. 7.   House plan: Jiang village. Residential pattern before
           division (2 married sons)   161
Fig. 8.   House plan: Jiang village. Residential patterns after
           division (1 married son)   162
Fig. 9.   House plan: Jiang village. Division of single suite of
           housing   163
Fig. 10.   Kinship organisation Jiang village   177
Fig. 11.   Plan of kinship organisation: Jiang village   178

PREFACE

The research for this book was undertaken while I was a Fellow at the Contemporary China Institute from 1974 to 1977. It is primarily concerned with the processes of change within the institution of marriage in the People's Republic of China, the economic and ideological factors responsible for differing degrees of change and the contest between the generations and between political and kin or neighbourhood groups which projected changes have occasioned. It is based on both documentary sources and a brief period of interviewing in China in 1977. This book, which employs an anthropoligical approach, is a revised version of an original manuscript which was presented as a Doctoral thesis in the Department of Anthropology at the School of Oriental and African Studies, London, in January 1978. I would like to thank Dr James Watson of the School of Oriental and African Studies for his advice and encouragement throughout this project. He has on all occasions been generous with his time and I am grateful for his careful reading of the various drafts of the manuscript. In addition I would like to thank Professor A. Mayer, Dr D. Parkin and other members of the Anthropology Department who have taken an interest in this project both informally and in research seminars. My thanks are also due to Dr C. Howe and the Contemporary China Institute of the University of London, where as a Fellow I was provided with both financial support and research facilities. I am very grateful for both. I would also like to thank Christine Lyall Grant of Cambridge University Press for her careful reading and editing of the final typescript.

The introduction to the book contains some discussion of the broader anthropological interest of the study and particularly the applicability of the anthropological method to a documentary study of one of the less accessible societies. Until the last year or so most anthropologists of Chinese culture have been reluctant to turn their attention to the People's Republic of China, partly because fieldwork has been virtually impossible in China over the last few decades. The first two years of this project were planned on the assumption that no such opportunity would materialise, but in the third year I was able to undertake some limited but intensive interviewing, and a household survey, in a few selected rural and urban locations. Although this visit in no way constituted the normal definition of fieldwork, data from this source did enable me to elaborate on certain of the hypotheses which I had previously developed from documentary sources prior to my visit. The Contemporary China Institute, the Chinese Embassy in London and the Guangdong Branch of the China Travel Service all made it possible for me to visit China and collect some data for this study. I would like to thank the many persons both in London and China who helped me to make the best possible use of a very short time in the field.

The book covers a wide time-span, but because of the reduction in publications on the subject during and since the Cultural Revolution, the case studies illustrating contemporary trends and problems are primarily drawn from the early 1960s rather than more recent years. Interestingly, in the last year and since the revision of this study for publication, there have been a number of more contemporary references in the Chinese media to the problems of marriage and especially to the persistence of 'arranged and venal marriages' and 'feudal and superstitious ceremonies' (*Survey of World Broadcasts* 5 August 1978, 6 and 11 January 1979). It has been forecast that there may be some revisions of the 1950 Marriage Law in the near future (*Survey of World Broadcasts* 13 January 1979), and a new campaign to reform marriage was launched in the earlier months of 1979. It once again publicised the fact that marriage should be determined and controlled by the principals themselves, that they must oppose marriage on a mercenary basis, that they must marry at an appropriate later age and that they must refrain from extravagance and practise economy in the celebration of marriage. The media has provided recent negative examples of all the above to add to those given in chapters 2 to 6. The campaign has also reaffirmed the principle of 'free-choice' marriage and hinted that very real difficulties have hindered this process of change (*New China News Agency* 29 December 1978; *Survey of World Broadcasts* 6 and 11 January 1979; *Beijing Review* 30 November 1979; *Women of China* 1 January 1980). Although there is little analysis in the media of the obstacles to change of the type presented in chapters 8 and 9, the recognition and illustrations of the problems do add further evidence that many of the phenomena, suppositions and hypotheses put forward in this book remain valid in 1979.

Finally, I would like to express my personal appreciation to James Croll, who has taken an active interest in the project and shared in the care of Nicolas and Katherine.

September 1979   E.C.

NOTE ON ROMANISATION AND WEIGHTS AND MEASURES

In this study I have mainly used the Hanyu Pinyin system of romanisation. Where well-known personal and place-names are less recognisable in this form I have placed the more familiar forms in parentheses when first cited in the text. The exceptions are a few village names associated with existing anthropological studies which are already familiar to many readers in the Wade-Giles romanisation. Where these and Chinese authors and titles have been written in or translated into English, then they remain as they were presented in the original texts.

1 catty = 1 jin = $\frac{1}{2}$ kg = 1.1 lb

1 mu $\quad = \frac{1}{15} = \frac{1}{6}$ acre

1 li $\quad = \frac{1}{2}$ km = $\frac{1}{3}$ mile

GLOSSARY

anjia luohu	settle down permanently
bai jiuxi	marriage feast
biao	cousins of different surnames
boxiao jieji chushen	exploiting-class origins
buxiao erzi	unfilial son
caoshuai jiehun	hasty marriage
chengfen	class status
fenjia	household division
fumu baoban ernu hunyin	arranged marriage
hu	household
huangdao jiri	auspicious days
hunyin ziyou	free-choice marriage
jia/jiating	family
jiating chengfen	family background
jiazhang	head of the household
jiazhuang	dowry
jiehun yishi	marriage ceremony
jieshao ren	introducer
jindaide ziyou jiehun	free-choice marriage in the modern way
jinqin	close kin
lianai zhishang	supremacy of love
lichang	standpoint
luantan lianai	fickleness of love
maimai hunyin	marriage by purchase
meiren	matchmaker
mingmei zhengzhu	marriage properly conducted
pinjin	betrothal gift
qiantu/chuxi	future
qiuhun	proposal of marriage
shidu	appropriate
shijie guan	world viewpoint
tan lianai	courtship
tang	cousins of same surname
timian	pride, 'face'

xiii

Glossary

wanhun	late marriage
xianhua	gossip
xiaodao	filial
xiaxiang	sent-down-to-the-countryside youth
xixin yanjiu	to like the new and to oppose the old
xuanze airen di biaozhun	norms for selecting a spouse
zaohu	early marriage
zhao duixiang	choose a spouse
zhaosan musi	changeability and untrustworthiness
zhengzhi diwei	political status
zhitong daohe	to be of one mind and purpose
ziyou jiehun	freedom of marriage
zu	lineage
zunzhong/zongbai	social status/respect

1

INTRODUCTION

On 1 May 1950 the government of the People's Republic of China announced the abolition of all laws upholding 'arbitrary and compulsory feudal marriage' and introduced a marriage contract based on 'freedom of choice'. The negotiations of marriage or procedures of mate selection in any society are normally distinguished by the degree to which persons other than the parties to the marriage, the bride and groom, participate in the selection and enter into the negotiations of marriage. Article 1 of the first chapter of the new Marriage Law rejected 'arranged marriage', or marriage negotiated between the kin groups or persons other than the bride or groom, and outlined the principle on which the new marriage contract was to be based:

Article 1: The feudal marriage system based on arbitrary and compulsory arrangement and the supremacy of man over woman, and in disregard for the interests of the children, is abolished.

The new Democratic marriage system, which is based on the free choice of partners, on monogamy, on equal rights for both sexes, and on the protection of the lawful interests of women and children, is put into effect.

Freedom of marriage (*ziyou jiehun*) or free-choice marriage (*hunyin ziyou*) was defined as 'the provision of full rights for the individual to handle his or her own matrimonial affairs without any interference or obstruction from third parties and without regard for social status, occupation or property' (KMRB 27 February 1957). It constituted the 'fundamental principle on which the new Marriage Law was based, the foundation for the establishment of new family structures and relations and the weapon for releasing the people, especially the women, from the suffering caused by feudal marriage' (KMRB 27 February 1957). The politics or redistribution of power involved in the substitution of free-choice marriage for arranged marriage and its consequences for the authority and controls exercised by interested generations, primary groups and the State is the subject of this book.

The study, based on documentary sources and a brief period of intensive interviewing in the People's Republic of China, examines the process of change within the institution of marriage in terms of the procedures and controls of negotiation, the criteria governing choice of spouse, the age of marriage and its ritual and ceremonial forms. It is a study of the new marriage patterns as they have evolved in contemporary China from 1950 to 1975, and an analysis of the specific economic and ideological variables working for and against their social change. The study of the new marriage patterns in contemporary China raises a number of interesting questions to do with conceptualising marriage and its relation to familial and kinship structures and the role of economic and ideological variables in 'modernising' marriage, family and kinship structures. The government of the People's Republic has not only redefined the institution of marriage, but has invested it with a new significance for the individual and for domestic, kin and other social groups.

MARRIAGE REDEFINED

Underlying all the policies to do with marriage is the assumption that it is a necessary and 'natural' step for each individual (RMRB 29 May 1959; Lu Yang 1964: 7). It is often stated that once young people reach an appropriate age, 'it is necessary that they find a life's companion' (ZQ 14 September 1962) and it is 'rational and irreproachable that they should get married and have a family of two children' (ZQ 1 October 1963). The normal concept of marriage is of a stable union lasting the lifetime of the parties,* and the placing of the negotiations of marriage within the control of the individual parties and the resting of the marriage bond exclusively on the congeniality of the parties was to invest marriage with a new significance for the bride and groom. As one article emphasised 'viewed from the perspective of an individual's life, love and marriage are important matters in a person's

---

* Although divorce by mutual consent is also allowed by the new law, it was more common in the early 1950s when many marriages arranged in the traditional manner were dissolved. Since the mid-1950s however, it seems that divorce has become much less common. Certainly all the educational materials to do with marriage assume that if a marriage partner is carefully chosen at an appropriate age and on appropriate criteria, then there will be little need for, or likelihood of, divorce.

life-cycle'. 'Choosing a life companion', it continued, 'can never be said to have no significance' (ZQ 14 September 1962). It constituted a serious political task for the individual.

Perhaps more than any other 'social drama' (Turner 1957) or socio-drama (Duncan 1968), the redefinition of the procedures and symbols of marriage was the vehicle by which the State intervened and attempted to articulate major changes in the social relations between the sexes and the generations within domestic and kin groups. The marriage bond constitutes the foundation of the domestic group, which continues to be the basic social unit of society (ZQ 16 December 1956). As one article pointed out:

The family, as a form of joint life of the two sexes united in marriage, we may definitely say will never be eliminated. The existence of this form of joint life is dictated not only by the physiological difference of the sexes, but also by the perpetuation of the race. Even in Communist society we cannot conceive of any objective basis and necessity for the 'elimination of the family'. (HRB 8 April 1959)

Marriage was to remain the foundation of the domestic group, but equally its redefinition was designed to effect some rearrangement of social relations within these familial and kinship structures. The strengthening of the marital bond as opposed to all other kin bonds had repercussions for familial and kin relations within and between households. The relations between the parties based on free choice and congeniality might thus be expected to affect the balance of power between the generations and the sexes and especially that between mother-in-law and daughter-in-law.

The redefinition of the procedures and symbols of marriage to represent interpersonal relations between equal partners of the opposite sex, rather than intergroup relations based on the interests of and the exchange of women between these groups, amounts to a rejection of both the alliance and descent models of marriage which underlie anthropological attempts to conceptualise marriage. In these two models, marriage is either conceived as the primary means by which domestic groups are reproduced and maintained (Fortes 1971), or as the primary mechanism whereby women are exchanged between men or groups of men (Lévi-Strauss 1969). In traditional China, marriage had been destined to accomplish both these aims. The old definition of marriage had described the purpose of taking a wife as the begetting of children to 'worship at the ancestral temple and continue the family line' (PR 8 March 1960). The other main purpose of marriage was

3

to establish alliances advantageous to the interests of the descent group of the respective parties as a means of socio-economic and political mobility. The Book of Rites, dating from the second century A.D., which was held to embody the rules defining correct social behaviour, declared that the purpose of marriage was to unite two families with a view to harmonising the friendship of two lineages. The redefinition of marriage as an institution symbolising interpersonal relations between equal partners of the opposite sex was not part of a theoretically based rejection of common anthropological theories. Indeed the materials to do with the reforms make no explicit references to anthropological theories as such. But the redefinition itself and the arguments cited in favour of reform make it possible to identify a contrasting model of marriage.

Although it is recognised that marriage has the natural aim of begetting children, no longer is the primary object of marriage seen to be the reproduction of the unilineal descent group. The new definition of marriage rejects sterility as grounds for divorce. Not only is the absence of children no longer an unfilial act, but in the new socio-economic conditions of collective land-ownership and collective welfare, there was seen to be no need to 'bring up children in anticipation of old age' or to ensure 'the inheritance of family property' (HRB 8 April 1959). The new definition of marriage also rejected the establishment of advantageous alliances between kin groups, which had exerted a substantial influence on the controls over the negotiations and choice of marriage partner. In the new ideology marriage is defined and designed to add a new facet to male–female relations, which has consequences for the structures of domestic and kin groups and for the position of women.

The new marriage contract with its emphasis on free choice of partners is one of the instruments charged with reducing systems of stratification. The exercise of free choice 'without regard for social status, occupation or property' (KMRB 27 February 1957) was meant to establish an open-marriage system in which the only persons unequivocally proscribed as marriage partners were those to whom the incest taboo was extended. In many societies, anthropological studies of what are commonly conceived to be open-marriage systems suggest that in fact marriage choice usually remains structured by such factors as social class, ethnic origin, religion and education, with a strong endogamous or preferential in-group trend characterising some status groups. The growing literature on mate selection in North America, for instance, suggests a preponderance of homogamy, or assortative mating, in which persons choose spouses of similar characteristics over heterogamy. Wide disparities in the status of marriage partners are in fact very infrequent (Hollingshead 1950; Kerckhoff 1963–4). The role of marital choice in accentuating or confirming patterns of stratification have led anthropologists to hypothesise that to encourage random mating or at least preferential out-marriage would mean a radical change in the existing social structure (Goode 1959:475; Goody 1971:599). In China the principle of free choice without regard for property and other socio-economic factors has formed an important component of the new ideology of marriage and the media has frequently advocated heterogamy in an attempt to reduce the social divisions between the 'mental' and 'manual' and rural and urban social categories (WC 1 March 1962; SWB 14 February 1974).

In contemporary China, marriage reforms are conceived to not only have consequences for social structure, but also to themselves be a consequence of, or derive from and reflect, characteristics of the broader economic and political system. Marriage and familial forms are not only directly linked to particular stages of socio-economic development, but the movement from one form to another is a symbol of the degree to which social structures have been rearranged. In this connection two passages from Marx and Engels have been widely quoted in China:

with the development of social reproduction, there is evolved a state of marriage and family, which is in keeping with the existing state of society. (Engels, *Origin of Family, Private Ownership and the State*, HZX 15 December 1956)

where there is a certain stage of development of production, exchange and consumption, there will be a certain social system of family, grade or class organisation. (Marx, letter to B. V. Aninkov, RMRB 13 December 1963)

Recent histories of the institution of marriage published in China have followed the lead of Marx and Engels in identifying a sequence of forms from the 'most primitive period of free social intercourse and free marriage to group marriage within blood relations, group marriage without blood relations, the choice of mates and finally monogamy' and link them to a particular sequence of changes in the relations of production (ZQ 16 December 1956). In the People's Republic of China, monogamy based on the principle of free choice is taken as the form of marriage most appropriate to a socialist society and the substitution of arranged marriage by free-choice marriage can be taken to be one measure of the government's success in founding a new society resting on socialist princples. For instance, the degree to which the individual parties negotiated their own contracts may reflect a reduction in the influence of kin groups and in the exclusive controls of the older generation and of men over family affairs. The degree to which marriage partners are chosen 'at random' may reflect the extent to which the government has been able to introduce egalitarian policies and break down hierarchical relations through reforms affecting education, the incomes structure, the redistribution of land and capital and the ownership of the means of production.

The redefinition of marriage by the State and the intervention of the State in domestic affairs challenged the assumption common in China before 1949 that marriage is the private concern of the individual or domestic group. Marriage as a family affair has always belonged to that sphere of the social field articulated on informal and normative bases making use of kinship, friendship, ritual and ceremonial as opposed to the contractual and formal relations of society rationally based on bureaucratic lines (A. Cohen 1974:xi). Marriage which was formerly defined as a family or domestic affair has been reallocated to the social, public or political sphere. In emphasising the public and political repercussions of the new marriage forms, many of the educational materials in China emphasise that the marital bond which provides for the birth, training and education of a new generation makes it a matter of vital significance to society and not a personal affair or trifling matter of daily life (GRB 15 November 1962). In China it has become an object of public and political import: 'We must regard marriage not as a problem of the enjoyment of "private life", but as a "cell" of the entire cause of Revolution, as something important to the interests of the whole society' (TKP 22 December 1956).

MARRIAGE AND SOCIAL CHANGE

What differentiates the experience of contemporary China in introducing new marriage reforms from that of many other societies is the conscious and planned nature of social change towards certain defined

6

and explicit social goals. The State has intervened and implemented reforms in marriage as part of a broad process of planned social change affecting all social institutions. It is primarily as a field for the study of this process of planned and conscious social change that social scientists have been particularly interested in the study of the People's Republic of China. Indeed it has been argued that the scope and intensity of planned social change is greater in China than in that of other social systems on which most contemporary social scientists focus (Greenblatt 1968:4). The anthropologist Maurice Freedman thought that the recent history of social engineering in China provided an ideal opportunity for anthropologists to test their ideas about social change and the degree to which a society is able to be transformed. He thought that social scientists could examine the series of experiments in China and assess the extent to which pre-existing modes of behaviour reasserted themselves within institutions deliberately designed to exclude them (1963:15; 1969:8). G. William Skinner argues that it is the 'modernisation' of China which is of special interest to social scientists studying change, not only because it was proceeding under the aegis of communism, but because of the extraordinary longevity, consistency and stability of the social system at the onset of the relevant change. He suggested that 'the very process of modernisation with its necessary disorganisation and reorganisation of the total system and the likely persistence of traditional forms whenever pressure for social change is relaxed should commend its study to social scientists concerned with the processes of change in the contemporary world' (1964:521).

The reform of the marriage system in China has been based on a dual strategy to promote a new ideology of free-choice marriage and at the same time create new and appropriate socio-economic conditions. A number of economic policies were introduced which strengthened the bargaining power of the younger generation and especially of the women. These policies provided the basis for their economic independence in the event of conflict with family and kin groups over the negotiations of marriage. In the first instance, land reform or the redistribution of a share of land to each individual member of rural households could potentially provide a source of independent livelihood for each member of the household. Measures following on from land reform were designed to remove the property base of the individual household and substitute collectivised production units for individual peasant producers. The introduction of cooperatives

7

and communes in rural areas and the establishment of joint State–private enterprises, cooperatives and neighbourhood-owned factories in urban areas were all to effect the separation of production from the individual and private household and provide employment for the younger generation away from the controls of the household head. It was anticipated that such policies would eliminate the traditional interest of the older generation in controlling the negotiations of marriage and in exchanging women to the socio-economic and political advantage of the domestic group. However, while the new economic policies might provide the appropriate socio-economic conditions for the new patterns of marriage, the movement or campaign to establish free-choice marriage has itself been primarily conceived in terms of effecting ideological change.

As early as 1953, before the establishment of new economic relations, the government emphasised that 'the marriage campaign was to be largely directed against the remnants of feudal thinking'. It was defined as essentially a movement for 'ideological remoulding' to eliminate the influences of reactionary social customs within the consciousness of the people (PC 1 March 1953). The early campaigns provided a forum for intensive publicity and discussion 'to enable everyone to clearly demarcate the differences between the old and new marriage systems and to eliminate the influence of the social customs within the consciousness of the people' (RMRB 20 March 1953). The movement to introduce new marriage patterns has been generally described as a 'battle in which new ideas were pitted against the old' or 'a struggle to get people to change their ways of thought' (PC 16 November 1957; RMRB 13 December 1963). In this struggle the government has concentrated on 'consciousness raising' on the grounds that once people become aware of the meanings behind the marriage symbols and rituals they will of their own accord reject traditional customs. In this respect the government in China is sharing an assumption with some anthropologists, that once the social functions of symbols become manifest the symbols lose a great deal of their efficacy (A. Cohen 1974:8).

This strategy for marriage reform incorporating both economic policies and the development and communication of a new ideology raises a number of questions to do with the relationship of ideology to economics in bringing about social change. The function assigned to ideology and the emphasis placed on its communication in

8

introducing and maintaining the momentum of social change reflects the quite central belief in China that ideology and organisation can serve as substitutes for the development of material forces, at least within certain limits and until material conditions allow for a further development of the economic base. The Chinese analysis of the important and complex relationship between the economic 'base' and its ideological superstructure not only rejects the crass determinism of the base on the superstructure, but allows for the possibility that under certain circumstances ideology has its own power or effectivity to determine the base. Thus the specific guidelines for the establishment of new marriage patterns in their every aspect, from pre-marital and marital negotiations to the appropriate age, ceremony and criteria for choice of spouse, have been constantly and consistently elaborated and publicised in the media from 1950 to the present day. It might be said that no government has been as assiduous as the government of the People's Republic of China in educating the younger generation in preparation for marriage. Yet the government has also admitted in the media that the area of marriage and family relations has proved to be one of the most difficult in which to introduce change (RMRB 13 December 1963). As well as identifying the variety of marriage patterns in China, this book attempts to isolate the specific ideological and economic variables not only working for, but also against, the establishment of new marriage patterns in China.

THE ANTHROPOLOGICAL METHOD

To approach a study of marriage patterns in the People's Republic of China from an anthropological perspective raises problems of methodology. Indeed, there have been few detailed studies of marriage patterns as they have evolved in the People's Republic of China. Freedman remarked in 1969 that there had not been, as there might have been, an anthropological enquiry into the institution of kinship and marriage, the new norms governing interpersonal relationships, the reorganisation of local groups and the change in the nature of property. Both C. K. Yang (1959) and M. J. Meijer (1971) have undertaken comprehensive documentary studies of the purposes and objectives of the Marriage Law of 1950 and the measures which were taken to implement the new laws. They both expressed some reluctance to survey the effects of the Marriage Law on the marriage patterns

9

in the country as a whole and changes in attitudes towards marriage which may have resulted from the introduction of the law until it is possible to conduct sociological investigations under better circumstances than those that prevailed in China. The factor which, more than any other, has detracted from the People's Republic of China as a field of anthropological study was the closing of its borders in 1949 to foreign scholars. The number of excellent first-hand local and national studies of marriage and related familial institutions, which had been undertaken in Republican China (1911–49) came to an end and the anthropologist has been left a data base made up of numbers of policy documents, discussions of the subject in the media and collections of descriptions of marriage thinly spread over a wide range of geographical locations and periods of time. Another problem arises from the scale of the society under scrutiny with its vast size and variety.

Anthropologists normally have a certain reluctance to embark on a macro-study of a whole society which embraces many millions of inhabitants dispersed over a large area. They may argue that the demands of fieldwork and processing and analysing the data from a study of the social system of a single community of a few hundred persons is considerable, and that it is absurd therefore to attach any scientific value to the findings of those who make generalisations about large complex societies. Before 1949 anthropologists in China thought that the most suitable unit for study was the village, both because most Chinese lived in villages and because it was possible for one or two fieldworkers to make a fairly detailed study in a year or so (Radcliffe-Brown 1936). However, it has been pointed out by both Skinner (1964:50) and Freedman (1963:4) that the confinement of attention to the local community in Republican China was to miss the very characteristic of Chinese society which made it so interesting to anthropologists, that is, its scale and complexity. This is an even more appropriate comment on the People's Republic of China, where it can be argued that the State has intervened and played a more crucial role than ever before in uniformly changing social structures and integrating primary and informal groups into new and larger systems. As this book illustrates, to have taken a small single unit of analysis, even if it had been methodologically possible, may have missed the very range of variables out of which the hypotheses put forward here have been derived. That said, the macroscopic approach to the study of marriage patterns in China does have its limitations.

Ideally it should be possible to document changes through time (historically) and from place to place (situationally). However, the materials available for study do not easily provide data comparable through time. The discontinuities in coverage of a particular problem in the media, for example, may mean that it has ceased to exist, merely become less visible or has lost its salience at a particular conjuncture. This problem is particularly pertinent in assessing the effect of the Cultural Revolution on the procedures of mate selection. Many of the policies of the Cultural Revolution had direct relevance for some of the problems revealed by the correspondents before the Cultural Revolution, but because magazines such as *Zhongguo Funu* (Women of China) and *Zhongguo Quingnian* (Chinese Youth) ceased publication at that time, and the other media have been conspicuously silent on some of these problems, it is impossible to do more than conjecture on their implication for some marriage reforms. The case studies can normally be located geographically, but the collection of descriptions of marriage are thinly spread over a wide range of geographical locations. This has meant that it has been possible to concentrate on the larger differences between the rural and urban social fields rather than the variety of patterns which must exist within either the rural or the urban social fields themselves.

APPROACHES TO THE STUDY

The materials used for these studies are mainly drawn from two primary sources. A statement of the goals, aims and policies of marriage reform can be found in the law, government policy directives, abstract discussions and statements in the media and educational material in all its forms, together with a study of the public reference groups or role models. The latter are a particularly common didactic form in China and they take the shape of personal documents or life-histories of people, either compiled in face-to-face interviews or written up by the respondents themselves (Sheridan 1968). They represent types or specimens of exemplary behaviour rather than the statistical average (Hong 1956:39). For instance, the publication of life-histories of young men or women who defy their parents, friends and neighbours and choose their own marriage partner, wait to get married until their late twenties or choose a marriage partner regardless of their socio-economic status do not necessarily suggest that these are common practices. Rather, they have been selected for publication in the media as positive models for emulation. An examination of all those educational materials designed to publicise and familiarise readers in the new forms of marriage illustrates the assumptions and propositions on which policies are based and how they are to be implemented.

The second type of materials which furnish information for the basis of this study is the case studies drawn primarily from the press – books, periodicals, newspapers and monitored radio broadcasts. These consist of interviews, life-histories and descriptions of marriage practices for a particular area or enterprise and letters to the editor which appear in the press from time to time. The didactic nature of the press has been commented on many times (Vogel 1969; Oksenberg 1969). In the discussion of the press as a source of information, Oksenberg concludes that it tends to play a heavy exhortatary role and informs the scholar more about how things ought to be done and ought not to be done rather than how things are (1969:594). This is certainly true of the abstract discussions of goals and policies relating to marriage, although even here and for role models too it can be argued that they reveal a certain concern with contemporary practical problems.* This may seem a surprising statement to make about role models, but they usually involve a sequence and relate the details of life-passage from 'real to ideal' states of behaviour. They assign major importance to the social norms by which the models choose to interpret their experience, the response of the model to a particular dilemma or choice of behavioural patterns and the role passage or sequence of experience in the movement from one stage to another. In displaying these characteristics they are akin to the life-histories or personal documents recommended for anthropological study by Kluckhohn (1945) and Langness (1965). However, within the media this study has taken as its primary source of information that provided by the letters to the editor in the correspondence columns which

---

* In an interview with Edgar Snow, Chou En-lai has suggested that where there is an article published in the media about a particular problem it is an indication that the social attitudes demanded of those in the article are precisely those things which some people still find hard to accept. 'When we encourage the good and criticise the bad, it means that bad things surely still exist and good ones are not yet perfect' (Snow 1972: 228–9).

periodically feature in magazines such as *Zhongguo Funu, Zhongguo Qingnian, Gongren Ribao* (Workers' Daily) and various regional newspapers. For instance, numbers of letters concerning the age of marriage were published in *Gongren Ribao* in 1962 and *Nanfang Ribao* (Southern Daily) in 1962, the types of marriage ceremony in *Nanfang Ribao* in 1964–5 and choice of marriage partner in *Zhongguo Funu* in 1963–4 and *Hunan Ribao* (Hunan Daily) in 1956–7.

Letters to the press may provide a useful source of information for anthropological enquiry into problems caused by the pressure of conflicting norms and belief patterns (Kluckhohn 1945:105), and the letters used in this study* have revealed the existence of dilemmas occasioned by competing and conflicting values and customs. They delineate the forms conflict is likely to take for sub-groups in Chinese society as well as the status and power relationships involved. One of the disadvantages of this type of material is that the scholar has to be content with such information as the informants choose to give about themselves. Most of the letters do however provide references to the sex, socio-economic background of the correspondent and his or her family, their class affiliation and location of residence; all of which make it possible to identify certain spatial and social contexts in which particular types of conflict might be found. What is perhaps more important, the letters usually describe informal group activities and glimpses of individual thought processes. For example, many refer to the expectations and advice of those around them, be they peers, parents, kin or neighbours, which may be said to reflect the norms governing interpersonal relations. Many letters also reveal the thoughts of correspondents as they enter into conflict situations or individual rationalisations as they resolve them. For example, a correspondent might follow one of a number of thought sequences such as 'I thought to myself...' or 'if I follow this advice then the result will be...but if I follow that course of action the result will be...' or 'I know I should do this, but I really think I shall do that because...'. But, however interesting these letters, no inferences can be derived from their study that the problems which they identify are representative or in any sense typical for China as a whole.

The principal weakness of this type of source material has to do with

---

* Letters to the editor have formed the data base for two previous short surveys of social attitudes and behaviour associated with marriage and the family in China by Chin Ai-li (1948) and Huang Lucy Jen (1962).

the method of sampling or the processes by which the letters are selected for publication. In the first place the magazines chosen are likely to draw correspondents from certain age groups and a certain sex and there must be a variety of motives involved in writing a letter to the editors of any one of these magazines. Generally the motives may well fall into one of two categories, those who primarily wish to appear in print and those who are asking for help with a personal problem. Some of the letters merely reflect socially approved behaviour in that they express official policies or goals and describe how they have put them into practice, although even this very process can be informative. The bulk of the letters relate to definite problems and dilemmas in which the correspondent is in effect asking 'What shall I do?' and some of the letters also expressly refute the goals and premises on which official policies rest. It is impossible to know the criteria used by editors in their selection for publication, although sometimes the editors will publicly estimate the number of letters they have received on a particular subject and summarise their general contents before choosing to publish a number. It is also a possibility that the very choice of letters published will influence the kind of letters which are submitted for selection. Although there can be no positive assumptions as to the representative qualities of the data, a lesser assumption can be made in that, unless otherwise indicated, the features revealed by the case studies used in this study are probably not grossly atypical.

The lesser assumption rests on comparisons of numerous additional accounts by internal and external observers drawn from alternative sources of materials. Oksenberg has argued very cogently that research on the People's Republic of China requires the use of different types of sources in order to draw on the advantages and escape the limitations of any one type of source material available to the scholar (1969:578). Comparative material has been drawn from a number of sources. There are the accounts of internal observers. It has been pointed out by Greenblatt, for example, that although untrained in sociological and anthropological methods, writers of articles in the Chinese media have shown themselves to be keen observers of behavioural patterns (1968:3). Certainly there have been numerous articles in the media which identify the range of general problems to do with marriage and generate abstract discussions on the factors apparently inhibiting marriage reform. There have been a number of external studies on subjects allied to marriage which are the result of interviews with those formerly resident in the People's Republic of China and who are now in Hong Kong. These include the study of *xiaxiang* youth (i.e., youth sent to the countryside) by D. Gordon White (1974) and a short survey of the family in rural areas by William Parish (1975). Both of these contain useful comparative material for this study.* In the last two decades there have been a few village studies undertaken by both Chinese and foreigners which have been based on some kind of direct observation. Jan Myrdal's two volumes on Liuling, a small Chinese village, is rich in the biographical data which it contains (1967; 1973), William Geddes (1963) undertook a brief survey of one of the villages originally studied by Fei Hsiao-tung, David and Isobel Crook recorded their observations of the life of a rural commune in the late 1950s (1966) and Jack Chen, a cadre (official) from Peking, has recorded the events of a year in a production brigade in the 1970s (1973). Each of these, and particularly the latter, have provided data which has been very useful in this study. Indeed, it was the observations of Jack Chen in the 1970s which were partly responsible for the initial interest in this subject. In addition to these, there have been a number of pertinent observations drawn from a variety of travelogues published as the result of visits of varying duration to the People's Republic of China. What has often surprised scholars working with these different types of source is their fundamental agreement. Although there are some subtle differences among the sources, usually they have been found to supplement each other and to converge on certain broad generalisations and trends (Vogel 1969; Oksenberg 1969; Whyte 1974).

There is one last comparative source which stands out from the others in that it is based on first-hand observation. Although it has not been possible to undertake fieldwork in the People's Republic of China (at least prior to the time this book has gone to press), it has been possible to visit China for three or four weeks at a time. I undertook two of these visits in the summer of 1973 and in April 1977. The first trip followed the usual pattern of visiting a wide variety of social institutions in a number of locations in the surrounds of Beijing, Nanjing (Nanking), and Shanghai and the northern provinces of Liaoning and Shandong. Trips of this nature do not provide the

---

* A valuable book belonging to this category is William L. Parish and Martin King Whyte, *Village and Family in Contemporary China*, University of Chicago Press, 1978. I much regret that this very important and extensive study became available only after this manuscript was completed.

opportunity to gather quantitative information from or systematically investigate a representative sample of institutions or range of informants, but it is a valuable experience. It does enable scholars to gather data in certain limited and selected institutions and it is possible to gain considerable insights into a number of concrete and specific cases which may or may not reinforce qualitative impressions drawn from previous research findings.

The second trip in April 1977 was of a completely different nature. It provided an opportunity to visit China in an individual capacity to undertake ten days of concentrated interviewing on the composition of the household, marriage and kinship relations in a selection of rural villages and urban neighbourhoods in the environs of Guangzhou (Canton) in Guangdong (Kwangtung) province.* In one village (Jiang village), however, what began as a highly selected sample became an all-inclusive sample when at my own request a return visit was arranged. During this second visit I was particularly fortunate to be able to interview members of each of the twenty-seven households and make a complete survey of the household composition, marriage and kin relations within the village (Croll 1977). Because of the problems of relating the form which social institutions have traditionally taken, and still take, in Guangdong to the rest of China, I have

* Locations: Jiang village, like the other rural villages visited, is to be found in the densely populated rice-growing region of the Pearl River Delta. The small village, which was entirely surveyed, and which I have called Jiang village after its common surname, had a population of 147 residents in April 1977 and was the largest of three villages which made up production team no. 11 (230 pop.). In turn it was one of the 322 teams which constituted the 31 production brigades of Huadong commune. Hua commune in Hua county is 40 km north of Canton and it has 71,000 mu of peanuts and has some forestry, animal husbandry, fisheries and sidelines occupations some sideline occupations. Yue village (585 pop.) composed number one production team of the 299 teams which made up the twenty-five production brigades of the Renhe commune. This commune is a suburb of Canton and 24 km north of the city centre. Renhe has 67,000 mu of agricultural land and mainly grows paddy rice, peanuts and has some forestry, animal husbandry, fisheries and sidelines occupations. The third village, Hao Mei village (480 pop.) is one of the 343 production teams that make up the nineteen production brigades of Dali commune which, like Renhe, is also a suburb of Canton. It is located 15 km south of the city and mainly grows paddy rice, vegetables and fruit. In addition to these three rural villages, comparative data was also drawn from interviews conducted within two urban housing estates in Canton. One was the factory housing estate attached to the Canton Heavy Machinery Plant which was composed of blocks of flats and single-storey bungalows, and the other was a housing estate on the banks of the Pearl River which was a resettlement area now inhabited by former boat people usually considered to be a distinct ethnic group (see Ward 1965). In each of these locations I followed a sequential list of questions on the household, primary groups and marriage which gave all the interviews a common structure.

added the findings from this second visit to the other case studies from documentary sources to illustrate problems, patterns and trends in the negotiation of marriage. During this visit I specifically set out to test the correlation of differing patterns of marriage with the structure and function of households and primary groups which I had already developed from documentary sources. In chapters 8 and 9, devoted to the relationship of marriage to the structure and function of domestic and kin groups, I have used the materials from Guangdong extensively.

On this data base it has been possible to express the range and variation in the procedures of marriage by means of a number of models which set out their characteristics in summary or clustered form. In the People's Republic of China there is a very well-defined model of marriage based on the new Marriage Law and presented in the media as the ideal form, and it is possible that this clearly defined ideology of marriage has tended to obscure the variety of social practices existing within China today. In a social field like China, perhaps the most obvious problem facing the anthropologist is that suggested by Lévi-Strauss, who thought that the problem of assessing the accuracy of the culturally produced or conscious model of a society was a particularly difficult task where there was a clearly defined ideology representing social structure, processes and social relations as they 'ought to be' (1953:517). In order to overcome the problem of identifying varieties in social behaviour, this study followed the example of Barbara E. Ward, who thought that scholars would do well to recognise the existence of a number of different Chinese ideal patterns varying in time and sequence with historical developments and the demands of particular occupations and environments. She concluded from her study of south China fishermen that there was no single conscious model, but a variety existing in their minds which can and should be contrasted (Ward 1965). She distinguished between ideological and immediate (home-made) models. The ideological model was based, however remotely, on uniform literati* practice which varied little from sub-group to sub-group. Because of its wide applicability she termed it the ideological model. This is the model of the participants' social and cultural system as they believe it to be.

* 'Literati' is a term often applied to the elite Chinese social group because of the emphasis on proven literary qualifications as a pre-requisite to membership of that group. For instance, to draw attention to the importance of the connection between education and polical power in China, Weber used the term to describe the whole Chinese privileged upper group (1951:107–41).

In comparison to the ideological model, the various immediate models of different sub-groups may well be expected to show wide variations. The details of an ideological model may be found in legislation, government policy statements, authoritative theoretical statements in the media and educational materials. The immediate models deriving from patterns of social behaviour common among sub-groups in society may be revealed by the subjects themselves in autobiographies, letters and interviews. For each sub-group, changes within the informal face-to-face communities can be expected to be reflected in the norms governing these interpersonal sets and by the role expectations expressed within egocentric networks.

BACKGROUND TO THE STUDY

In 1950 a new ideological model of marriage was introduced into China which was designed to substitute an existing range of conscious models already operating during the Republican period (1911–49). It has been argued by Freedman (1967) and Ward (1965) that marriage rites before the twentieth century could be represented by one basic model. Although there might be some variation in the ceremonial details according to locality and wealth of status, this single model was to be identified by its chief characteristic: that the marriage contract was entirely negotiated and controlled by the heads of the household (*jiazhang*) and the couple had no active role in the negotiations. By virtue of his authority over the individuals of the household, the senior male was entitled by law to select a marriage partner and negotiate the marriage of any member of the household without the consent or even the knowledge of that member. A broker called the *meiren* (literally matchmaker or go-between) was normally engaged for the purpose of conducting the negotiations, but it was the head of the household who finally arbitrated the choice, decided the ceremonial expenditure and put his name to the marriage contract. The practice of arranged marriage (*fumu baoban ernu hunyin*) and employing go-betweens to negotiate the marriage contract was said to have become such a time-honoured custom that it had crystallised into the belief that all marriages were brought about by the 'command of the parents and the words of the go-between' (Levy 1949: 101).

In the Republican period (1911–49) new marriage patterns had begun to emerge which no longer reflected the unqualified dominance of this one basic model. Influenced by social practices in Europe and North America, the urban-educated younger generation had begun to demand the free choice of marriage partner or the non-intervention of parents or third parties and the establishment of independent households (*hu*) on marriage. A variety of new marriage procedures emerged in the cities in the earlier decades of this century. Commonly, couples met and courted each other and after an interval made their vows to each other in a very short and simple ceremony in the presence of a few friends and family. Alternatively, they merely made an announcement at a small dinner-party, by post or in the newspapers that they had signed a marriage contract and changed their address (Waln 1933:129; Chao 1970:193; Tyau 1922:72–3). Many young persons who had met others to their liking requested the consent and support of their parents; some even went through traditional ceremonies as if they had not met before the marriage. Wong Su-ling and a fellow-student both agreed that although they had independent means of support, they 'desired to have his father's consent and blessing' to the marriage, for only the acquisition of this would 'square the matter with the requirements of Chinese custom' and enable them to feel that they 'were really engaged' (Wong and Cressy 1953:367). Others, fearing familial conflict or dissuaded by the distance and difficulties of communication involved, did not request parental consent and proceeded directly to marry of their own accord. Frequently the new procedures required two important pre-conditions. First, the young people were often forced to defy their families and break betrothal agreements formerly arranged by their families, and secondly they had to select a partner of their own choice in a society where there were few opportunities for the association of the sexes outside of the new institutions of education.

Arranged marriage remained dominant in the Republican period and almost entirely in the rural areas. All the village studies undertaken during this period, and even in 1948–9, describe arranged marriage as the local custom (Fei 1939:40; Lang, 1946:122–3; Gamble 1954:379; Osgood 1963:273). By the mid-century though, some villages were becoming aware of an alternative form which was rumoured to be practised elsewhere but was certainly not in keeping with current customs (M. Yang 1945:103–22). In one village located on the outskirts of Guangzhou in south China, C. K. Yang found that even in 1948–9 parents still controlled the marriage negotiations and there had been no modifications. Although the villagers lived too close to a large city not to have heard of marriages in which young people had chosen their own marriage partners, they regarded the new form as another of those 'strange fashions characteristic of strange modern urban living especially among the foreignised rich city folks' and certainly they had no thought that it might one day modify their own village customs (1959:83, 176). By 1949 however, free-choice marriage was practised in the cities and in some provincial towns by College or high school students and returned students from abroad who later entered the professions (Chin 1948:1–2; Fried 1953:40, 58). Even within these groups, many who adhered to the new form in principle eventually bowed to their parent's wishes and entered into an arranged marriage (Lang 1946:122–4, 215). Among other urban social categories, from landlords and rich merchants to factory workers, the majority still thought that marriage was a family affair and that sons and daughters should obey their parents. In her investigations of marriage patterns among factory workers in the 1930s, Olga Lang was greeted with remarks like 'This new idea is something for the rich people like modern dress and umbrellas'; 'Modern marriages are improper'; 'We don't have such things in our native village'; 'As for modern marriages public opinion frowned upon them for it was shameful to choose one's own mate'; 'Children should be married as their parents were' (Lang 1946:123, 266–7). She concluded that although they were familiar with the new forms these seemed remote from the realities of their own lives. Over much of Republican China, then, the traditional ideological model remained the dominant conscious model and none of the new models which had been adopted by minority social categories and negatively formulated in terms of deviancy from, or rebellion against, the traditional custom of arranged marriage achieved the status of a new ideological model of nation-wide applicability. It was not until the establishment of a new government in 1949 that a new ideology of marriage, based on the principle of free choice, was formally introduced and developed on a nation-wide scale. At this time it began to provide for, and actively encourage, widespread competition and conflict with the traditional ideological model.

The main aim of the government in 1950 was to introduce a new ideological model as a universal measure of social behaviour by familiarising every household in urban and rural areas with its details (PC 1 June 1952). The new law only established the principles on which the new model was to be based, and the specific guidelines for its practise were elaborated and publicised in all forms of educational materials which were popularised by government personnel, the Youth League, the Women's Federation and other mass organisations. After the promulgation of the law all aspects of the media were marshalled in its support. There were articles and short stories in the press, periodicals and wall newspapers, it was featured in films, drama, travelling picture exhibitions, rhymes and songs and it was the subject of classes in schools, in winter schools for peasants, in factories and on the radio. Two years later an intensive and nation-wide campaign to once again familiarise the people with the details of the new model was planned for March 1953. The government decreed that this month was to be set aside for a special family-by-family and street-by-street campaign to conduct education in the new form of marriage. The Vice-Chairman of the Commission leading the campaign described it as a period of intensive publicity and discussion designed to inform, educate and explain the general outlines of the Marriage Law in order to enable everyone to clearly demarcate the differences between the old and new marriage systems (RMRB 20 March 1953). At the conclusion of this campaign, the government thought that it had introduced a new ideological model to compete with the old model and it estimated that overall it had effectively acquainted a high proportion of the country's population, perhaps 70 to 80 per cent, with the details of the new model, but it also recommended that education in the details of the new model should continue on a regular and nation-wide basis (CR September 1953; NCNA 5 March 1955).

Since these early campaigns there has been a steady flow of educational materials directing attention to some aspect of the new ideology. There have been two exceptions to the general emphasis on education, and these have both occurred in 'left' or 'radical' periods.* During the Great Leap Forward (1958–9), there was more attention given to the economic strategy to do with the reorganisation of the relations of production and the reduction of the role of the household as a unit of production and consumption, which had obvious implications for the reform of the marriage system. The Cultural Revolution (1966–9), on the other hand, was much more concerned with the

---

* It has become increasingly common to debate the implemention of policies in China in terms of cyclical or circular patterns of 'left' and 'right' or 'moderate' and 'radical' oscillations (Skinner and Winckler 1969; Winckler 1976).

rearrangement of social strata and class relations, and although the policies seldom directly encompassed those to do with marriage and domestic affairs, they certainly had repercussions for all of them. Since the Cultural Revolution, and especially in the movement to criticise Confucius and Lin Piao (1973–5), the flow of educational materials has resumed, although in much reduced numbers. Perhaps this reduction is due to the continuing absence of the magazines *Zhongguo Qingnian*, *Zhongguo Funu* and *Gongren Ribao* which had formed popular channels for the educational materials before 1966.

SCOPE OF PRESENT STUDY

This study takes as its starting-point the introduction of the new mariage contract as outlined in the first two sections of the 1950 Marriage Law,* which cover the negotiations of marriage, the age of marriage, choice of marriage partner and its ritual and ceremonial forms. The first chapters are devoted to the process of change within the institution of marriage itself. They include an examination of the degree to which arranged marriage and the institutional intervention of kin and brokers in the procedures of mate selection have been substituted by free-choice negotiations based on mutual volition (chapter 2) and the extent to which courtship has replaced betrothal as the dominant pre-marital ritual form (chapter 3). Chapter 4 examines the age of marriage and chapter 5 assesses the qualities of the preferred mate. They ask how far the age of marriage has been raised and how far a narrowly defined field of eligible mates, based on the pursuit of class status and power, has been replaced by a broad field of eligibles characterised by the negation of such socio-economic criteria. In chapter 6 an examination of the ritual and ceremonial forms of marriage reveals the extent to which these have been simplified both procedurally and symbolically. For each of these processes the varieties in patterns are identified and attributed to broadly defined sub-groups in Chinese society.

Chapter 7 summarises the variety of marriage patterns identified in the first chapters and assesses the degree of social change which has taken place within marriage over the past twenty-five years. It discusses previous analyses of social change or the 'modernisation' of marriage and kinship structures in China, and suggests that analogies

* For the text of the Marriage Law see Meijer (1971) or Croll (1974).

drawn from the comparable social fields of China during the Republican period, and post-1949 Taiwan, which primarily attribute 'modernisation' in rural areas to economic variables to do with industrialisation and urbanisation, may not be appropriate when considering the case of the People's Republic. The subsequent chapters offer an alternative explanation for the variety in marriage patterns and suggest that economic policies in rural China may have had precisely the opposite effects on marriage patterns to those in China in the Republican period and post-1949 Taiwan. Chapters 8 and 9 explore this possibility in greater detail by correlating the variety of marriage patterns with both social and economic relations within the household, and between the household and primary kin or neighbourhood groups in China; they put forward two hypotheses. The first suggests that the degree of parental participation or authority of the older generation in the negotiations of marriage can be directly correlated to the structure of the household. In the second hypothesis, the degree of parental participation or control of the negotiations by the older generation varies directly with the degree to which individual households are encapsulated by overlapping primary groups. The final chapter concludes the analysis of the specific ideological and socio-economic variables working for and against social change within marriage and kinship structures. It suggests that there is a degree of competition, tension and conflict operating in rural China between the demands of the new ideological model of marriage and socio-economic policies. It is the attempt to mediate the two which has been responsible for the development and crystallisation of the variety of marriage patterns in China today.

2

THE INITIATION OF NEGOTIATIONS

The Marriage Law which placed the negotiations of marriage within the control of the individual parties and allowed them full rights to initiate their own negotiations without any interference or obstruction from third parties brought free-choice marriage (*hunyin ziyou*) into direct conflict with arranged marriage (*fumu baoban ernu hunyin*). Out of this competition and conflict there has arisen a variety of patterns which characterise marriage in China today. An examination of the social behaviour and role expectations exhibited in the case studies reveals the operation of at least four conscious models, two coinciding with the old and new ideological models and two involving combinations of elements from each of the ideological models. If the procedures constituting marriage are broken down into three stages: (1) the initiation of the negotiations or selection of partner, (2) mechanisms providing for consent by third parties and (3) the conclusion of the negotiations, then the range of marriage patterns in China today can be represented by the conscious models given in table 1. The models may be distinguished according to the patterns of authority and controls which they exhibit. These range from model (1), in which the negotiations, from their initiation to their conclusions, are entirely monopolised by the elder generation or parents, to model (4), where the controls are exclusively operated by the parties to the marriage negotiations. There is evidence to suggest that it is this range in patterns of control which have distinguished and continue to distinguish conscious models in the People's Republic of China.

A small number of case studies follow model (1), or the traditional ideological model, and display a parental monopoly of controls of the marriage procedures. That is, the older generation initiate the negotiations and conclude the marriage arrangements without consulting with, or requesting the consent of, the principal parties. The negotiations which they undertook consisted of selecting a likely

24

Table 1. *The range of conscious models in the People's Republic of China*

	Initiations of negotiations	Consent	Conclusion of negotiations
Old ideological model (1)	Parents	—	Parents
Immediate model (2)	Parents	Parties	Parents
Immediate model (3a)	Parties	Parents	Parents
(3b)	Parties	Parents	Parties
New ideological model (4)	Parties	Political associations	Parties

spouse, fixing the amount of the betrothal gift and the date of the ceremony. The negotiations were normally conducted through a third person, sometimes a professional go-between, but more often a member of kin or a neighbour, who have offered their services. The go-betweens are now usually given the name of *jieshao ren* or 'introducers' to distinguish them from the traditional brokers or go-betweens whose services were now outlawed. A number of letters and broadcasts show that young people, even in the 1970s, suddenly found that their marriages had been arranged without their prior knowledge.

In 1963, for example, two letters were written to magazines by young people whose marriages had been arranged in this manner. One young girl returned home to work in the countryside after graduation from primary middle school to find that her mother had initiated marriage negotiations with the prospective groom's family. The young people had not been consulted and, despite the girl's objections that she had never met, and that she knew nothing of, the prospective groom, her mother proceeded to finalise the marriage negotiations (ZQ 26 November 1963). Another young girl suddenly learned that she had been betrothed for six years and that the marriage arrangements were due to be concluded in the near future – all without her knowledge, let alone her consent (ZF 1 February 1966). The newspaper *Anhui Ribao* (Anhui Daily) reported a case as recently as in March 1974 in which a young girl had been betrothed without her knowledge. The negotiations had been conducted by a matchmaker and with the approval of her parents. The young girl said she was shocked when she first learned of the news and returned home at once to reject this marriage arrangement. She met with no response from her parents, who said that they were adhering to the old maxim that 'the parents' orders must be obeyed and the words of a matchmaker must be heeded'. In this belief the parents proceeded to prepare for the marriage ceremony and disregarded both their daughter's wishes and the criticisms of some of the local commune members. After consultation, the families of the bride and groom agreed to hold the wedding on 15 December 1973. On that day the groom's family used every possible means to take the struggling bride to the home of the bridegroom (SWB 21 March 1974). The case studies in which this model persists more or less intact are relatively few, and they almost always occur in the countryside and cause some conflict between the generations and among commune members.

The second conscious model incorporates characteristics of both the old and new ideological models. The parents take it upon themselves to initiate the marriage negotiations and the terms are agreed much as in model (1), but the parties are also introduced to each other and the conclusion of the marriage agreement is dependent upon their consent. Parents no longer have the monopoly of the negotiations. The case studies which illustrate these marriage procedures usually begin with the parents' search for suitable mates. As young people approach marriageable age, parents approach kin, friends and neighbours and in rare instances even employ professional brokers to aid them in the search for a suitable mate and in conducting the preliminary negotiations leading to a proposal of marriage (*qiuhun*). A tentative choice, or in rare instances a short-list of suitable candidates (e.g. CR 1 September 1953), is presented to the son or daughter to solicit their opinions and consent. This stage of the procedure seems to be no mere formality. In one village study conducted in 1970, parents involved in marriage negotiations considered several prospective mates for their son and several times the match seemed very suitable in every respect, but each time the negotiations were abruptly ended when the young people turned down the idea, either as the result of prior knowledge of the partner from schooldays and reports of mutual acquaintances or as the result of a meeting. In one case the couple who had known each other as school mates turned down the match, and in another case in the same village, the school teacher and her prospective partner had several talks together and it was said that she put him through several tests before giving her consent to the match (J. Chen 1973:72–86).

That the consent of the young people was an institutionalised prerequisite to the conclusion of the negotiations in model (2) is evidenced by the great disappointment or even helpless anger expressed by parents if that consent was not forthcoming. The parents of one girl found an acceptable suitor for their daughter through introductions conducted by an elderly woman neighbour. To their fury the daughter rejected not only him, but a subsequent number of very desirable partners including an army officer, a cadre and a technician. They were each rejected in turn. Although the parents were very angry, it is noticeable that they did not consider either the use of coercion or proceeding to the conclusion of the negotiations on their own initiative (ZF 1 May 1964).

In contrast to the two previous models, in the third conscious model the young people themselves select their own marriage partner, ask for their parents' consent, and the marriage negotiations are then concluded either by the parents and/or the principal parties. Where the younger generation takes over the initiation of marriage negotiations, the negotiation process takes on a new form. The principals usually come to a decision to marry after a period of courtship. Third persons play a much less conspicuous role. Young people might continue to be and usually were informally introduced to each other by workmates, friends or relatives, and there are a number of cases where government organisations are reported to have intervened and played 'matchmaker' to couples who have been shy or fearful of openly admitting their initial interest in one another. For example, young couples might be reluctant to express their affections because they either feared ridicule or were anxious about the likely opposition to their match. In these cases, leaders of the women's organisations or Youth League or Party cadres might give them encouragement and provide the opportunities for them to openly advertise 'their relationship' (e.g. WC 1 March 1962; ZF 1 January 1966). The conclusion of the negotiations might take either of two forms. In some cases parents take over and conclude the negotiations as in models (1) and (2) by settling the form of exchange between the two families. In other cases the parties, or the parties and parents combined, might disregard traditional procedures and arrange the ceremony as in the new ideological model (see chapter 6). In any event it is the control of the initial negotiations by the parties which primarily differentiates this model from others.

Parents adhering to model (3) might bring considerable pressure on their sons and daughters to marry, but they did not themselves proceed and initiate the negotiations on the behalf of the young people. Rather the older generation accepted the right of the younger generation to choose their own marriage partners, and even in cases where the young people were to delay the decision for some years, the parents did not seek to take the initiative and conduct negotiations on their sons' and daughters' behalf. What parents do seem to have expected, though, was that they be given the opportunity to give their consent and that this be viewed as a necessary prerequisite to the conclusion of the negotiations. Letters to the media indicate that some couples who were wishing to marry were worried by the fact that their parents disapproved of the match and were withholding their consent. In these cases the refusal of consent by the parents was often enough to cause either or both of the young people to doubt the wisdom of the match and break off the negotiations. The parents of one girl strongly opposed their daughter's decision to marry a cadre who worked in a government office. At first the girl was not unduly worried by her mother's attitude, for she thought that her mother would surely see reason and come round to giving her consent with time. But after a short interval her mother was still vehemently of the opinion that the match was not suitable and accused her daughter of ingratitude. These accusations had the effect of causing the girl to have 'the feeling of being in a dilemma'. She began to feel anxious and depressed and uncertain about whether she should proceed with her plans (NFRB 12 May 1962). In the case of another young couple planning to marry, the refusal of the girl's parents to give their consent caused the boy to think that the relationship between them had come to an impasse and he himself began to contemplate breaking off the negotiations (ZQ 27 November 1962). Both the initiation of the negotiations by the parents and the consent of the parties – model (2) – and the initiation by the parties and parental consent – model (3) – indicated a degree of shared control of the marriage negotiations. In model (4) the marriage negotiations are exclusively controlled by the parties themselves.

The last conscious model, model (4), coincides with the new ideological model introduced on a nation-wide scale in 1950. In this model the parties to the marriage initiate the negotiations for marriage, allow no obstruction or intervention of the older generation to stand in their way and, despite any withholding of parental consent, they proceed with the help of political associations to conclude the negotiations themselves. Most of the role models or public reference groups selected for emulation in educational materials fall into this category. The case of Chen Meiying was published in the women's magazine *Zhongguo Funu* to illustrate the new ideological model and to remind the readers that the struggle for freedom of marriage is in effect a struggle against traditional forms of familial authority. Chen Meiying chose her own marriage partner after a period of courtship, but her decision met with combined opposition from the members of her family and particularly from her father. The long-drawn-out struggle which followed only served to strengthen the resolve of Chen Meiying and her partner to conclude their marriage arrangements themselves. When finally the parents began to talk of bestowing their consent but at the same time to impose conditions on the young couple, such as the amount and constituents of the betrothal gift which they knew the groom couldn't possibly meet, the young couple disregarded their opinions and demands. Their marriage took place not at home with the support of the older generation, but at the factory where they both worked and only afterwards were their parents informed of the event (ZF 1 October 1963). What the case studies which reveal this sequence have in common is that political associations came to the aid of the couples, the older generation of the family were usually informed that the negotiations had been concluded after the event and at the ceremony itself the young couple were often praised for adhering to the new ideological model or holding the 'correct viewpoint in choosing life's companions, for daring to fight against the old thinking and for the way in which they had handled their wedding arrangements' (ZF 1 October 1963). The history of their negotiations was often circulated in the media to encourage their peers to defy opposition and to practise the new ideological model.

THE DISTRIBUTION OF MODELS

Any attempt to quantify the distribution or degree of adherence to any one model is handicapped by the fragmentary nature of available and appropriate statistics. An attempt was made to assemble figures for free-choice marriage in the early 1950s, but it is immediately apparent that the statistics available can hardly provide the basis for any comparison according to either area or time period. The figures for arranged marriage usually refer to the operation of model (1), but the figures for free-choice marriage may refer to any of models (2), (3) or (4). There is therefore no means of assessing the relative weight of the controls operated by parents and parties which distinguishes models (2), (3) and (4). In the absence of national and useful statistics, it has been necessary to rely on impressionistic data collected over a period of time from a number of media sources. There is a remarkable degree of coincidence in these sources in favour of models (2) and (3). These two syncretic models combining old and new elements seem to represent a high proportion of the selection procedures. All the available evidence suggests that model (2) probably determines most role expectations and therefore social behaviour in rural areas, and model (3) represents the most common procedure in the urban social field.*

It was estimated at the end of the first campaigns for marriage reform that in most rural areas, the marriage system was at the stage of 'individual decision and introduction by others or semi-voluntary in form' (Kan 1965:4). One report in the mid-1950s stated that in the greater number of villages, the people stand at the stage of social revolution where marriage is arranged through the introduction of another person. The report went on to estimate the proportions for one province, Shaanxi, where 10–15 per cent of the population were said to follow the new ideological model, 5–10 per cent adhered to the old model, and 80 per cent combined old and new models (CNA 13 May 1955). It must be remembered that Shaanxi (Shansi) was a part of the old Soviet base where the new ideological model had at this time been in operation for approximately 20 years, albeit in low profile because of the war conditions of that period. There is every evidence to suggest that the predominant models in operation in rural areas have continued to combine elements of the old and new ideological models. In 1964 a village reader pointed out that young people were commonly introduced by friends and relatives (Lu Yang

* It is difficult to draw a precise line between rural and urban China. It would have been preferable, if the materials had allowed, to refine the usual rather simplified distinction between 'urban', which usually refers to the major cities and industrial towns, and the 'rural' social field which includes villages and local market centres. Marketing towns and minor cities of the type distinguished by Skinner (1964–5) probably fall somewhere between. It is probably preferable to think of the simplified categories of 'rural' and 'urban' as forming the poles of a continuum.

1964), and, in the 1970s, a participant observer of rural social life in the late 1960s noted that this type of marriage was still common in rural areas (J. Chen 1973:186). Certainly my own impressions from Guangdong confirmed this impression. When I asked how a couple had met, in nearly every case it was through the introduction of a mutual acquaintance, relative, friend or neighbour. That initiation by the parties and parental consent, or models (3a) and (3b) (see table 1) was viewed as the most acceptable norm of behaviour in urban areas is suggested by the number of references to it as a common pattern in the case studies and by the redefinition of the new ideological model to approximate its form.

Both these immediate models seem to have been such common procedures that they have each become widely accepted as forms of marriage by 'self-determination' or free-choice marriages and have been officially promoted as such. Even model (2) has been defined as a form of free-choice marriage (*ziyou jiehun*). In 1955 the Central Committee of the Movement for the Thorough Implementation of the Marriage Law issued a statement to this effect. It said that marriage contracts in which the principals were first introduced to each other by third parties and then expressed their own agreement to the match were to be recognised as a form of marriage by 'free-will'. 'It is incorrect,' the statement concluded, 'to consider that the introduction by a third party means an arranged marriage' (NCNA 5 March 1955). Apparently this pattern was often referred to as marriage by free-choice and was distinguished from model (3), which became known as 'free choice in the modern way' (*jindaide ziyou jiehun*). As Jack Chen, living in a village in Henan, noted in the 1970s, the former was considered to be the accepted custom or standard of behaviour in the village and in other villages of its inhabitants' acquaintance. Although at the same time they were dimly aware that somewhere else in China there might be alternative patterns of marriage, they did not accept these as appropriate to 'their way of doing things' (J. Chen 1973:72).

Equally, although model (3), in which the parties initiated the negotiations but the conclusions were dependent upon parental consent, did not entirely conform to the new ideological model, it became a constantly recommended form of behaviour in the educational materials published to give guidance to young people. These normally took pains to state that the taking of advice and consulting with parents did not in any way constitute parental interference in marriage negotiations or mean that a marriage was not to be categorised as 'free choice' (ZQ 16 December 1956). Advice columns recommended that young people in urban areas should indeed consult with their parents. If they opposed the match, the young couple were advised to patiently persuade and reason with them even if it meant delaying their marriage for quite some considerable time in order to win their consent (ZQ 27 November 1962). Only as a last resort and at a much later date were the couple advised to disregard the wishes of their parents and conclude the marriage negotiations themselves (NFRB 12 May 1962). Although models (1) and (4) have the status of ideological models, the new ideological model has been informally redefined to incorporate the immediate models (2) and (3). It is these two models which commonly constitute the recommended procedures of marriage and determine most role expectations and therefore social behaviour. In turn, these new and immediate models derive from patterns of social behaviour or strategies which were widely evolved to accommodate to varying degrees both the old and new ideological models and to mediate the conflict between them.

THE THREAT TO THE OLDER GENERATION

The case studies suggest that the conflict between the two models has largely been played out between the older and younger generations and that this conflict has centred on the rights and authority of the older generation to control affairs within the domestic domain. The new Marriage Law demanded that they should relinquish this power. Even the development of immediate models (2) and (3) demanded that both generations share the control of the marriage negotiations, and the persistence of these models over time has required the continual concurrence of both the parents and the parties in some form of power sharing. The form that the immediate models have taken suggest that the older generation has worked to maintain its control of the initiation of marriage negotiations in rural areas, and, at the very least, to retain their consent as a prerequisite to the conclusion of the marriage negotiations in urban areas. In both rural and urban areas the older generation rightly foresaw the consequences of the Marriage Law for the traditional distribution of power within the household. Formerly, the reputation of the *jiazhang*, or head of the household, rested on the orderliness of the affairs within the domestic domain and his ability to exercise authority over the members of the household. This exclusive control over the marriage arrangements of the younger generation contributed to the power base of the older generation and it is evident that the conflict between the old and new forms of marriage was viewed as a facet of the struggle for hegemony within the household.

That the parents felt their controls to be threatened by the new law is evident from the following poem:

> With freedom of marriage,
> Gone is the father's prestige;
> Now comes the Marriage Law,
> Mothers are no longer held in awe. (CR 1 July 1962)

From the case studies, it is clear that parents frequently perceive the operation of free-choice marriage to be a direct attack on their authority, and they express their hostility to the new practices accordingly. The young people's initiative in the marriage negotiations is commonly interpreted as a direct expression of disobedience or rebellion against parental authority that threatens their power base within the household and therefore causes the loss of their dignity or 'face' within the community* (ZF 1 October 1963). When a young girl was courting the boy of her choice, her mother, who only indirectly heard of the matter, was furious. She harassed her daughter with the words, 'What kind of nonsense is this? It's downright rebellion. A young girl goes out and looks for her husband, see if I won't break her legs'. The neighbours and government cadres had to intervene to prevent physical injury (Chen Hsu 1952). The father of another girl who had chosen her own spouse in a rural village refused to give his consent on the grounds that 'This free-love business, it's nothing but losing-face business' (RMRB 12 January 1957).

In later case studies, in the 1960s, parents often expressed their hostility less directly; instead they resorted to delaying tactics to compensate for their loss of direct control. The most commonly cited reason for withholding consent was their disapproval of the qualities of the chosen partner. Sometimes before they would give their consent, parents imposed conditions on the parties, such as the demand for

---

* In her fieldwork in Taiwan, Margery Wolf enquired of villagers what constituted having or losing 'face'. She was informed that when no one was talking about a household you could say it had 'face' (1972:40).

certain goods and payments which they knew to be either unacceptable or impossible for the parties to meet. In a case published in *Nanfang Ribao* in 1962, the mother of the prospective bride, seeing that she could not change her daughter's mind by employing 'tough or soft tactics', demanded that the groom should send her 'gifts' such as ten crates of rice grain, ten catties each of chickens, ducks, pork and peanut oil and 100 yuan in cash before she would consider giving her consent. The young couple could not and would not oblige; but the mother continued to press her demands until the Party committee intervened (NFRB 6 October 1962).

Whether they expressed their hostility either directly or indirectly, the older generation often invoked traditional moral and ritual obligations and mobilised the support of kin and neighbours in support of their threatened authority. The alarmed and angry reactions of the parents of young people who had chosen their own marriage partner were often expressed in terms of filial piety, or the obedience and obligations of the young to the elders and their ancestors. Just as the older generation had an obligation both to the ancestors and to future descendants to arrange the marriage of the younger generation, so sons and daughters had an obligation to obey their parents in this most important matter. As the father of a girl who had chosen her own marriage partner saw it, 'such goings-on not only tarnish his good reputation, but are an insult to his ancestors'. He is adamant; 'tradition demands obedience' (PC 1 March 1952). The older generation not only called upon filial obligations in their support, but also time and again they mobilised kin and neighbours in support of their traditional controls of mate selection. Parents turned to kin and neighbours for help in the search for suitable mates (indeed most go-betweens usually turned out to be either a relative or a neighbour) and to exert pressure on the young should they prove recalcitrant and cause conflict within the household. Collective pressure from this source was often brought to bear on a son or daughter to reinforce moral and ritual obligations invoked by parents. In one case, a girl reported how she had come under the combined pressure of parents, kinsmen, friends and neighbours to get married once she had turned 23 years of age. Her parents, anxious to see her safely married to a suitable mate, continually warned her that an older girl just would not get a good husband. At their bidding and in their support, villagers and kin also urged her to get married, and began to talk in her hearing of the difficulties which older girls have in finding suitable mates and the pleasure her marriage would bring to her parents in their old age (ZQ 1 August 1964). Many letters written by young people to the newspapers and periodicals reported how difficult they found it to defy the combined pressure of parents, kin, neighbours and friends (GRB 27 September 1962; 9 October 1962).

THE CONCURRENCE OF THE YOUNGER GENERATION

The persistence of the new immediate models also required the concurrence of the parties in sharing rather than appropriating the controls of the negotiations. The case studies suggest that many young people had allowed their parents to substantially retain their traditional controls by having them initiate the negotiations or by making their consent a prerequisite to the conclusion of the negotiations. Many seem to have been openly reluctant to defy the traditional authority of their parents. Despite the fact that the Marriage Law rejected arranged marriage as an expression of blind obedience to the unreasonable demands of parents, the traditional obligations of duty and gratitude continued to influence the behaviour of young people and caused them to concur in the continuation of old patterns. This is evident from the study of letters written by those who had been accused of disobedience. The obligations of filial piety (*xiaodao*) still seem to have invoked feelings of anxiety and guilt among a number of girl correspondents who felt that they should follow the wishes of their parents, who had taken the trouble and expense to bring them up and were now losing them to another family (NFRB 12 May 1962; ZQ 26 November 1963). Young men did not have the same economic reasons for a daugher's gratitude in that they could be expected to support their parents in their old age, but for them the ideal of filial piety had traditionally been especially instilled in them from an early age. The accusation of 'unfilial son' disturbed one young man. He had rejected an arranged marriage and was thus accused of disobedience by his father and relatives who said that a 'filial son' should 'follow the wishes of his father whatever the consequences and even if he has something to lose'. After one year elapsed, the young man wrote to *Zhongguo Qingnian* to ask for advice. During that year he had had no cause to change his mind, but he felt very disturbed because some people still thought of him as an 'unfilial son' (*buxiao erzi*). 'The problem weighs heavily on my mind', he says, and 'I cannot concentrate on my study and work. Comrade editor, what does filial piety really mean? Am I an unfilial son because I turn my back on an arranged marriage?' (ZQ 12 February 1963).

The degree to which the younger generation might appropriate the control of their own marriage negotiations was directly linked to the number of opportunities for social interaction between the sexes and the introduction of new selective procedures. In rural areas in China the opportunities for meeting and establishing relationships in the village continued to be limited by two factors, the tradition of lineage (*zu*), or surname exogamy, and segregation of the sexes. The former is particularly limiting in single lineage or surname villages where spouses traditionally had to be found beyond the village boundaries. Although the number of marriage prohibitions has been reduced by the new law, it seems as if lineage exogamy may have continued to affect the opportunities for the likely interaction of potential mates within the same locality (see chapter 5). More widespread in influence, however, are the traditional norms segregating the sexes. The influence of the ancient maxims that there should in effect 'be some distance between men and women' has continued, especially among the older members of the rural communities. Although peasant women were not always secluded to the degree expected by the traditional Confucian ideology, segregation of the sexes was practised to the extent that the mixed social life of young people was circumscribed. In the 1950s the 'under-developed social intercourse' (WC 1 May 1950) and the 'lack of collective life' (CNA 13 May 1955) were specifically identified as conditions making for difficulties in introducing free-choice marriage in rural areas. Twenty years later, both Chinese and foreign commentators have observed that social relations in rural villages still displayed a certain degree of segregation. Although young men and women worked together in small teams, propriety still demanded that an adult be in charge of these groups. 'In point of fact', one observer noted, 'the girls chaperone themselves. In rest periods for example, they sat slightly apart and the boys would not be so forward as to intrude upon them.' It was the impression of the same observer that if a young man found that he could approach and make friends with a girl rather easily, be would be wary of marrying her himself or advising any of his friends to do so (J. Chen 1973:77).

The tradition of segregation and absence of precedent for the phenomenon of courting caused many young people to write to magazines expressing the wish that the Youth League would take a more active part in 'introducing' young people. The Youth League did indeed form one of the more obvious opportunities for mixed gatherings, but the political organisations have expressed a certain reluctance to meet this request. They point out that it was not their aim to replace traditional go-betweens by their modern equivalents, which would have the similar result of ultimately removing the responsibility from the young people of initiating negotiations themselves (ZQ 1 November 1956). Instead, and because the new patterns of marriage demanded the prior introduction of new opportunities for mixed social interaction, the government set out to establish youth clubs and organisations which would facilitate mixed social activities.

A NEW CATEGORY OF SOCIAL RELATIONS

There is some evidence that the institutionalised encouragement of a new category of social relations between young people of opposite sexes which were neither those of avoidance or marriage aroused some hostility among the older generations of the rural village. It was not unknown for the Youth League to discourage its members from openly fraternising with the opposite sex for fear that this might harm their reputation and draw attention to their affairs in a derogatory way (ZQ 1 April 1955; 1 November 1956). A young girl wrote to *Zhongguo Qingnian* in 1964 complaining that in her village young girls continued to be banned from the activities of the recreational clubs, reading-room and spare-time cultural work groups. Regardless of their daughters' feelings, the parent kept them at home and prohibited them from attending any meetings or taking part in certain activities. In defence of their actions the parents put forward reasons such as, 'when young people get together nothing good can happen', and the young people 'may not behave properly and may even ruin family reputations' (ZQ 27 October 1964). Two years later another young girl similarly complained to *Zhongguo Qingnian* that the activities of their village club were spoilt by the suspicions which they aroused (ZQ 16 April 1966).

In this atmosphere of continuing suspicions and segregation, individuals, if they did meet and attract each other, were often afraid to express their affections openly to each other in private or in public. They feared that they would become the subject of talk, gossip and

37

rumour, and would lose their reputations. Young people who had the effrontery to be seen together, let alone to embark on a steady courtship, were often severely censured. Couples remained shy, and, fearing disapprobation, were often reluctant to come out in the open and express their affections. In one village when a couple did finally meet alone 'by contrived accident', the young man stammered out to the girl that he had been wanting to speak to her for almost two years now. Although she felt the same for him, she dared not do more than stay and talk for a few minutes (CR 1 September 1953). Several cases in the media report that after young girls were seen alone with a young man they frequently thought they were automatically compromised and were therefore compelled to marry him (ZQ 1 May 1956). It was often the lack of an alternative opportunity to meet and develop a relationship with an eligible mate that demanded a high degree of courage among those who dared to defy the norms and play these furtive games of hide-and-seek. It was certainly true that those who did initiate their own marriage negotiations in rural areas were very often those who had access to extended networks beyond the confines of the face-to-face community. It was the young activists, the Young League members, Party members, members of locally renowned drama groups and those rewarded by the political authorities as 'good commune members' who had occasion to attend meetings, conferences and festivals outside the village. They enjoyed the opportunity to meet and become attracted to a partner of their own choice and were thus motivated to reject the immediate models of their community (PC 1 December 1951; RMRB 12 January 1957).

The lack of widespread institutional opportunities to meet and select their own marriage partners encouraged many of the younger generation to support parental authority and control of the initiation of negotiations. The young people in the rural areas lost their new legal right by default, as it were, in comparison to young people resident in urban areas. Although here, too, a few workers in specialised all-male and all-female occupations found it difficult to meet members of the opposite sex. For example, male city engineers who were frequently posted to distant worksites for short periods (ZQ 1 April 1955), and workers in all-female factories of some 20 li outside the city limits (RMRB 15 November 1956) both complained about the problems of gaining access to mixed gatherings. On the whole though, in urban areas young people had not only a greater number of opportunities for association in work enterprises and in better-developed recreational activities based on the neighbourhood, but the norms encouraging segregation no longer dominated the informal relations of the urban social field.

A CONFLICT OF INTERESTS

Those who did meet a partner of their choice and consequently opposed the traditional controls of the marriage negotiations exercised by the older generation, either at their initiation or conclusion, were often forced into a prolonged and heated conflict with their parents. In rejecting parental authority, the younger generation had access to legal resources and political associations and could turn to them for support. The Marriage Law's unequivocal declaration in favour of 'freedom of marriage' provided the younger generation with the legal right to reject the old pattern of family arranged marriage. Its clauses were often used as a weapon in verbal arguments, but normally sustained defiance depended on the support of one of a number of political associations. In nearly all the case-histories of conflict presented in the media, the young people had turned to government cadres, the Women's Federation, the Youth League or the Communist Party for support in maintaining their position and exercising their new rights (NFRB 6 October 1962; ZF 1 October 1963). These associations cooperated to persuade parents and kin of the advantages of the new form and in cases of violence took the young couple into their protection. The juxtaposition of the old and new ideological models occasioned by the Marriage Law has not only brought the younger and older generations into direct conflict, but has also brought the resources and sanctions of the kin and neighbourhood or informal groups into competition with those at the disposal of the new political associations or the formal social field. The forms which the new patterns of marriage would take to a large degree reflected the degree to which the resources or sanctions at the disposal of parents or kin were outweighed by those at the command of political associations.

Marriage patterns in contemporary China cannot be represented by one dominant model, for the new ideological model of free-choice marriage has not simply substituted the old ideological model of arranged marriage; instead, a number of immediate models containing characteristics of both have arisen to mediate the conflict between the

Table 2. *The initiation of marriage negotiations*

	Model 1	Model 2	Model 3a/3b	Model 4
Initiation	Parents	Parents	Parties	Parties
Consent	—	Parties	Parents	Political associations
	rural		urban	
	informal sanctions		formal sanctions	

old and new ideological models, and these have persisted to the extent that there has even been a tendency to redefine the new ideological model in their direction. The conflict between the generations for control of the marriage negotiations has been temporarily or permanently resolved in favour of shared controls, in favour of the older generation in the rural areas and partial to the younger generation in urban areas. In evaluating the relative weight of free choice and parental participation in negotiating the marriage contract, and thereby distinguishing the varieties of marriage patterns, the main dividing line on the continuum lies at the point where the parties take over the initial negotiations or where 'free choice' is distinguished from 'free choice in the modern way'. All the available evidence suggests that this point tends to roughly coincide with the division into rural and urban social fields and where the sanctions at the command of political associations begin to outweigh those at the disposal of parents and kin. This can be represented as in table 2. The point at which the initiation of negotiations is taken over by the parties will also be shown to coincide with radical changes on similar continuums for pre-marital rituals, choice of marriage partner, age of marriage and the forms which the conclusion of the negotiations take.

3

PRE-MARITAL RITUAL FORMS

The first phase of the negotiations of marriage was traditionally concluded by the exchange of a formal betrothal contract prepared at the behest of the heads of the two households concerned, and by the passage of the betrothal gift (*pinjin*) from the prospective groom's family to the future bride's family. The form and amount of the betrothal gift was normally negotiated by the heads of the families through a go-between, and usually involved the transfer of clothing, jewelry, household goods, food and money. The value of the prestations varied according to the resources of the individual households, but for all families it represented a major outlay. These formalities and transfers which constituted betrothal were entirely negotiated by the older generation and both represented and reinforced parental control over the marriage negotiations of their offspring. The introduction of a new form of marriage based on free choice required transformations in pre-marital ritual forms. The new Marriage Law made no reference to betrothal as a procedure of marriage. Indeed, Article 2 of the Marriage Law expressly prohibited the exaction of money and gifts in connection with marriage.

At the time of the passing of the Law, Shi Liang, the Minister of Justice, explained that the absence of betrothal in the Communist Law was due to the fact that it was associated with the negotiation and arrangement of marriage by persons other than the parties concerned. It was the occasion for payments of the money and gifts now banned by the new law (Pan Dunzhi 1950:43–8). Since it marked the first step in the series of marriage prestations it was hoped that its prohibition would establish a precedent and render subsequent monetary transactions unnecessary. The symbolic character of the payments was also stressed. It was argued that betrothal represented a business transaction or a metamorphosed form of marriage by purchase. An editorial in *Zhongguo Qingnian* stated that 'betrothal gifts'

41

were nothing but 'a pretext for the buying and procuring of women with money and other goods' (ZQ 19 November 1964). The practice was thus said to have symbolised the exchange of women between groups of men and to have harmed countless numbers of women by reducing their independence of movement and their status in society. According to the new ideology, betrothal was not only an outmoded custom in economic terms, but its symbolic meaning was also seen to be irrelevant in the new society which supported the equality of women. Instead, the new ideology prescribed a period of courtship (*tan lianai*) as a necessary prerequisite to marriage by self-determination or free choice.

In China, with its history of segregation and arranged marriage, courtship had always been negatively sanctioned; the very institutionalisation of this form of social behaviour would have posed a threat to the authority and controls of the older generation. Now the new ideology positively sanctioned and encouraged courtship as a 'natural, expected and proper prelude to marriage' (GRB 22 November 1962). In *Zhongguo Qingnian*, perhaps the foremost educational forum for young people, it has been stated time and again over the past twenty-five years that courtship was a necessary constituent of the new negotiation process and a prerequisite for the introduction of new forms of marriage. The main function attributed to courtship was the development of mutual understanding between potential marriage partners. In 1962 an article, written in response to queries about the proper length and functions of courting, stated that many problems in marriage could be avoided if the couple had developed a prior understanding of one another. It went on to list the functions of courtship:

Before a man and a woman get married, they should thoroughly understand each other. One must make a careful analysis and judgement of the political stand, ideological quality, attitude towards labour, habit of living, disposition and likes and dislikes. It is necessary to see whether or not in the future they can live together and live in happiness. This kind of understanding cannot be just reached through impressions gained within a very short time, but it must grow through a comparatively long period of contact and observation. Nor can you depend upon a third person's introduction. It is necessary for you to contact each other directly and know each other. Only mutual understanding, respect and confidence can produce deep love – and then you can talk about marriage (ZQ 14 September 1962).

42

Table 3. *Pre-marital rituals*

	Model 1	Model 2	Model 3a/3b	Model 4
Negotiation of marriage				
Initiation	Parents	Parents	Parties	Parties
Consent	–	Parties	Parents	–
Pre-marital rituals	Betrothal	Betrothal (courtship)	Courtship (betrothal)	Courtship

A booklet written two years later to advise cadres on the recommended forms of pre-marital behaviour again stressed the necessity to establish the new custom of courtship as 'an absolutely essential stage in the procedures leading to new forms of marriage.' Cadres were thus to encourage young couples to court each other openly and over a considerable period of time in order to facilitate sustained contact and promote their understanding of one another (Lu Yang 1964: 19). Courtship represented the new status of the individual parties in the marriage negotiations and a rejection of the controls of their elders and kin groups.

The new ideology thus discouraged betrothal and prescribed a period of courtship initiated by the young couple themselves as a prelude to free-choice marriage. Today a wide range of pre-marital rituals characterise the preliminary procedures of mate selection. It is not only that the old and new pre-marital rituals of betrothal and courtship are frequently to be found side by side within contemporary China, but commonly preliminary negotiations include multiple rituals so that the modalities of betrothal and courtship may coexist within the one set of negotiations. It seems as if the form which the pre-marital rituals take primarily depends on who initiates the negotiation of the marriage contract; see table 3.

BETROTHAL

Despite its discouragement, betrothal continues to function as an important social institution in the People's Republic of China. It is a feature of the negotiation of marriage in numerous case studies (e.g. ZQ 30 August 1956; ZF 1 January 1966; SWB 21 March 1974). Observations in the media also refer to its continuation as a widespread custom in rural China. A village reader published in the 1960s admitted that though betrothal neither received the protection of the law nor existed as a prerequisite demanded by the law, it still remained a custom in some areas of China (Lu Yang 1964:32). In the 1970s, Song Qingling (Soong Ching-ling) included it in a recent list of traditional customs which were still in current practice in rural China (PR 11 February 1972), and there have been some references to its persistence in China in the recent anti-Confucius campaign (XyP 10 January 1975; NCNA 7 March 1975). Long after the introduction of the new Marriage Law, the transfer of the betrothal gift to the bride's household or kin continued to signify the successful initiation of the marriage negotiations between the two families. In many case studies, individuals acknowledge its prohibited status, but with custom on their side they felt there was no need to press for its demise.

In many areas in China there was reported to be a general consensus that the custom should continue, although where the amount of the betrothal gift was excessive it had come under some attack. Its persistence was rationalised by 'these old rules which had been handed down from one generation to another and which nobody could now do without' (ZQ 19 November 1964). But it was also clear from some reports in the mid-1950s that where the custom had come under direct and government-sponsored attack, a number of strategies had developed to provide cover for the prestations in order to escape likely censure. In Shanxi (Shensi) province, a survey conducted in 1956 reported that betrothal payments there were camouflaged by various terms and procedures. For instance, cash deals were concluded by parents behind the backs of matchmakers, or two sets of matchmakers were employed, one to negotiate the payments and one to handle the marriage registration and give evidence that no payments of any kind were involved in the negotiations. Payments were often made in kind, such as in personal clothing and furniture that could pass as permissible voluntary gifts, rather than in the form of the outlawed 'cash deals'. New titles were formulated such as 'engagement gift', 'money for tobacco' or 'personal-use money' to replace the traditional 'betrothal gift' or payment (ZQ 30 August 1956). Some parents just kept their negotiations very quiet in the face of likely criticism. For example, in one case study the mother of a young girl who was a Youth League member and a leader of a production team just waited until the girl was absent from home and attending a meeting in a nearby town

before she opened negotiations for betrothal presents with the prospective groom's parents (ZQ 26 November 1963). It was more
common, however, after the initial campaigns in support of the
Marriage Law, for the transfer of gifts from the bridegroom's kin to
the bride's kin to remain an open and tolerated procedure of the
betrothal negotiations.

The betrothal gift has usually consisted of a combination of gifts in
kind and payments in cash. In some case studies it was shown to be
entirely composed of a cash sum, but more often it included household
and personal items for the kin of the prospective bride and for the bride
herself. The normal amount of cash in rural areas seems to have
averaged about 300 yuan in the 1950s and 1960s. In 1958 it was
estimated to range from 100 to 300 yuan with the average nearer to
300 than 100 (Kan 1965:8). In the process of computation it is evident
that there was room for bargaining and hence for the introduction of
some competition. It was not unknown for families to simultaneously
negotiate with several suitors in order to see who could furnish the most
attractive betrothal gift (ZQ 30 August 1956). In rural areas of Shanxi
in north China, for example, the sum generally ranged from 300 to
400 yuan and at times it reached 1000 (NCNA 31 January 1953).
Another estimate for the rural areas in Shanxi province put the
average amount at 500 yuan, with a minimum of 200. Some were said
to reach more than 1000 yuan, but these were unusual. In one of the
villages cited there were twelve betrothals recorded for 1954–5, and
gifts fell somewhere between 300 and 500 yuan (ZQ 30 August 1956).
In parts of south China in 1965 it was reported in *Nanfang Ribao* that
betrothal payments were not less than 300 to 400 yuan, and might
reach as high as 600 or 700 plus gifts of food (NFRB 18 January 1965).

By the 1970s the available figures for one village in Henan province
suggest that by this time there had been some reduction in the value
of the gifts. There the betrothal gift might consist of movable
property such as a bicycle, a sewing-machine and a clock, or
household items valued at a total of from 60 to 80 yuan together with
a small amount of cash (J. Chen 1973:80–5). In my own work in
Guangdong, it was difficult to question how far the custom of
betrothal gifts had persisted. Certainly both the bride's and groom's
family contributed to the expenses associated with marriage (see
chapter 6). In each case presented to me, the groom's household
contributed gifts to the new conjugal fund, but whether these were

at any point sent to the bride's household as part of the initial negotiations and could therefore be defined as betrothal gifts was difficult to ascertain; documentary evidence would suggest that this was probably so.

Some case studies have included detailed inventories of the contents of the betrothal gifts, and these show some small changes between the 1950s and the 1960s. From north-east China a case was reported in the press in which a bride's father had made a list of the presents his prospective son-in-law was expected to contribute. They included items of summer, autumn and winter clothing, leather shoes, cloth, gold and silver ornaments and cash (CR September 1953). Simultaneously the parents of a girl residing in Xinjiang (Sinkiang) province demanded gifts which included two suits of cadre uniforms, one of which was cotten padded, one gold ring, one pair of gold earrings, one pair of silver bracelets, two pairs of shoes, 160 feet of white cloth and 1000 yuan in cash (NCNA 9 February 1953). In comparison, in the 1960s there were no references to jewelery for personal use by the bride as a constituent of the betrothal gift, although clothing for her personal use remained a popular request. At one meeting of young people in a rural village, several of the participants described the demands of their parents. One girl reported that she and her parents had demanded a bicycle, a sewing-machine, a big leather chest and a quilt with a silk surface as part of a list of twenty household and other personal items. Another had asked for a bicycle, two or three silk dresses and a pair of leather shoes (ZQ 22 February 1962). In the 1960s likely constituents included a cash payment of about 300 yuan, household items such as furniture, sets of bedding and a sewing-machine, items of personal clothing and perishable goods including chickens, fish and meat (ZQ 19 November 1964; ZQ 16 January 1966).

It was evident from an examination of the contents of the betrothal gift that not all the items negotiated were eventually intended for the use of the young couple, or the conjugal as opposed to the familial fund. Some were obviously intended to directly benefit members of the bride's household. In one case an elderly man used the occasion of his daugher's betrothal to furnish himself with a superior coffin. He asked for 1200 yuan and a good coffin, but he later called off the arrangement when he found the coffin to be of inferior quality (ZQ 30 August 1956). There was the odd case where the kin of the bride clearly benefited from the dissolution of a betrothal, and the household accumulated capital and possessions in this way. In 1958 *Zhongguo Qingnian* referred to case studies where families profited by negotiating betrothal agreements many times over (Kan 1965:8). Another report in 1970 from Henan province referred to a case in which a very desirable young woman was said to have found betrothal gifts good business. It was revealed at a meeting that she had broken no fewer than three betrothals and was even now embarking on her fourth. The observer reported that he thought that this would be the last because of the publicity now attending her case (J. Chen 1973:187). It is much more likely, however, that the criticism aroused by the retention of the gift normally caused it to be returned on the breaking of the betrothal, and it was the problems associated with the return of the payments and the subsequent disruption of the economy of the bride's household, which would be caused by the dissolution of a betrothal, that led to pressure on women to remain betrothed.

MECHANISMS FOR CONSENT

Where the parents monopolised the negotiations, as in model (1), courtship played no part in the procedures of selection, but where the consent of the parties was a prerequisite to the conclusion of the negotiations, as in model (2), courtship rituals might play a small part as a means by which the young couple might become acquainted and give their consent to the match. Following the betrothal feast in one village in the 1970s at which the couple were given the first opportunity to get acquainted, it was observed that after a short talk they decided that they apparently liked each other's company. As a symbol of their consent to the match, they arranged to go to the county town the next day to have their photograph taken together and to do some shopping. This trip had apparently become the custom for newly betrothed couples signifying their consent to the match. The two or three hours they took to walk there and back was thought to give them ample time to talk about 'this and that' (J. Chen 1973:83–4). It might be inferred from this that a period of courtship would follow and occupy the interval between parental negotiation and consent by the parties and the marriage ceremony, but it seems this was not so, or certainly not in this village. Within a fortnight of their expedition, the young man took some eggs to his ailing mother-in-law, as he already called her, but for weeks thereafter it was observed that he seemed to forget his

47

prospective bride completely, though she was a local girl and they had attended the same school. It was explained by his parents that it would not look 'proper' were he to go visiting too often (J. Chen 1973:83–4).

Both Chinese and foreign observers in rural China have noted that betrothed couples can rarely be identified by their behaviour in agricultural work or in recreational activities within the village. William Hinton noted in a record of his interviews with workers on a State Farm that betrothed couples never thought of speaking to each other unless they had work to do together. It seemed as if this would have constituted a breach of the young couple's code of behaviour, 'which allowed for no outward sign of recognition between couples in public and especially while at work'. Signs of mutual affection were considered by the local community to be the proof of immorality, and it was only when they travelled away from the farm, on shopping trips on Sundays, that they felt free to disregard such restraints (CR September 1953). From more recent case studies, it seems as if such restraints may have been reduced, but they have continued to inhibit the development of courtship rituals among betrothed couples within rural villages.

Where the parties themselves had initiated the negotiations, as in model (3), betrothal gifts were still sometimes exacted by the girl's parents as a condition of their consent to a free-choice match. The mother of one young girl, on hearing of her affections for a young man, said to her, 'Before you are married into his family, we have to ask for something from them. So you can wear something nice at your wedding. We will not ask for many items. All we want from his family is 300 yuan in cash, together with a set of furniture, two complete sets of bedding, four dresses and a sewing-machine' (ZQ 16 January 1966). Sometimes items were demanded by the girls themselves, but generally the transfer of betrothal gifts at the behest of the kin of the bride or the bride herself was a much less common procedure where the young couples had themselves initiated the negotiations. An investigation conducted into the custom in the State-owned Fourth Cotton Weaving Works in the north-east provinces showed that, as early as 1953, in only 18 out of 40 cases was the groom required to make gifts of cash, cotton yarn, oxen and clothing (NCNA 31 January 1953). Where the parties initiated the negotiations themselves, courtship was likely to become the predominant pre-marital ritual, but in both rural and many urban areas courtship has constituted a new form of social behaviour. There has not only been some opposition to its introduction which involved the breaking-down of the traditional norms of segregation, but there has also been some uncertainty and confusion concerning the form which the new ritual should take.

COURTSHIP

In both rural and urban areas courtship rituals were frequently simplified and foreshortened into a few hasty meetings. Where rural couples themselves undertook the initiation of negotiations it was rarely the result of a sustained period of open courtship, but rather it was often the result of a number of rushed and secret encounters. A brief stroll in each other's company and in the absence of others often sufficed to enable couples to make their promises. Many a couple got to know each other in the company of mutual family friends and only then did they take a stroll together 'to say what was on their minds' (Chen Hsu 1952). In one village a couple were not so fortunate in having mutual friends, and it was many months before they found the courage to meet alone and admit their feelings for one another. They passed notes to each other and she gave him a towel to mark their new relationship, but it was not until three months later and at the village fair that they met again and talked of marriage. Still they did not keep each other's company, even though they had each asked for the consent of their parents to the match (CR September 1953). Over the past twenty-five years it has frequently been observed that older villagers were just not accustomed to the idea of courtship, and a young couple walking or talking openly together was enough to attract attention and imply a commitment embarrassing to the young couple at such a tentative stage of the relationship. Even the sustained contact of individuals of the opposite sex through work was enough to cause gossip in a village and draw comments such as: 'They are always together, and they are not yet married!' (PC 16 June 1949; ZQ 27 October 1964). The widespread introduction of the bicycle may have affected courtship rituals, and in villages within walking or cycling distance of towns with their theatres, opera shows, restaurants and shopping centres, couples may have more easily kept each other's company away from the controls of the village. Despite the new ideology and frequent encouragement of young people to reach an understanding and build a new relationship of congeniality based upon a period of courtship, in rural areas courtship continues to be characterised by its restrained nature, even in the 1970s.

Courtship has been more of an urban phenomenon and here the rituals are more elaborate. A stroll in the park, visits to the theatre, opera or movies, eating in a restaurant and visiting friends are all part of the courtship rituals, but even in towns courtship is not uniformly institutionalised. In the first decade after 1949 there was constant criticism of couples who had rushed into rash or hasty marriages (*caoshuai jiehun*) without taking the opportunity to get to know each other in a period of courtship. Courtship patterns were rituals often foreshortened into a brief series of occasions, or even to a single visit to the theatre, an opera or movie before marriage took place. An article in *Renmin Ribao* in 1957 reported the results of a sequence of enquiries at street offices in Tientsin where marriages were registered, and there it was found that some couples had rushed into marriage after the cursory acquaintance of one dance, one or two movies or a few strolls in the park (RMRB 9 March 1957). Other articles have reported the cases of couples who embarked upon marriage after a brief encounter at the movies or even in a railway ticket-office (KMRB 27 February 1957). The stroll, visit or entertainment had itself become a symbol of courtship signifying a level of understanding on the part of the couple which often was not present. In the larger cities today, observers report that it is not an uncommon sight to see young couples enjoying each other's company. On my first trip to Guangdong in 1977 I was greatly surprised by the amount of free association between the sexes in Guangzhou, where couples were openly to be seen in the streets or in the park. According to my own observations and those of others, this intimacy of association contrasts strongly with that evident in the cities of the north of China and in rural areas. In rural areas, pre-marital rituals more commonly take the form of a betrothal, and even where courtship has become the dominant pre-marital form in the cities it remains at a low level of institutionalisation.

THE PERSISTENCE OF BETROTHAL

A number of rationalisations for the persistence of betrothal are revealed in the case studies. Marriage continues to be conceptualised as a contract between the kin of the bride and the groom and the betrothal gift expresses the intergroup relations. In the case studies, the most frequent explanation given by the older generation for the continuing transfer of the betrothal gift was that it took the form of compensation paid by the wife-receivers to the wife-givers. It compensated the bride's parents for the expenses of the girl's upbringing. Indeed, some parents stated that after many years of raising a daughter they thought they ought to get a handsome sum in return (e.g. ZF 1 October 1963). Negotiations were broken off because the gift did not offer sufficient compensation for the loss of a daughter. In one case study a mother, who had just rejected a betrothal gift because of its low value, exclaimed to her daughter: 'I have raised and brought you up and do you think this little sum of betrothal is enough? In the days of the past at least twice this amount would have been asked for!' (ZQ 19 November 1964). In cases of conflict arising over the value of the gift, the requests of the girl's parents often received the support of most of the village. One girl's parents were greatly dissatisfied with the proffered gifts, saying that they 'had taken great pains for many years with the upbringing of their daughter, and were they now to be given in return so small a present that it was not even enough for the exchange of a pig?' Many of their fellow-villagers thought that the parents were being 'quite reasonable' in their approach, for surely it was not too much for them to ask for a reasonable betrothal present in exchange for a daughter whom they had brought up. In this case the villagers concluded that it was a 'matter of convention' that when a daughter was to be given away in marriage, the groom's parents should give a betrothal gift to show their gratitude to the bride's parents for having raised their future daughter-in-law (NFRB 25 December 1964).

That the older generation felt that investments in daughters should be recouped at marriage is borne out by the fact that it is the parents of daughters rather than those of sons who more often insist on compensation in the form of betrothal gifts. Although some parents of sons thought that the parents of the daughter should be compensated for their loss (ZQ 19 November 1964), many were only too pleased to adopt the new form and thus be relieved of their obligations. One mother of sons said she was very pleased when her son married in the new way for it meant that she didn't have to pay a penny for her son's bride (PC 1 June 1951). Many parents operated a dual standard. Families who insisted on gifts in return for their daughters often encouraged their sons to marry in the new way. Jan Myrdal, in his interviews with one father in Liuling village in the early 1960s, recorded the words of the father who had paid dearly for his wife and who certainly intended to get some of it back when his daughter married. He exclaimed, 'Look at the cost of a daughter!' The same father, however, had allowed all his sons to marry in the new way for this had meant that he did not need to pay anything for his daughters-in-law (Myrdal 1967: 289–90). A similar rationalisation for the persistence of the custom was offered by the future brides themselves. Many appear to have believed that even if they had initiated the negotiations themselves, they should accept betrothal presents to show gratitude to their parents, who had fed and supported them for up to sixteen or twenty years (ZQ 24 April 1962).

Another explanation forwarded for the persistence of the custom was that it had traditionally confirmed the permanent exchange of women between domestic or kin groups. It was claimed that only the transfer of the betrothal gift to the bride's parents could guarantee a sufficient measure of stability in a marriage. This was especially so when the groom's family felt themselves to be disadvantaged in negotiating an alliance. What qualities they lacked could be compensated for by raising the value of the betrothal gift. In areas of poverty and agricultural infertility, the parents of boys had customarily been forced to give large betrothal gifts in order to secure wives for their sons (PC 16 November 1957). In one mountainous area of north Fujian (Fukien) province which had a reputation for its bitter quality of life, the parents of the groom felt most uneasy when the parents of the girl refused to accept the proffered gifts. They feared that the bride would not stay in the mountainous area very long (ZF 1 February 1966).

A more widespread rationalisation, however, for the persistence of the betrothal gift was that in its present reduced form, with its lower value and with the establishment of new economic relations in Chinese society, it had now lost much of its original symbolic meaning and function. What meanings and functions had been implied by the betrothal gift were no longer applicable or valid in contemporary China. Now, it was said that incomes were higher and more secure and the expenditure involved in the betrothal gift was less, therefore the economic pressures on the household were less and the debts incurred to meet the costs of marriage were fewer. Moreover, even the poorest now had access to wives and the costs of betrothal and marriage no longer prejudiced the entry of the poorer families into the marriage market. The persistence of betrothal practices was thought to no longer harm countless numbers of women by holding them responsible for the debts so incurred,* and nor was it considered to be insulting to their status in the new society. Women, equal, economically independent and with new rights to individually contract a free-choice marriage, could no longer be likened to bought goods or to 'a form of private property' to be exchanged at will. Under these circumstances many wondered why they should not indulge in a 'warm pleasantry', merely symbolising good relations between the two families (ZF 1 February 1966).

Even in the 1970s some young people were quoted as saying, 'With bumper harvests in the past two years and with plenty of money and grains, why shouldn't we accept some betrothal gifts?' (RMRB 24 January 1972). Some young people have thought that in the circumstances of better times and lower-value gifts, they would be rather foolish not to ask for something. 'What is wrong in asking for a few gifts from the fellow's family or a small dowry for one's parents?' (Lu Yang 1964:32). Others saw material and social advantages in the persistence of the custom, and while it continued to be the local custom they did not want to be the only ones missing out. 'If when I get married, I ask for betrothal gifts and a dowry, others will not criticise me, but if I wait until after I marry then it won't be so easy to get anything' (Lu Yang 1964:32). Some young women were quoted as saying: 'If other people have all asked for this or that and if I decline to accept anything, will it not reflect on my family's social standing and avoid doing things in a grand style?' (ZQ 19 November 1964).

Against this popular defence, educational materials continued to argue that it still symbolised the 'buying and procuring of women with money and other goods' (ZQ 19 November 1964), and that the meaning attributed to the custom cannot be altered despite the fact that what is now demanded in exchange has sometimes changed in form. The demand for money and jewelry may have become a demand for watches and bicycles, but these gifts, even if voluntarily given, were still seen to be substitutes for the value of the women being exchanged

* In the past many bridegroom's families had been forced to borrow heavily in order to find a sum several times their annual income, and many a bride was said to have received silk in her betrothal gift only to find herself eating chaff after her marriage in order to pay the interest on the debts so incurred.

in marriage (Lu Yang 1964:42–3). Opinion has continued to be divided and the rights and wrongs of the practice debated. When one young girl did reject a betrothal gift she reported that, although she was praised in the media, opinion was somewhat divided in her own village. Some said she had set a good example to other girls, but others thought she was 'foolish' because she didn't take the opportunity to ask for a few sets of clothing as a gift from her husband's family (RMRB 24 January 1972). In 1975 the women in one production brigade described how in 1974 they had still taken the practice for granted as a 'warm pleasantry' or harmless custom. It was not until the anti-Confucius campaign of 1974, when there was a renewed attack on the custom, that they came to recognise that it did liken them to a commodity to be valued and exchanged. As women of new China now engaged in independent economic, political and social activities, and enjoying equal rights with men, they thought this custom, a form of marriage by purchase, should now be broken. To demonstrate their new consciousness of the meaning of the custom, twelve girls of this brigade went in person to return the betrothal gifts to the families of their betrothed but without cancelling their engagements (NCNA 7 March 1975; XyP 10 January 1975).

OBSTACLES TO COURTSHIP

In the competition between the customary and newly recommended pre-marital ritual forms, not only have a number of economic and symbolic explanations rationalised the persistence of the betrothal gifts, but a number of factors have worked against the institutional-isation of courtship as the dominant pre-marital ritual. Some of these factors are inherent within the very definition of the new institution itself. The definition of courtship as outlined in the educational materials following up the law seems to preclude it either as a form of recreation or as a procedure of mate selection, the two commonly held functions of courtship in other cultures. The process whereby individuals awaken their interest in the opposite sex is frequently and cross-culturally viewed as a form of recreation, which at the same time provides opportunities for a trial-and-error intimate and personal acquaintance with a number of potential suitors (Burgess and Locke 1945). Although it does have significant consequences for marriage patterns where mate selection is highly personalised, it may not have any necessary connection with marriage (Lowrie 1951). In contemporary China, however, 'love is a prelude to marriage', and the definition of courtship seems to preclude it both as a recreational form or as a process of mate selection.

Although the new ideology advocates the development of mutual understanding and congeniality in courtship, it recommends that these should be based on the foundations of encouraging each other and helping each other in production, work and study rather than in recreation or through the exchange of gifts. The role models portrayed in the media may conform to this prescription, but it is in their leisure time that most young couples have sought to differentiate courting relations and invest them with a significance distinguishable from the new general ideals of comradeship or friendship. The bases for the bonds of friendship have been described in articles on social relations (ZQ 21 August 1962). One booklet suggested that 'friends ought to be comrades in our socialist society. Sentiment between friends is lofty, and the relationship between one and the other is equal and cooperative, full of solidarity and love. Common ideals, common interests, and common lives of labour and war have bound us tightly together and have created a brand-new comradely relationship between us' (Lu Yang 1964:17). The relations of romantic love and courtship have had to be given a characteristic of their own over and above these ideal 'work-share activities'. How was courtship to be distinguished from the common friendship of comrades? This was the question put to the editors of *Zhongguo Qingnian* by Xing Fei of Heilongjian (Heilungkiang) province (ZQ 16 May 1956). Most young people, resident in urban areas, who have described their courtship in the letters to the media have almost entirely referred to leisure or recreational activities such as taking walks, visiting parks, the cinema, the theatre and sightseeing (GRB 11 September 1962; 5 October 1962; 9 October 1962).

Courtship has also come to be associated with the exchange of gifts, perhaps in the tradition of betrothal practices, to express and differentiate this personal relationship from others. An article in *Zhongguo Qingnian* in 1962 suggested that spending money on amusements or gifts was very common and had come to be associated with the state of 'being in love'. There was even a saying, 'invite the loved one to the restaurant today and the provision stores tomorrow' (ZQ 1 January 1962). One young man in a machinery plant who was courting a fellow-worker found it an expensive business. His girlfriend began to hanker for gifts which she said would publicly express his love for her (GRB 18 September 1962). A boy in Guangzhou who made frequent trips to other provinces was encouraged and indeed expected to bring gifts to please his girlfriend. 'I bought her cotton cloth bags and woollen sweaters from Beijing, fragrant toilet soap and plastic products from Shanghai, a silk umbrella from Hangzhou and an embroidered quilt cover from Changsha'. 'Each of these', he said, 'she received as a token of my love, saying "You truly love me"' (ZQ 1 January 1962). The bestowal of gifts seems to have played no small part in winning consent. A girl worker in a department store was much taken by a young man who bought her some woollen dress material. 'Things like these', she said, 'impress me greatly' (ZF 1 May 1964). It was the common association of courting patterns with recreational activities and the exchange or bestowal of gifts which seems to have led to some censure of the courtship rituals.

In educational materials a high degree of concern with recreational activities was often interpreted to mean a preoccupation with the individual and the private, both of which detracted from the social contribution of young people to the public and the collective, and to the construction of a new society (Qingnian Chubanshe 1953:30). In all the educational materials, participation in study and production took priority over recreation, and public and collective activities took priority over the individual concerns of love and marriage. The sayings, 'Compared with revolutionary work, marriage and love is really a small matter' (ZQ 14 September 1962), 'An individual must try and place love in a secondary position to the revolution in one's life' (ZQ 1 April 1955) and 'Compared with the undertakings we have been called upon to do, marriage after all takes second place' (ZQ 2 February 1963), are all representative of the emphasis of the educational materials. Tensions between the ideal of the educational materials and common practices in courting are revealed in the letters of young people to the media.

Young couples, and especially students, seem to have experienced some conflict between personal and political priorities and find it difficult to distribute their time and attention to both sets of activities. Frequently they experience some disquiet as they embark on courtship and they look for ways to resolve the conflict. For example, one couple found they just could not participate in so many collective activities if they were to see and get to know each other. They felt 'it was better for us to be alone together', even though this meant that they were segregated from the other students for much of the time. A second couple who spent much time together said that they had to constantly remind themselves not to spend too much time on courtship or it would detract from their studies. A third couple found it difficult to concentrate on any activity which did not involve the other. They tried to limit their meetings to once a week, but the male partner reported that though 'his eyes might be on the book, his heart was already at the theatre or the park' (ZQ 16 June 1963). Sometimes the conflict in priorities seems to have made for dissension between the courting partners and eventually to the dissolution of the partnership. A girl working in a store became dissatisfied with her courting partner once he had shown a certain reluctance to continuously keep her company by strolling in the park or attending the cinema. He thought such activities would inevitably affect their work. He was soon replaced by a young man who better knew 'how to please me!' He constantly took her out to restaurants or for a stroll in the street or the park (ZF 1 May 1964).

Courting behaviour also implied a certain degree of commitment on the part of the couple. This was not only the result of its novelty as a pre-marital ritual and the exaggerated amount of social recognition which it received due to the gossip, talk and joking which it aroused, but also because it was officially conceived of as less a procedure of mate selection than as a form of anticipatory socialisation for marriage. In courtship, young couples were exhorted to develop the habit of practising thrift in anticipation of marriage and establishing a household, and to derive mutual satisfaction and support in solving life-long occupational, livelihood and study problems. One educational article in *Zhongguo Qingnian* stressed that love and courtship were only the prelude to marriage or the common life of a man and a woman, and above all that life companions needed to develop a relationship which would enable them to find mutual support for a long and not entirely smooth life after marriage. The lines of a Russian poem were quoted to illustrate the ends of courtship:

> Life is not idling under the bright moon,
> Nor is a sigh on a long bench.
> Anything may happen! There'll be mud as well as wind or snow.
> For it will take a whole lifetime to live together.

Love is just like a beautiful song,
But this song is not so easy to compose.

(ZQ 14 September 1962)

The expression of these sentiments is indicative of the tendency to play down the significance of courtship as anything other than preparation for marriage itself. For instance, as one article stressed, the mystification of romantic love was to be avoided and no encouragement was to be given to the full enjoyment of the sweetness of love for its own sake (GRB 22 November 1962). This direct link between courtship and marriage has led to a curtain amount of tension among young people as to the degree of commitment implied by embarking on the rituals of courtship. The procedures for choosing a marriage partner from several candidates, or courtship with more than one partner, were sometimes confused with 'fickleness of love' (*luantan lianai*) or a tendency to swing with the wind and 'abandon the old and embrace the new' (*xixin yanjiu*): both were constantly criticised forms of social behaviour. For instance, a girl in Shanghai, cited as having 'courted' as many as five or six young men in one year, was criticised for the habit of 'loving the new and abandoning the old' (ZQ 16 May 1956). A worker in Nanjing who apparently advocated courting a number of girls 'so that he could pick a loved one to his liking from a great many prospects' was given the nickname of 'one toying with love' (GRB 5 October 1962).

A lengthy case-history of a courtship cited in *Zhongguo Qingnian* in 1956 became the occasion of widespread debate on the stability to be ascribed to courtship and its relation to marriage. The debate was occasioned by a letter which a couple wrote to the editor describing how they had both been the subjects of 'criticism'. She, because after promising to try and cultivate her love for another man and finding she couldn't, had fallen in love with the young male correspondent. She had therefore been accused of taking the new as she got tired of the old. The young man had been criticised for butting in and edging his rival out or sabotaging the love of another, which was metaphorically stated as 'undermining the foundation of the wall'. Apparently *Zhongguo Qingnian* was flooded with letters as a result of the publication of their case-history. Many questioned the definition of courtship as a permanent relationship leading directly to marriage. Was this not abandoning the principles of 'free will' or voluntariness which were the foundations of the new form of free-choice marriage or marriage by self-determination? To carry an initial decision through however much it had turned sour was surely no different from the feudal concept of 'virtue' based on the premise that 'love should never change'. Surely it was not wrong to change one's mind even though an initial choice had been made? Other letters countered the above arguments and suggested that a change of mind was indeed wrong and that the girl should be criticised for changing her mind after promising to try and love another young man. Some admitted that they frankly did not know which view was correct: to hold to a given promise, carefully or carelessly made, or to correct an error and make a new choice (ZQ 16 May 1956). A village reader on love and marriage published in 1964 did recognise two possible outcomes of courtship, one that led to marriage and another that led to its break-up. In a forced relationship, the author said, it is often the case that 'the melon that is gathered by force is not sweet' and that the rejected often feel cheated as a result and suffer. In these circumstances a break in relations should not be averted. But the same booklet then immediately went on to criticise 'fickleness of love' which was characterised by changeability and untrustworthiness (*zhaosan musi*), thereby hardly failing to associate change with frivolity (Lu Yang 1964:19).

Common patterns of pre-marital behaviour are characterised by a recognisable combination of elements of both betrothal and courtship. In the rural areas certain factors have encouraged the persistence of the betrothal rituals and gifts, although these have been slightly modified by mechanisms providing for the consent of the parties. In the urban areas, courtship has become the dominant pre-marital ritual although, despite constant encouragement, it has mainly remained at a low level of institutionalisation and its form has been modified by the persistence of betrothal, the history of segregation and the tensions within the definition of courtship itself. In both rural and urban areas the shapes which the pre-marital ritual forms take directly reflects patterns of control of the marriage negotiations. Where the older generation and kin groups initiate the negotiations, their preliminary phases usually take the shape of betrothal; where the younger generation personally take over the initiation of the negotiations, courtship, albeit often at a low level of institutionalisation, becomes the dominant pre-marital ritual. The forms which the pre-marital rituals take are not only a reflection of these controls, but at the same time the rituals serve as a means to emphasise and endorse the dominant patterns of generational controls.

4

AGE AT MARRIAGE

'When a man is old enough, he should get married; when a girl is old enough she should be given away' (Lu Yang 1964:23; ZQ 12 April 1962). This old maxim, said to have been handed down from generation to generation during the past several thousands of years, is reported to have a new meaning in China today. A most important component of marriage reforms has to do with raising the age at which marriage takes place. The advocacy of late marriage (*wanhun*) has become a major state policy, with consequences for demography and the reforms of other social institutions which have been recognised and encouraged by the government (RMRB 30 January 1971). At a provincial conference held in 1974 it was emphasised that:

After establishing a socialist mode of production, late marriage along with planned parenthood constituted a profound revolution in the realm of the superstructure. Since it was a matter of fundamental importance in changing existing habits and customs and transforming China, undertaking this reform was of great and far-reaching significance for the individual and the nation. It has constituted a set policy of the Party for the period of socialist revolution and construction. (SWB 20 November 1974)

Of the policies designed to introduce reforms into marriage, no aspect has been so widely publicised as the new age of marriage.

The new ideology distinguishes between the statutory age of marriage and the appropriate (*shidu*) age of marriage. The Marriage Law stipulated that 'a marriage can be contracted only after the man has reached 20 years of age and the woman 18 years of age'. The new legal age contrasts with previous codes and was an increase of two years over the most recent legal code, the Family Law of 1931 which had stated that marriage between a male under 18 and a female person under 16 was voidable (Article 980). The new statutory age of marriage was reported to have been worked out by the government as a compromise between the principle of opposing early marriage and due regard for the consciousness of the population, who had long been socialised into practising early marriage. It has often been said by the government that one way of raising the age of marriage would have been to simply alter the statutory age, but this solution was rejected by the government on the grounds that to raise the legal age of marriage was to raise it beyond the level of awareness or consciousness evident in Chinese society. As one article explained, 'If we go beyond the consciousness of the masses by fixing the marriage age at too high a level, that will also be improper' (GRB 7 November 1962). The legal age was thus established as the minimum age of marriage and was contrasted to the 'appropriate' age which was defined as 'the age worked out by the young men and women themselves according to their own circumstances and in full awareness of the advantages of late marriage and the disadvantages of early marriage' (GRB 7 November 1962).

The government has frequently stated that the custom of early marriage (*zaohun*) was unlikely to disappear of its own accord or within a short period of time, and the aim of the educational materials circulated during the campaigns to raise the age of marriage has been to persuade people of the advantages of late marriage. The tone of these materials was to be persuasive rather than forceful, and wanton interference or intervention in the affairs of others was not to be encouraged. As one article remarked 'this is a problem of their own and the young people must handle it themselves,' and 'It is absolutely incorrect to look upon love as if it were a criminal act and penalise lovers or obstruct young people's wedding plans as this would be nothing but a reflection of the feudal concept' (ZX 3 April 1956). Instead;

it is up to each young person himself or herself to, or not to, get married or to be in love. Provided two people's love is moral, provided they are both willing to get married and provided their marriage is in accordance with the provisions of the Marriage Law, nobody should normally interfere with or obstruct them. Nor should people discriminate against or jeer at young people who are already in love or who are already married. (ZQ 1 June 1962)

The first aim was to raise the levels of awareness and consciousness in order that young people would delay their marriage consciously and willingly. Although the advocation of late marriage is linked with the campaign for birth control in articles on population, in the educational materials for young people the advantages of late marriage are nearly always stated in terms of individual benefits to do with education, choice of marriage partner, physiological development and economic independence. Qualitatively the appropriate age of marriage is associated with the age of physical maturity, the age at which education and training may be completed, the ability to provide a reliable and adequate basis of material support and the age at which a thoughtful exercise of marital choice may occur.

THE APPROPRIATE AGE OF MARRIAGE

Now that marriage is to be negotiated on the basis of self-determination and free choice it was considered to be imperative that young people approach it 'with a great deal of care and in all seriousness' (SRB 8 March 1958). A certain maturity was deemed to be necessary if partners were to sufficiently concern themselves with each other's thinking, personality and character and make a mature assessment of desirable qualities. It was argued that young people just out of school were less likely to know their own minds so that 'a proposed mate might be ideal today, but not be so tomorrow' (ZX 3 April 1956). Moreover they may be tempted to indulge in romantic love based on the principle that 'love is supreme' (*lianai zhishang*) or is the central and primary purpose of life. They may simply regard marriage as a means of self-gratification and such a relationship, based on no common interests and goals, was not easily consolidated and developed (Henan ACDWF 1955:69; ZQ 6 September 1956). The younger the marriage partners, the less likely they were to be economically independent. Many may be still studying and receiving no wages, and those who were in employment were likely either to be apprentices or among the less skilled, whose incomes barely covered the living expenses of a single person. They were warned that marriage inevitably entailed an increase in living expenses, no matter how small the new family might be, and that financial difficulties could seriously affect family relations and lead to discord.

Young people were also encouraged to delay their marriage on physiological grounds. Numerous articles have suggested that those who have reached the legal age of marriage have not yet attained the age of full physical maturity. An old proverb was quoted which said that at 22 and 23 one leaps a little (grows a little in height) and at 24 or 25 one blows a little (grows in strength). Although women might enter puberty at 12 to 14 years and men at 14 to 16 years, the articles point out that in the case of young girls neither the endocrine system nor the calcification of bones was complete and for both sexes the formation of the epithelial cells of the cerebrum might not be completed until 23 to 25 years of age. A second group of reasons for delaying marriage had to do with the claimed impairment to health of excessive sexual activity at a young age (ZQ 12 April 1962). Youth was said to be a time when the sexual impulse is relatively strong and the power of restraint relatively weak, and this was thought to have serious consequences for sexual compatibility and harmony in married life and for physical well-being and growth.

Late marriage has primarily been linked to the regulation of fertility and is widely quoted as a means of limiting population growth (Lu Yang 1964: 30), but there is also much emphasis on the benefits of late marriage to the health of the mother and child. The old saying that early and too many childbirths are harmful to mothers, that they are 'weak and feeble before they are really old' was said to have a scientific basis (NFRB 15 May 1962). If children were born to mothers of immature physical development, not only the health of the mothers but also that of the children would suffer. Several eminent physicians have written articles stating that from the standpoint of obstetrics and gynaecology, the most suitable age for childbirth was 25 years (ZF 1 April 1957; ZQ 21 July 1962). In making this statement they were directly countering the popular belief that childbirth was more difficult after the age of 20 and conception was more difficult for women in their thirties (J. Chen 1973: 87).

Above all though, youth is portrayed as the 'golden age' of an individual's life-cycle, when all of its physical advantages make for the easy acquisition of knowledge and skills. Just as the best moment for making a plan for a day is in the morning, and the best season for making a plan for the year is in the spring, so the best moments for formulating a life's plan is reckoned to be in youth (ZQ 10 May 1962). Young people are exhorted to concentrate on learning skills and techniques, reading books and seeking truths, and are reminded that without solid foundations, significant mansions cannot later rise (GRB 15 November 1962). When energetic youth have all the opportunities to develop their individual skills and political understanding and contribute to socialism, why should they choose early marriage and be tied down to children and household affairs? (GRB 22 November

1962). Early marriage was thought to direct the previous energy and attention of young persons, and especially young women, away from work and studies and towards the interests of their 'narrow family' and domestic cares. Besides young women, students also have been singled out as a group especially liable to suffer from the burden of an early marriage. They were reminded that the annual expenditure of one university student is equivalent to the fruits of labour of six or seven peasants toiling throughout the whole year (ZQ 21 July 1962). They were thus encouraged to avoid marriage at a time when they 'were energetic and eager to learn and could devote themselves to their studies in an effort to master more knowledge, be concerned with the political life of the country, cherish their own ideals and train and advance themselves in every possible way' (ZQ 1 June 1962). One national heroine who had delayed marriage was said to have established the correct priorities for all young people. 'In the past', she said, 'there was a proverb which said "found a family and establish a career"'. She felt that young people ought to reverse this order and 'establish a career' first and then 'found a family' (Lu Yang 1964: 10).

The literature circulated to young people to persuade them of the advantages of late marriage cited the experience of numerous negative models who had been once energetic and active in studies, at their work or in political study, but who after marriage had been beset by domestic, familial and physical problems. For instance, those who were studying suddenly found after marriage that household chores prevented them from concentrating in classes or studying after classes or during holidays, and that their once-good study records and relations with other students declined. Others lacking sufficient financial support to clothe, house and feed themselves were forced to turn to relatives for help (SRB 8 March 1958). Still others who married young found that early and excessive sexual activity affected their central nervous system, resulting in neurasthenia, low spirits, headaches and discomfort (ZQ 12 April 1962). Underlying all the literature on the age of marriage is the assumption that childbirth will very closely follow on from marriage and it is this which will primarily affect the ideological, educational progress of young people, increase their domestic burden, harm the health of both mother and child and stretch financial resources to their limits. The advocacy of late marriage is usually stated qualitatively in terms of these concrete conditions and by listing its advantages, but on several occasions the

Table 4. *Recommended ages of marriage in the People's Republic of China*

Years		
Men	Women	Source
25–26	23–24	ZQ 6 September 1956
28–32	22–26	GRB 28 June 1962
25–29	23–27	ZQ 12 April 1962
25–29	23–25	ZQ 21 July 1962
25–29	23–27	ZQ 9 May 1963
25–30	23–28	Lu Yang 1964: 28

educational materials have provided quantitative guides and stated the recommended age of marriage.

These figures (table 4), which are well above the legal age of marriage, indicate that the minimum recommended ages of marriage have not noticeably increased over the years, although there has been a gradual increase in the upper limits. They show some differences in the recommended ages for men and women. The average recommended age for men is 28 to 29 years, which is three to four years older than the average age of 25 years recommended for women, which may suggest a recommended age difference of approximately 3 years between spouses. What is perhaps the most impressive factor about these figures is the breadth of their range. The range for women is a total of seven years between 22 and 28 years of age and for men a total of eight years between 25 and 32 years of age. This width of range may possibly be accounted for by the difference in appropriate ages given for young people in urban compared to rural areas. It is general policy that people in the cities must be urged to marry even later than those in the countryside (SWB 20 November 1974), and more recent figures given to visitors in China suggest that a range of 23 to 25 years in rural areas and 25 to 28 years in urban areas is recommended (Keeson 1975: 19; Johnson 1976: 45). This difference is also reflected in the ages of role models. For instance, Weng Yujiao and Wen Jinxiu were village girls who delayed their marriages until they were in their late twenties (ZQ 1 August 1964; RMRB 12 June 1973), whereas factory worker Yi Shizhuan was 33 years old at marriage (ZF 1 June 1963).

The advocacy of the 'appropriate' age of marriage has brought the

Table 5. *Age of marriage in Republican China (Percentage distribution)*

Years	Male	Female
Under 14	4.8	5.4
15–19	40.3	66.8
. . . . .	. . .	. .
20–24	39.4	25.4
25–29	10.1	2.3
30 and over	5.4	0.1
Total	100.0	100.0

(Source: Chiao 1934:28)

newly recommended ages into conflict with customary ages of
marriage, in that the age of marriage in the past seems to have
predominantly coincided with the new legal age of marriage rather
than with the newly defined appropriate age. Field studies in the early
part of this century record much variation in the age of marriage from
village to village,* and the age of marriage doubtless varied according
to sex, local custom and socio-economic status. But overall, surveys
conducted in China in the earlier part of this century suggest that the
average age of marriage may well have coincided with the new legal
age. In one study of persons married between 1929–31 in 12,456 farm
families in 22 localities and 11 provinces in China, the average age
of marriage for China as a whole was calculated to be 20.78 years for
boys and 18.47 years for girls (see table 5). In the families resident
in north China it was found that marriage was at an earlier age than
in south China, where 62.2 per cent of men and 79.6 per cent of
women, compared to 46.4 and 67.5 per cent respectively, were
married before the age of 19 years (Chiao 1934:28, 31). According
to the same survey, 45.1 per cent of men and 72.2 per cent of women
were married close to the new legal ages, and only 15.5 per cent of

* In Kaihsienkung village 92 per cent of the girls and 75 per cent of the boys were
married before 16 years of age (Fei 1939:40, 52). In Phenix village the girls were
married at an average age of close to 19, while boys were a little younger (Kulp
1925:170, 175). In Taitou village the average age was about 20 for both boys and
girls, with no cases of boys under 19 or girls under 17 recorded or known to the author
(M. Yang, 1945:113). In Kao Yao the average age of marriage ranged from 14 to
20 (Osgood 1963:279). In West Town the lowest age approved for marriage was
17 years for males and 16 for females, but the majority of boys and girls married two,
three or four years later than that (Hsu 1948:88).

men and an even smaller proportion of women married at the approximate average age recommended in the new ideology.

In the absence of recent national statistics, it is necessary to turn to more localised and impressionistic data, such as local surveys and case studies reported in the media, to ascertain both the actual age of marriage in China today and, most important, the ages at which the young people feel they are expected to look for a spouse.

AGE AT MARRIAGE

The first surveys of the 1950s reflected the traditional custom of child and early marriage. For instance, in 1953 it was reported that in a village of nearly one hundred households in one county in Hunan province, with the exception of one eighteen-year-old girl, all the girls above 13 years of age were married (NCNA 9 February 1953). In 1956 at the time of the first campaign against early marriage, it was reported that by and large young people got married as soon as they reached the legal age of marriage. The average age of marriage in a factory in Beijing (Peking) was a little more than nineteen years of age and some students were barely out of middle school when they started their wedded life (ZQ 6 September 1956). One teacher taking a third-year class in a junior department of a girl's school in Wuhan municipality reported that out of forty students aged from 15 to 19 years, two were married and six or seven were talking of marriage (ZQ 16 November 1956). In the same year, the magazine *Zhongguo Qingnian* undertook a survey of the age of marriage among factory workers. It made the general observation that although very few young persons got married below the legal age, many got married as soon as they reached the legal age. A survey of workers from a cotton mill and from a chemical plant showed that forty-three out of fifty-five, and twenty-four of the twenty-nine female workers were married before they reached 21 years of age. The average age of marriage was reckoned to be 19 years of age. The survey concluded that an absolute majority of young people married early, and that this tendency was especially marked among female workers (ZQ 6 September 1956).

By the 1960s certain patterns of behaviour began to emerge which differed for urban and rural areas. In rural areas young people seemed to marry at or near the legal ages or somewhere between these ages and their early twenties. After a campaign for late marriage in one village it was reported that girls tended to get married between 22 and 24 years of age, although circumstances sometimes encouraged earlier marriage (Myrdal 1967:111). In other villages in 1964 it was reported that it was quite rare for girls in their early twenties to remain unmarried and that most girls were married and had one or two children by the time they were 23 years of age (ZQ 1 August 1964). In a Henan rural village in the 1970s, marriages were still negotiated early or nearer the legal age (J. Chen 1973:80). In one case a couple were married although the boy, at 19 years of age, was still below the legal age. Despite the refusal of the government administration to register the marriage, the boy's mother had encouraged the couple to live together as man and wife (J. Chen 1973:78). A county cadre in Guangdong province told two Canadian anthropologists that in the country as a whole, about one-third of the couples married near to the recommended ages of 23 and 25; in one-third of the cases one of the pair is younger, and in the remaining one-third, neither one of the couple has reached the recommended age (Johnson 1976:45).

JIANG VILLAGE

In Huadong Commune in which Jiang village is located, there had been no special campaigns to introduce late marriage, but informants thought there was general support for raising the age of marriage. One of the leaders of the commune thought that now, young people were married around the ages of 24 to 26, and certainly no earlier than 24 for men and 23 for girls. When the age of marriage was surveyed in the one village, of all those now resident there and married in the 1970s, the average age of the ten couples was 26.3 years for men and 24.4 years for women. These figures (in table 6) are higher than the average age of marriage for previous decades. The age of marriage was obtained for all those men and women under the age of 60 years and a comparison by decade would seem to suggest that there has been a general increase in the age of marriage; see table 7.

Where both partners were still alive it was possible to compute age differences between spouses for the previous thirty years. The average age difference was 2.8 years and in all cases except two the wife was younger than the husband. The age differences between spouses had not altered significantly over the past three decades; see table 8. In many households there were sons and daughters living at home in their early- to mid-twenties who were not yet married; see table 9.

Table 6. *Age of marriage: Jiang village*

Year of Marriage	Age	
	Male	Female
1977	29	29
1974	30	26
	27	26
1973	25	26
	26	22
1971	24	20
1970	24	21
	26	22
	26	23
1970s	28	28

Table 7. *Age of marriage: a comparison by decade: Jiang village*

Decade of marriage	No. of marriages	Average age (male)	Average age (female)
1970s	10	26.3	24.4
1960s	9	25.0	21.2
1950s	3	22.1	21.1

Table 8. *Age difference of spouses: Jiang village*

Age difference (years)	Numbers
0	2
1	7
2	3
3	5
4	4
5	2
6	3

Table 9. *Age and marital status: Jiang village*

Age	Single	Married	Widowed	Total
0–9	39	–	–	39
10–19	23	–	–	23
20–29	23	12	–	35
30–39	–	22	1	23
40–49	–	8	–	8
50–59	–	8	3	11
60–69	–	2	4	6
70–79	–	–	1	1
80 and over	–	–	1	1
	85	52	10	147

In the other two villages where interviews were undertaken, the average ages of the six couples married in the 1970s was 26.3 years for men and 24.5 years for women. These figures all seemed higher than previous documentation on the age of marriage would have suggested, and the actual ages of marriage largely fell within the appropriate age categories. The fact that the sample is made up of wealthy communes in the Pearl River delta and ranges between 15 and 40 km from the city of Guangzhou may have some bearing on their average ages of marriage.

In the urban areas it seems that young people might well wait until their mid-twenties before they get married. Most of the role models either wait until their late twenties or early thirties to initiate marriage negotiations, but many letters to the media indicate that urban correspondents are more likely to marry when they are in their mid-twenties. The most significant correspondence on the age of marriage was aroused by the publication of educational articles advocating late marriage in *Gongren Ribao* (Workers' Daily) in 1962. The editors of that paper revealed in November 1962 that they had received in response to their articles nearly five hundred letters weighing up the advantages and disadvantages of late marriage, and subsequently they published a selection of these in a discussion entitled 'Is it good or bad to get married early?' In these letters, the urban correspondents were divided between those who had got married at 23 and 24 years of age and those who at the ages of 25 and 26 remained unmarried and think that this age is still too young for marriage (GRB

18 September 1962; 5 October 1962). From my own personal observations among cadres and professional workers in their late twenties in the summer of 1973, it was evident that many of this group were still unmarried at this age. During my second visit to China, questions on the age of marriage were asked of those who lived in a Canton factory housing complex and an urban housing estate and who were married in the 1970s. The average age of the four couples was 28.5 years for men and 25.75 years for women. The available evidence does begin to allow for a continuum to be drawn up between the legal and appropriate ages of marriage and to begin to correlate actual ages of marriage with rural and urban social fields. However, the dominant feature of correspondence columns in newspapers and magazines is that in both rural and urban areas young people experience considerable pressure to marry as soon as they reach the legal age of marriage, and continue to feel this pressure until they have actually married.

PRESSURES TO MARRY

Many correspondents refer to the pressures of public opinion and particularly to those from parents, kin and neighbours in favour of early marriage, or at least against the delay of marriage or late marriage. In many cases the young people described the pressures that they experienced once they reached their early twenties. One correspondent noted that all young people over the age of 20 become the subject of gossip if they remained unmarried (GRB 9 October 1962). One young man who was 25 said he had reached the age when he had become 'desperate about the possibility of remaining a bachelor if he did not settle down fast' (RMRB 15 November 1956). Many of the role models who delayed their marriage until their late twenties said that they had been under constant pressure to marry since their early twenties (ZF 1 June 1963; ZQ 1 August 1964). Several correspondents generalised from their own experience and referred to the importance of this social pressure in preventing a rise in the age of marriage. They reported that from their experience and observations it was very difficult for young people to withstand the persuasive influence of others, particularly that of friends, parents and kin.* Several described how relatives and friends had exerted such

* In a few cases young people experienced unidirectional pressures in that the influence of parents and kin in favour of late marriage coincided with the recommendations

pressure. Three young factory workers wrote that they had discussed the question at length and concluded that the policy of late marriage might theoretically rest on sound ideological and economic foundations, but in actual practice waiting until the age of 30 for the man and around 25 for the woman was just not acceptable to most persons. 'Although some people think of getting married later', they said, 'a number of persons around them will often chide them, put pressure on them, or jeer at them and express pity as if they have done something wrong' (GRB 18 September 1962). Another correspondent warned that in his experience the difficulties of withstanding social pressures exerted in favour of early marriage should not be underrated (GRB 27 September 1962). The pressure from parents, kin and peers has continued into the 1970s, and in 1973 cadres from Guangdong province suggested that the pressure of parents in favour of early marriage was still a major deterrent against instituting late marriage (Johnson 1976:45).

Although young people in both rural and urban areas experienced social pressure against delaying their marriages, the sources of this demand differ. In rural areas the pressure was predominantly exerted by parents who, with the support of kin and neighbours, wished to find wives for their sons in order to acquire the services of a daughter-in-law or to enjoy their grandsons. Parents often expressed their opposition to late marriage in terms of their desire to 'drink a cup of tea provided by a daughter-in-law' (Johnson 1976:45), or with the folk-saying, 'plant seedlings early and you will enjoy a rice crop early; have a daugher-in-law early and you will enjoy happiness [grandsons] early' (GRB 11 September 1962). Indeed, parents and kin often encouraged young people to marry early in the hope of enjoying their grandchildren, and particularly grandsons. One 23-year-old boy, the only son of quite elderly parents who were increas-

of the new ideology. The parents of a 20-year-old road maintenance worker who was courting persuaded him not to have a girlfriend too early for it would only divert him from his studies. They had said, 'What girl would love you if your work is poor and your thought backward?' After listening to them and giving the matter some consideration he felt that their advice was very reasonable and that they really cared for him (GRB 11 September 1962). In another case it was the older brother who attempted to persuade his younger brother to postpone his pending marriage and concentrate his efforts on study, although the younger brother did reject his advice in the end (GRB 27 September 1962). These cases, though, are far outweighed by the number in which parents, kin, neighbours and peers exerted pressure in favour of early marriage.

ingly worried about his marriage prospects and the birth of grandchildren, described how they and their relatives and friends had zealously introduced him to a number of girls they knew well (GRB 9 October 1962). Another young man reported that he had been unable to withstand the influence of his parents and had got married at an early age. His family had openly wanted a male child early in line with the custom of 'finding a wife for one's son early so that one can enjoy a comfortable life early' (GRB 27 September 1962). In Upper Felicity village in 1970 it was the ardent wish of the boy's mother to have a grandson which caused her to defy the law and the government administration and bring a wife into the household for her under-age son (J. Chen 1973:78).

Some parents expressed their preferences for early marriage in terms of bringing another labourer into the household. One mother initiated early marriage negotiations on behalf of her son on the grounds that it was time she had some extra help in the household (J. Chen 1973:80). A transportation worker who was less than 19 years of age reported how he was encouraged to marry despite his young age by kinsmen and friends, who, 'seeing that he was without help in everyday life', introduced him to girlfriends and persuaded him that it was time 'to set up a small family' (GRB 14 July 1962). It was not only sons who were pressured to provide descendants; girls too found their parents often became anxious as they approached marriageable age and expressed their preference for early marriage in terms of a wish for grandsons (ZF 1 June 1963).

By far the most important factor operating in urban areas against the adoption of the appropriate age of marriage is the fear that, unless young people find a prospective spouse early and while they are young, they will indeed miss out. Age itself is perceived to be an important criterion in mate selection. Many of the letters reveal a great deal of anxiety, among both those of the appropriate age who now find difficulty in searching for a suitable mate and among the younger correspondents who fear a declining field of desirable mates as they get older. These fears are often induced by parents, kin and especially peers. The following examples of this type of pressure are taken from several different letters. 'You are not very young, you should start looking for a mate' (GRB 16 October 1962). One twenty-year-old was advised by his workmates to look for his girlfriend right now. 'When you grow several years older, you will find it difficult to get one' (GRB

73

11 September 1962). One 26-year-old correspondent reported that he and his friends felt greatly pressured by the folk-saying: 'a man cannot find his mate when he is old, and a woman is no longer wanted when she is old' (GRB 18 September 1962). A similar folk-saying, that a 'woman past the age of 20 and men past the age of 25 need no longer think of finding suitable and compatible mates', was reported by one girl to be commonly cited in her factory (*ibid.*). A 24-year-old technician with a number of skills and educational qualifications was constantly told that 'it will be too late to get married when one is a little older, nobody will be after you when you reach the age of 30' (*ibid.*). One set of parents advised their 21-year-old son, 'You must grasp the right moment for handling your marriage problem. When you grow older, the young, beautiful and progressive girls will have boyfriends already so you will eventually be unable to find an ideal wife.' These words sounded very reasonable to the young steel-worker and as a result he was very much worried that if he delayed his marriage he might not be able to find his ideal mate in the future (ZQ 28 July 1964). These types of social pressure were commonly cited and some young correspondents reported that as a result of conflicting pressures they had become preoccupied with their mating problems. One young boy said he had become so bewildered and confused that he was finding it difficult to study in the daytime or to sleep well at night (*ibid.*).

The conflict between the demands of the new ideology and the influence of peers, parents and kin is particularly acute among those who had been influenced by the educational campaigns and were determined to postpone their marriages, that is until the problems of those older than themselves who were still looking for a mate caused them to question that decision. Where the correspondent's reference groups include such a category, the correspondent experiences much anxiety and is greatly tempted to reconsider the original decision to postpone his marriage. Some of the letters merely imply the influence of such a reference group. The older workmates of one twenty-year-old kept telling him that he should look for his mate now as it is much more difficult to look for a mate later (GRB 11 September 1962). Another letter, however, states the problem particularly clearly. The young male writer says that after having read some of the educational articles in the papers he has learned that many advantages can be reaped from late marriage, 'yet', as he goes on to say:

in my mind there is still some worry and anxiety that I may not be able to get a wife when I grow old. Many of my male comrades around the age of 30 have already built for themselves a certain foundation either with respect to work or study or economic power, and conditions really permit them to fall in love and get married. As a matter of fact, they do want to fall in love and get married. However, girls do not wish to fall in love with men at their age. Girls are unhappy when they are told that their boyfriends are men of around thirty. 'Who would marry a man who has already lived half of his life?' they would say. Unable to find a wife, these men become pessimistic and disappointed, and regret they have wasted their youth. I am going to be 26 soon, and I still feel it is a little bit too early to get married at that age. I want to think of my marriage when I reach 30. Yet I am worried that I may be like these comrades. What should I do? (*ibid.*)

Another correspondent expressed similar fears. He was nearly 26 and, though he thought it seemed a bit early to get married, he and a number of friends had lately all become vexed and worried by the difficulties experienced by those who were older than themselves in finding a suitable mate. 'What shall I do', he says, 'if I fail to find my mate when I grow older year after year? After pondering the matter, I am in conflict with myself and do not know what to do' (GRB 18 September 1962).

The correspondence columns reveal that it is not so much the fear of remaining single that influences young people so much as finding an 'ideal' or 'suitable' mate or a 'good prospect'. They rarely elaborate in this context what they mean by 'ideal' or 'suitable', although the words young, beautiful and progressive feature regularly. (For common definitions of 'ideal' and 'suitable', see chapter 5.) There is some indication that the conflict between raising the age of marriage and age as a criterion of choice has brought the older and younger youths into competition for a common pool of girls. One correspondent, herself a school teacher, complained in the media that older government cadres and members of the army constantly sought out girl students as objects of their attention and looked upon schools as a source of potential mates. She thought that because they were older and therefore experienced more difficulty in finding a mate, they were tempted to court younger girls who would be less discerning or discriminating than their older and more culturally advanced counterparts (ZQ 16 November 1956). College students certainly felt that there was cause for anxiety if they had not found a mate among the many boys and girls at college. They thought it would be much more difficult to find a suitable mate once they had been assigned to a work place (ZQ 16 June 1963).

It seems that the anxiety invoked by the fears of finding a suitable mate was particularly acute in urban areas. In the cities the increasing practice of young people taking the initiative in negotiating their own free-choice marriage has meant that they themselves felt the responsibility of making the choice of a suitable marriage partner. There is probably much less anxiety about finding a suitable mate among the young people in rural areas as this choice is still very much the responsibility of the elders of the household, who exercise greater control over the negotiations of marriage. Moreover in urban areas, the gradual abolition of betrothal and its replacement by informal pre-marital courtship has left no system of spouse reservation that is given social recognition. There was thus no means other than marriage to allay the fears of young people that they would not find a good mate or, if they did find one, that they would not lose him or her unless they have actually married. Again, this contrasts with social practices in rural areas where the custom of betrothal, to which there was no legal age barrier, continued to operate a system of reservations which is given social recognition. The custom of betrothal and the fact that marriage negotiations in the rural villages were likely to be concluded nearer the legal than the appropriate age meant that they did not experience the longer period of anxiety expressed by urban correspondents between the legal and actual ages of marriage.

ALTERNATIVE STRATEGIES

In urban areas young people have sometimes reacted to the conflicting demands of the new ideology and the social pressures from peers and kin by adopting alternative strategies. An option commonly mooted was that of falling in love early but delaying marriage for a few years. This resolution was seen not only to allay the anxieties about finding a suitable mate, but, if the courtship was handled well, it would surely also fulfil the aims of the new ideology to promote progress in work, study and political consciousness (GRB 5 October 1962). Several correspondents advocated 'falling in love early'. One did so in order that he might pick a loved one to his liking from a great many eligible mates. 'This time of youth', he said, 'was an opportunity one must not miss. A very good opportunity that may not come again and should be prized' (*ibid.*). Another felt that young people were caught in a dilemma between following the recommendations that they devote their time and energy to work and study and the risk that they may not be able to find suitable mates when they were older. He concluded that the only way out of the dilemma was to fall in love early and handle courtship according to the prescriptions set down in the educational materials (GRB 9 October 1962). The only disadvantage of this strategy was perceived to be the lack of guarantees in this informal arrangement, that is, that one of the partners might change their minds in the intervening period before marriage. A 26-year-old factory worker who wanted to postpone his marriage found that his prospective spouse did not approve of his plans. She feared that he would change his mind in the meantime. If she didn't make sure of him now she might miss out later (GRB 5 October 1962).

A few urban correspondents rejected the idea of late marriage altogether and continued to openly advocate early marriage. One young man who could not withstand the pressures in favour of early marriage got married at the of 20 (ZQ 28 July 1964). This solution was rationalised by another correspondent, who thought that early marriage at least brought peace of mind early and since one is going to get married anyway, does it matter if it is early or late (GRB 16 October 1962)? The assumed correlation between early marriage and early childbirth in the educational materials caused some to think that delayed and planned parenthood would alleviate many of the disadvantages of early marriage (ZQ 1 June 1962; 7 July 1962). One correspondent thought that personal solutions to the problem depended upon individual circumstances. 'It was probably all right', he thought, 'for those who possessed skills and who were drawing higher wages to remain single until they were older, but it was impracticable for those without qualifications' (GRB, 18 September 1962). Others were more sceptical. They suggested that the whole policy of late marriage was thought up by persons who were already married and did not have to worry about getting a wife themselves! 'They just want to comfort us and make us bachelors happy' (GRB 11 September 1962). All the advantages linked to late marriage were said by another correspondent to 'simply give some consolation to those of us who were still single' (GRB 18 September 1962).

Despite such sentiments, one of the most important influences cited by the correspondents to be working in favour of raising the age of marriage has been the campaigns conducted in its support. Most of the letters to the media illustrate that the correspondents were familiar with the advantages of late marriage and especially its implications for study and political progress as listed in the educational materials. Moreover, the emphasis of the educational materials has been adapted to alleviate newly identified fears and anxieties of young people, such as the potential difficulties of finding a mate when older. The educational articles have begun to stress that the more young people devote themselves to study and work, the more they themselves will fall into the category of 'desirable' or 'ideal' mates, and, as more and more young people follow the recommendation to marry late, the less will the fields of desirable mates narrow with age. One letter written in support of late marriage quoted a saying now said to be common in Zhejiang province that just as 'there is a hole for each snail so there is a mate for each person' (GRB 9 October 1962). The influence of the educational materials on young people is mainly implicit in their letters, although in one letter a correspondent explicitly states that at a time when he was wavering in his opinions the educational materials printed in the media were influential in determining his final decision (GRB 18 September 1962). Perhaps the negative examples of those around them were equally influential, for several of the correspondents quoted how they had been influenced by personal acquaintances who had got married, borne children and become preoccupied and burdened with household matters to the detriment of their work and others interests (GRB 11 September 1962; 9 October 1962).

The policy of advocating late marriage has brought the recommended and 'appropriate' ages of marriage into competition with the customary age of marriage. This competition has brought about a wide variation in the actual age at which marriage takes place and has been responsible for the considerable degree of latitude in the designation of the appropriate age of marriage. There is also sufficient impressionistic evidence to suggest that the overall age of marriage is probably increasing, and certainly the data obtained from Jiang village would support this view. The impressionistic evidence also begins to allow for a continuum to be drawn up between the legal and appropriate ages of marriage, and a correlation to be made of actual ages of marriage with patterns of generational control and with rural and urban social fields. In rural areas where the older generation still largely control the negotiations, it seems as if the age of marriage has generally stabilised towards the lower end of the spectrum of 'appropriate' age. In urban areas where the younger generation are more likely to select their own marriage partner, a wide range in the age of marriage has evolved with a significant category of persons waiting until they have reached the recommended ages before they marry. Both patterns represent some rise in the age of marriage. However, the dominant impression to be derived from the data is the considerable degree of disquiet experienced by young people as they reach the statutory age of marriage which is not alleviated until they have actually married. This must provide some measure of the pressures which continue to be exerted against the implementation of the new ideological model.

5

CHOICE OF MARRIAGE PARTNER

Since the establishment of the People's Republic of China, the government has aimed to create an open marriage system in which the only group of persons unequivocally proscribed as marriage partners are those to whom the incest taboo applies. The new Marriage Law attempted to remove as many restrictions as possible from the marriage field in order to establish a broad field of eligible mates and increase the range of choice for each individual. The marriage prohibitions outlined in Article 5 of the Marriage Law thus reduced the number of kin restrictions in a society where the number of prohibitions has been so large that surname exogamy was once the rule. Previously a person was forbidden or at least discouraged from marrying another of the same surname no matter how distant the relationship or different the *zu*, or lineage. Since the number of surnames has been estimated at approximately 500, this rule had succeeded in substantially circumscribing the field of eligibles.* The new Marriage Law of 1950 reduced the exogamous group to lineal blood relatives. In contrast to the Ching dynasty (1644–1911) and the Nationalist Civil Codes (1930), affines were now exempt from this rule. Similarly, collateral relatives by marriage were not included in the new reduced list of prohibitions. As to prohibiting marriage between collateral relatives by blood beyond that of brothers and sisters born of one or both parents, but within the fifth degree of relationship,† the law allowed the question to be determined by custom. This

---

* Although alliances with those of the same surname and with cross-cousins had been prohibited by law, there were some exceptions in practice. Both Freedman (1958:4–5) and Hsu (1948:80) point out that in some parts of China, marriage between persons of the same surname, though not of the same lineage, apparently occurred. Frequently, however, the surname of one of the parties might be slightly altered in the genealogies.

† The term 'five grades' (*wu fu*) includes four generations of paternal and maternal ascendants, four generations of ego's own descendants, and five generations of the descendants of the ascendants mentioned (Meijer 1971:166).

Choice of marriage partner

Table 10. *Preferential marriage in Republican China*

Village	Matrilateral cross-cousin marriages	Patrilateral cross-cousin marriages
Phenix[1]	Permissible	Taboo
Kaihsienkung[2]	Preferable	Permissible but discouraged
Taitou[3]	Permissible but undesirable	Permissible but undesirable
Kao Yao[4]	Preferred (first choice)	Desirable
West Town[5]	Preferred	Permissible

Sources: [1] Kulp 1925:167–8 [2] Fei 1939:50–51 [3] M. Yang 1945–119 [4] Osgood 1963:360 [5] Hsu 1948: 79–85.

concession to custom was probably designed to accommodate the cross-cousin marriage.

Within the prohibited five generations on the maternal side an exception was made from Ching times for the marriage between *biao*, cousins of different surname, such as children of mother's brother and father's sister. These *biao* cousins, as opposed to cousins of the same surname, *tang* cousins, were permitted to marry, and, it seems, may have been encouraged to marry in various historical periods and in certain geographical regions of China (Zhongyang Renmin Zhengfu 1950:98–102). A number of field studies suggest that different forms of cross-cousin marriage were allowed, preferred or discouraged and that matrilateral and patrilateral marriages were not always similarly categorised. The findings of these field studies can be presented as in table 10. It is based on summaries provided by Osgood (1963). In educational materials published after the promulgation of the new Marriage Law, Chen Shaoyu and Li Zuyin argued that *biao* cousin marriage was now allowed and that there was no need to maintain the prohibitions against intermarriage between collaterals. Socio-economic conditions would increasingly remove the conditions encouraging *biao* cousin marriage and in the meantime the matter could be left to custom (Meijer 1971:167; Chang Fan 1952:39–41, 58–66). The remainder of the prohibitions are to do with medical disabilities which might render a person unfit for marriage. Those specifically categorised as such include the sexually impotent, those who suffer from venereal disease, mental disorder and leprosy.

The government planned to broaden the field of eligible marriage partners not only by reducing the number of kin prohibitions, but also

81

by abolishing socio-economic criteria as factors governing the choice of marriage partner. After 1911, legal restrictions no longer prohibited marriage between persons of certain classes or social status, but, despite this legal change, village studies in the 1930s and 1940s suggest that families negotiating a marriage had continued to be guided by the old maxim that 'wooden doors should match wooden doors and bamboo doors with bamboo doors' (C. Yang 1959:29). According to a study of lineage rules and a number of field studies this rule of homogamy was more particularly interpreted to mean that there should be hypergamy for daughters (Fei 1939:50; M. Yang 1945:107; Liu 1959:79). From 1950, however, preferential mates were not only left socially undefined, but the new ideology specifically rejected socio-economic dimensions of preference. 'Freedom of marriage' included the freedom of each person to select or choose a spouse (*zhao duixiang*) not only without unreasonable interference from others, but also unhindered by traditional socio-economic criteria or 'social status, occupation or property' (KMRB 27 February 1957). A passage from Engels was often quoted in support of this aspect of 'free choice'. In *The Origins of the Family, Private Property and the State* he had pointed out that: 'Full freedom in marriage can become generally operative only when the abolition of capitalist production, and of the property relations created by it, has removed all these secondary economic considerations which still exert so powerful an influence on the choice of partner. Then no other motive remains than mutual affection' (1954:77; in RMRB 13 December 1963). Preferential mates were left socially undefined as part of a strategy that was introduced to reduce systems of social stratification. On the one hand, differentials in occupational rating, income and educational levels were to be reduced and on the other hand, socio-economic characteristics such as occupation, income and educational levels were to cease to be so influential in choosing a spouse. Plays such as *Choosing a Son-in-Law*, based on Hunan drama ballad and first produced in 1953, specifically applied these principles to mate selection. In it a mother inadvertently remarks to her daughter that she could never accept a tinker or one in such a menial trade as a son-in-law. 'I would never', she says, 'marry my daughter to a tinker whose face is as black as charcoal'. With a great deal of word-play and humour she comes around to appreciating the value of their contribution to society's welfare and accepting just such a person as a son-in-law (WC 1 February 1966).

Choice of marriage partner

In the new ideology, desirable or preferential mates were defined according to their state of political consciousness. The ideal marriage partners were those who were politically compatible and in ideological agreement (*zhitong daohe*) – literally to be of one mind and purpose – (Henan ACDWF 1955:29–36; Song 1957:9–16). What this new criterion for selecting a spouse (*xuanze airen di biaozhun*) meant in practise was spelt out in a number of educational materials published after the promulgation of the Marriage Law. As one article said 'In choosing a life partner, the fundamental thing is to have a common interest in politics as well as in ideology.' It went on to say that it is the quality of political thinking and attitudes towards labour that are important (ZQ 16 June 1963). A booklet written to advise on these matters stated that the most important condition is the character of the person; finding out whether he/she shares the same political standpoint, ideological views, class sentiments and revolutionary ideals. Therefore there is a need to understand clearly the person's political viewpoint, attitude towards work, style of life and quality of thinking (Lu Yang 1964:115). The preface to a booklet published in 1964 and entitled *Between Husband and Wife* again stressed that the individual parties to the marriage contract should 'respect and love each other' and that common levels of political consciousness should provide the exclusive basis of their relationship. 'In a socialist society', it said:

love between a husband and wife is built on common political thinking and on the foundation of struggling together for the revolutionary cause. The relationship between husband and wife is first of all comradeship and the feelings between them are revolutionary. By revolutionary is meant that politically he should take her as a new comrade-in-arms, in production as well as in work, he should take her as a class sister and labour together, at home he should regard her as a life companion, besides that a couple should respect and love each other, help each other, and encourage each other so as to achieve progress together. (ZF 1 October 1964)

All the recommendations have a common emphasis on the partner's *lichang* (standpoint), *shijie guan* (literally 'world outlook') or political attitudes defined in the broadest possible sense, and make no reference to economic criteria.

The newly prescribed field of eligible mates bounded only by minimal kin restrictions, and the categorisation of preferential mates defined only by their levels of political consciousness and without regard for the traditional socio-economic dimensions of preference,

83

were intended to establish a broad field of eligible mates for each individual and therefore an increasingly wider choice of mates, particularly for those previously disadvantaged in the marriage market for socio-economic reasons. As one article pointed out, 'now there is to be sweet grass everywhere' (ZQ 16 June 1963). However, despite the new law and educational programmes designed to establish a broad field of eligibles and to encourage random mating, a number of restrictions have operated both to limit the field of eligibles and to distinguish certain categories of preferential mates.

THE FIELD OF ELIGIBLE MATES

The principle of surname exogamy has now been formally abandoned, but all the available evidence would suggest that it remains the common practice. In the 1950s, William Geddes, in his brief anthropological study of Kaihsienkung village, did not discover any actual cases of marriage between partners of the traditionally exogamous lineage (*zu*), even though it is now legally allowed. He thought that *zu* exogamy might still be regarded as proper, although no longer obligatory (Geddes 1963:30). His impressions are supported by other materials. An article published in *Nanfang Ribao* makes reference to the fact that parents are sometimes reluctant to give their consent to marriage between members of the same lineage (NFRB 12 May 1962). In a more recent study in a village in Henan, the tradition of surname exogamy continued to reduce the number of eligible spouses in the proximity of the village (J. Chen 1973). In Jiang village in Guangdong that I visited, an informant thought that although it was more common for some young people in the commune to marry those of the same surname, it was still better to marry beyond the five-generation limit.* A survey of all the households in the village itself

* After the promulgation of the Marriage Law there seems to have been very little reference to marriage between *biao* cousins in the source materials, and any references seldom go beyond stating the law. There are one or two case studies in which young people come under parental pressure to marry a cousin (WC 1 June 1953), or in which young people have chosen a cousin as a marriage partner (ZQ 1 April 1955), but there is no further definition of the kin relation. The lack of material on this subject might reflect the fact that this custom is not viewed as a serious impediment to marriage in many areas, and, where it is, customary rules are disregarded as in traditional times. Equally, the lack of material may reflect the fact that in the new ideological model a great deal more attention is given to the positive selection of mates.

Table 11. *Source of wives: Jiang village*

Locality	Numbers
Within production brigade	–
Within commune	24
Different commune	3
Different county	4
Guangzhou	1
Total	32

showed that in fact only one of the thirty-two wives of the village had the same surname as their spouse.

The field of eligible mates is also bounded spatially by the probability of interaction between the spouses and their mutual networks and the norms of residential propinquity. Over the years, numerous sociologists have studied the relation of mate selection to residential propinquity, and it is generally accepted that there is a demonstrable tendency for it to occur within a bounded locality, with the likelihood of marriage decreasing markedly as the distance between the contracting parties increases (Bossard 1932:219; Stouffer 1940:846). In late traditional China, Skinner suggested that for the peasantry the endogamous unit may well have been the standard marketing community (1964:36), and in China today residential propinquity remains an important factor in mate selection. Wives were normally recruited from within a local radius defined by custom and distance.

My own work in Guangdong would suggest that wives were commonly recruited from within the commune and that the familiarity of this practice gave rise to propinquitous norms based on residence. Informants at the commune level suggested that most brides came from within the commune, although at the village level they suggested that they came from within the same production brigade. The survey data shows that the majority of wives were in fact recruited from within the same commune; see table 11. Where wives were recruited from beyond the commune either both spouses had kin, perhaps an aunt or older sister, who worked together and had introduced them, or mutual friends may have performed the introductions. Often the mutual friend of both spouses turned out to be the wife of the groom's friend who had introduced girlfriends from the same locality as herself.

On the whole there seemed to be a marked preference for local girls. One informant expressed this trend in normative terms when he suggested that it was 'better for young people to find spouses nearby because it would help mutual understanding between the couple'.

The data from the other communes visited in Guangdong reinforce the impression that most brides are recruited from within the same commune, although in the larger villages with more than one surname, a few of the wives came from within the village and certainly more came from within the same production brigade than in Jiang village. In one commune the majority of the wives came from a neighbouring commune, but in fact their villages of origin were closer in actual distance than most of the rest of the same commune. In urban Guangzhou, in each of the dozen households interviewed where wives had recently been recruited or were about to be recruited, brides had previously lived nearby. In the factory housing complex and the housing estate of the former boat people, the wives had come from within the same housing complex. To some extent propinquity of residence may be an index, even if rough, of cultural similarities and social characteristics. It can be observed in China too as elsewhere that there is some coincidence of spatial and social distances, but the operation of both new and traditional norms defining the criteria on which 'choice' should be based point to the location of preferential mates within a field of eligibles already bounded by surname exogamy and residential propinquity.

THE POLITICAL STATUS SYSTEM

The location of preferential spouses within the field of eligible mates results from the operation of two separate and competing status systems, one political and the other socio-economic. Although the new ideological model introduced in 1949 conceptualised political status (*zhengzhi diwei*) according to levels of political consciousness or 'political standpoint, ideological views, class sentiments and revolutionary ideals' exhibited by an individual, in practical terms political status is usually defined by the degree of formal recognition or honours conferred upon an individual by the government and the Communist Party. On this basis it is possible to identify a gradient of approval and disapproval based upon the differential distribution of political status. According to refugees interviewed in Hong Kong, those who were members of the Youth League, the Party or who were honoured as labour heroes or 'five good workers' of enterprises were held to embody the highest degree of political status in the new society (White 1974: 500). Of this group, those who were members of the Youth League and Communist Party formed a clearly bounded category of preferential mates. In the many letters and life-histories in which young people referred to the attractions and attitudes of their potential marriage partners, there were constant references to their political status measured in these terms. In the 1950s those who had a long history of participation in the revolution had acquired a certain romantic aura. One young girl described her husband as enthusiastic, smart and capable, but what had really impressed her from the start was his personal history of revolutionary activity. 'More valuable than these personal qualities', she said, 'was the fact that he had participated in the revolution since 1939 and was a member of the Communist Party. It was these things which put a spell on me' (ZF 1 November 1955). Another young girl said she just could not believe her luck when she met an attractive young man who 'laboured well, worked well, was honest and was a Communist Youth League member to boot!' (ZQ 22 February 1962).

There is some evidence to suggest that there was some competition for spouses who had achieved positions of political power and acquired public awards. One young bachelor in his mid-twenties who was an official in village government and a leader of the local militia was described as the 'object of purposeful attention from all the young unmarried women of the villages for 10 li around' (CR 1 May 1957). Another who had been elected a 'five good commune member' many times over had attracted the attention of the local girls, some of whom had 'come forward of their own accord and offered to marry him' (ZQ 22 February 1962). A survey of marriage patterns in the mid-1950s had suggested that the cases of girls marrying cadres in order to gain Party membership for themselves and win support of the leadership were unfortunately many (ZQ 4 January 1955). The competition for cadres, Party members and others similarly categorised seems to have aroused the resentment of those not similarly endowed. A discussion of the problem of mate selection in Hunan province in 1957 revealed that many young men were rather resentful of the way in which young women were attracted to cadres rather than to fellow-peasants and labourers (NCNA 2 July 1957). On another occasion young people complained that the desire to maximise political status through marriage was so high as to cause membership of the Youth League or Party to be almost a prerequisite to a 'good match'. In *Shaanxi Ribao* it was reported that some young people who were 'disappointed in love' blamed the leadership for not promoting them or the Party and Youth League for not accepting them as members. They complained that without either attribute they were 'just nonentities', 'unable even to get someone to love them' (SRB 8 March 1958).

The desire to maximise political status through marriage led to the odd case in which spouses freely exaggerated their access to political authority and influence. In extreme cases young men found it prudent to exaggerate their political credentials. One case of 'marriage by fraud' was reported in 1957. A young man was accused of fabricating a personal history of colourful participation in the revolution and of posing as a member of the Communist Party in order to win his girl, and in the court hearing which followed the discovery of the fraud, his wife admitted to having been attracted to him because he seemed to be 'a hero of the revolution' (XR 28 April 1957).

If political status, expressed in terms of individual political position or award or membership of political associations formed a clearly bounded category of preferential mates at the positive pole of the continuum of approval and disapproval, those who were said to be of 'exploiting-class origins' (*boxiao jieji chushen*) could be said to function negatively on the continuum. Below those rewarded individually and positively, political status seems to have been awarded collectively according to social origins and class status (*chengfen*). In 1949 or thereabouts, members of each household were categorised according to their class position, either on the eve of land reform in rural areas or on the public ownership of industry in urban areas. For instance, the rural population was divided into landlords, rich, middle-class, lower-middle-class and poor peasants according to the amount of land they owned and worked with their own hands and the number of implements in their possession (see Hinton 1966; C. Yang 1959). Landlords, rich peasants and urban capitalists, because they had hired labour to work their land or employed workers, were said to belong to the former 'exploiting classes'. Poor and lower-middle-class peasants and urban workers were said to be of 'good' as opposed to 'bad' class origins. Initially, in the 1950s, certain rules had been imposed banning intermarriage between the groups during periods of heightened class conflict.

In 1952, *Nanfang Ribao* stated that during land reform, marriage
between those of peasant and landlord background could not be
tolerated, for it was not unknown for landlords to marry off their
daughters to poor peasants in order to establish alliances that would
blur class lines and thus the class conflict (NFRB 13 February 1952).
Many local Party and Youth League organisations had similar rules
still in operation in the mid-1950s (ZQ 24 May 1956; RMRB 12
January 1957). These rules were later criticised in the media, and the
government has since stressed that levels of political consciousness were
not supposed to be predetermined by class origins or ascriptive
criteria, and that class origins should not therefore affect or influence
the choice of marriage partner. Rather, individual levels of political
consciousness should form the criteria for those of 'exploiting-class'
origins just as for other social categories. One piece of advice clearly
stated that there was a distinction to be made between members of
the exploiting class and those born of the exploiting classes, and that
young people, in considering whether they should fall in love and
marry those of exploiting-class origins, should appraise them according
to their behaviour and not their family background (*jiating chengfen*).
'As long as those young people wanted progress, were willing to
participate in politics and were committed to the goals of the new
society, then it is all right to fall in love and marry them' (GRB 6 May
1965).

Nevertheless, the government also warned against the influence of
ideas and standards of the former exploiting classes which might be
disseminated through friendships which crossed class boundaries (XG
16 October 1955), and not a few advice columns suggested, at least
by implication, that compatibility in marriage was often much more
difficult to achieve with members of the former exploiting classes (ZF
1 February 1963). Like the young man who expected his wife to be
a dependent and passive asset, they were thought to have unconsciously
and collectively inherited old family attitudes and opinions deriving
from Confucian and capitalist ideologies (ZF 1 May 1964). This put
the onus on the young people of exploiting-class origin to constantly
prove their revolutionary character or level of political consciousness.
Despite the recommendation that it was wrong to collectively discriminate against those born into families of the exploiting classes, there
was a certain tension between collectively allocated class origins and
individual levels of political consciousness in determining the
acceptability of the individual as a potential spouse. An examination

of the case studies in the media suggests that social origins had come to be associated with certain levels of political consciousness and that this correlation disadvantaged those of exploiting-class origin in the marriage market.

What those of 'good' class origins feared was a reduction in their own political status as a result of association or a marriage alliance with those of exploiting-class origins. Refugees interviewed in Hong Kong in 1970 all stated that family background or class origins had an important influence on determining a person's 'future' (*qiantu* or *chuxi*) and therefore their marriage prospects (White 1974:495). There were many letters written by the sons and daughters of those of the exploiting classes which expressed concern about the effect of their social origins on their political status and hence their relations or alliances with members of other social classes (NFRB 8 March 1965; GRB 7 November 1965; ZQ 16 October 1965). An observer living in Henan province in 1970 described the patterns of association in one village between those of so-called 'good' and 'bad' class origins. When working in the fields, he observed there to be 'no difference between them and other young people they are with. They chat, joke, laugh with everyone normally, but their friends naturally do not like to visit them at home.' But he then went on to describe how difficult it was for them to get married, although it was slightly easier for girls. The reasons for this slight difference were that girls were often better read and trained in housewifely skills, but more important was the normal post-marital residential arrangements, in which brides went to live in their husband's household. The patrilocal nature of marriage meant that the problem was especially great for young men who would take their wives into households that were to some extent taboo, and girls of poor and lower-middle-class peasant or even rich peasant families were understandably reluctant to accept such a proposal. He quoted one case in which class origins were the obvious cause or factor in the rejection of a marriage proposal. The girl involved was calculated to be ideal in every other way, 'she was an able housewife and agricultural worker and good-looking as well,' so that the negotiations soon came to centre around the question: 'Should a red-flag poor peasant get allied in marriage with a former rich peasant family?' The father of the boy decided that it was not only this particular match that had to be taken into account, but the future of the entire family, and he rejected the match (J. Chen 1973:74, 104). In another case, quoted in *Zhongguo Funu*, where the parents intended to negotiate an arranged marriage to the son of a rich peasant family, their daughter used the disadvantages associated with his 'exploiting-class origins' to convince them otherwise (ZF 1 February 1966).

Where the young people themselves initiated the negotiations for marriage, class origins were also found to be a factor governing choice of mate. Two correspondents writing to *Zhongguo Qingnian* and *Gongren Ribao* in 1965 were specifically concerned with this problem and their letters reveal the conflicting interests influencing the choice of spouse. One letter was about the dilemma of a young man who was a member of the Communist Party. He was attracted by a girl who was a middle school graduate teaching in an elementary school and who was quite active politically. There was one obstacle to their marriage; she was from a rich peasant family. According to some of their friends this was a matter of real concern affecting his 'future', but according to others he need not be unduly concerned as long as her level of political consciousness was high. Influenced by former attitudes, however, he wondered if he had committed an 'error' in his association with her because it might affect his 'future prospects'. His letter ended with the question, 'did love and marriage with youths from families of the exploiting classes entail loss of class stand or political status?' (ZQ 1 May 1965). The other letter suggested that even where individuals exhibited high levels of political consciousness, this was not enough to cancel out their class origins and raise their political status within their immediate reference groups. The fact that his girl was a member of the Youth League and had made considerable efforts to study politics did not soften the reaction of the boy's workmates when he informed them of his impending marriage. They told him that as a son of the family of the working classes, he would lose his 'class stand' by marrying a girl born of the family of the exploiting classes. The young man said that as a result he was very confused about the association of social origins and political consciousness in determining political status and he was also very anxious that he should not lose his own 'class stand' (GRB 6 May 1965). Indeed, it was the apparent association of exploiting-class origins and low political status and its importance in choice of marriage partner which caused a young man to contract a hasty marriage before his social origins could be discovered (ZF 1 February 1963), and caused a young high school teacher in Guangzhou, born of the family of a former landlord, to hide his social origins from his future spouse (Salaff 1971:322). In each instance the subsequent discovery of deception was said to be a factor contributing to the later breakdown of the marriage.

If the association of levels of political consciousness with class origins was responsible for placing those of exploiting-class origins at the negative end of the gradient, the association of high levels of political consciousness with 'good' class origins placed workers and poor and lower-middle-class peasants in the middle ranges of the political status gradient, directly below those who had been positively regarded for their level of political consciousness. Although the government has pointed out that those of 'good' class origins did not automatically assume high levels of political consciousness, there had been a tendency for the constituents of the 'revolutionary vanguard' or 'real proletariat' to take their ideological probity for granted unless there was some specific reason for assuming its loss. Any hint of misde-meanour, reprimand or punishment from the political authorities, for instance, could have the effect of cancelling out 'good' class origins. In one village in Henan, for example, a girl of poor peasant origin was thought to be a suitable match in every way, but there was one obstacle to the conclusion of the negotiations of the proposed match. Her father had been brought before the People's Court in regard to some affair that might have involved punishment at the hands of the court. Although the case against him had been dropped, it was clear that an explanation was thought to be due. In this case the matter had turned out well, but it was said at the time that had the matter not turned out well, and had he been jailed, this would certainly have affected the chances of his daughter in marriage (J. Chen 1973:81). Those of 'good' class origins had a definite advantage in the marriage market in that they began with a 'clean record', but to remain within the 'preferred category' they should not have a blemished political record.

Political status measured according to reward or by class origins is an important factor governing marriage choice, and under its con-siderable influence the traditional social status gradient has largely been reversed. The new criteria determined by levels of political consciousness was influential to the extent that the traditional status groupings of landlord, rich peasant and the urban wealthy have been replaced by new status groups of government cadres and certain skilled urban workers as preferential spouses (see fig. 1). But an

Choice of marriage partner

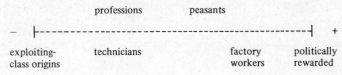

Fig. 1. Choice of mate: political status gradient

examination of the case studies suggests that socio-economic characteristics also remain important criteria in mate selection and in the
definition of those categorised as preferential mates.

THE SOCIAL STATUS SYSTEM

The term 'social status' refers to the distribution of social honour in
Chinese society or the extent to which individuals or groups receive
respect or esteem (*zunzhong* or *zongbai*). The distribution of social status
is revealed in the attitudes and expectations of their immediate
reference groups, such as relations, neighbours, fellow-workers or
friends. It was mainly allocated according to occupation with its
corollaries of level of education, income, life-style and degree of
mobility or 'future'. Traditionally, marriage was seen to be an
opportunity to maximise the resources of the household or kin group
through the negotiation of a suitable alliance, and there is evidence
to suggest that both families and the young people who themselves
undertook the negotiations have continued to view marriage as a
means of social mobility. They seek a partner who in the eyes of the
immediate reference group is considered to have 'future'. Some local
sayings, such as 'Ask not if he is a member of the Party, ask not if he
is a member of the Youth League, but ask only if he has money' (HZX
15 December 1956), or 'First, look to see over the house, second look
over the person, third look to see if he can earn one hundred per cent',
are said to indicate the criteria underlying mate selection in China
in the 1960s (Lu Yang 1964: 13). In letters and life-histories, young
people explicitly considered the occupation, the income, the likely
standard of living and the extent of the family burden of future spouses
(e.g. ZF 16 April 1959; 1 May 1959). A lengthy correspondence
conducted in the pages of *Zhongguo Funu* in 1963–4 on the subject of
mate selection indicated that the prospects for a 'good livelihood' after
marriage remained an important dimension in assessing the suitability

93

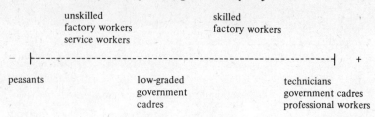

Fig. 2. Choice of mate: social status gradient

of a spouse. As one correspondent said, she hoped to choose a man who had high pay, a high position and who was young and smart (ZF 1 September 1964). Another congratulated herself on finding a good husband. His salary was not low and he had no heavy family burden, which made for a good livelihood (ZF 1 September 1963). Others, in aspiring for a settled and comfortable life, gave priority to men who had a high position and earned much income (*ibid.*).

Those with skills and high wages included specialist occupations in factories or the government bureaucracy, professional positions such as those held by engineers, professors and doctors, technicians, scientists and jobs of skilled industrial work which were rated highly in terms of remuneration and welfare benefits. They made up the positive poles of the social status gradient (see fig. 2). Within the rural social field, wealth is calculated generally according to local environmental factors which contribute to variations in the wealth of local areas and, more specifically, according to the ratio of wage-earners to wage-dependants, which affects the resources of individual households. In two case studies, parents were reluctant for their daughters to marry into mountainous areas because of the lack of facilities, such as uneven roads, less fertile land and unreliable sources of good food (PC 16 November 1957; ZF 1 February 1966). In order to maximise opportunities for a favourable marriage alliance, the accumulation of household status symbols was reported to characterise the period immediately prior to negotiations. In the village of Upper Felicity in Henan the purchase of a transistor radio, sewing-machine, bicycle or clock was said to be a sure sign that a family was embarking on marriage negotiations (J. Chen 1973:80–1).

An examination of the case studies suggests that there are in fact two competing status systems in operation. At times, government policies have contributed to the importance of each status system relative to the other,* and there has been some vertical jockeying for positions on each gradient, but the location of points of congruence or concurrence on both gradients defines the actual location of preferred marriage partners. Not surprisingly, the preferential mate was one who combined both socio-economic and political status and it was this combination which was much sought after. As one girl, in the midst of choosing a mate and faced by a constant discrepancy in political and social status, was heard to utter: 'Wouldn't it be wonderful if I could find a suitor whose thought was good and who earns more money?' (ZF 1 September 1964). Another girl described how she had always thought that she would like to choose a husband who had a high salary, a high position and who was young and smart. She fell in love with a 'deputy chief of a section at her place of work who was also a Communist Party member and rated as an 'activist' in study. She had some criticisms of him, but on the whole she concluded that 'it would be nice to have a husband like him...I felt that he would be a good husband in which I could take pride in the presence of other people!' Her neighbours and friends also advised her 'to stick with him' (*ibid.*).

This concept of the ideal mate who maximises both political and social status resources had by the 1960s been incorporated into the new ideology and modified the exclusive political criteria previously recommended in the educational materials. The combination of both political and socio-economic resources was included in the definition of the desirable mate in one booklet of advice on marriage and family matters. In answer to the question of what kind of marriage partner is most satisfactory in prospects, the reply was that political compatibility is of course the most important criterion. That is, political standing, ideological views, class sentiments and revolutionary ideals are listed as the first criteria in choosing a mate, but then follows a list of characteristics including economic situation, cultural level, appearance, suitability in age, taste, demeanour and compatibility in temperament, which were all to be taken into consideration, albeit as secondary criteria. 'In love and in looking for a partner', it said, 'considering the other's profession, whether he works well, how much

---

* For instance, at certain periods there has been more attention and recognition given to groups of high political status or greater 'red' qualities. At other times it is the technicians or the 'experts' with formal educational qualifications who have been rewarded.

his income is, the spaciousness of his home, and whether he is good looking – these cannot be considered wrong. The mistake lies in only considering these secondary issues' (Lu Yang 1964:12–17).

PREFERRED CATEGORIES OF SPOUSES

There were several social categories that were most likely to meet these joint criteria and a number of reports in newspapers have specifically identified the preferential mates. One report said that women workers in the cities preferred to marry technicians, army officers and factory managers rather than workers, and that in rural areas women preferred to marry factory workers (RMRB 23 August 1956). Another noted that young women in rural areas sought mates among army men, factory workers and cadres rather than choosing peasants (ZQ 1 November 1956). Yet another also referred to the preference of young girls in the rural areas for factory workers and cadres in the cities (KMRB 14 January 1957). In a summary of the views expressed in the media in Hunan province, a newspaper concluded that the young people in the rural areas sought mates who were either cadres working for the government or factory workers (NCNA 2 July 1957). In the correspondence columns of the 1960s the preferred category of spouses was again identified as government cadres and skilled industrial workers, that is those who ranked high on both political and social status gradients. In these case studies it is normally difficult to ascertain the balance of political and socio-economic criteria in determining the choice of marriage partner, but the letters and commentaries uniformly suggest that there are clearly defined status groups and that marriage is still viewed as an avenue of social mobility, and especially among young women (e.g. SRB 8 March 1958).

A folk-saying was declared to reflect the calculated socio-economic interests of women: 'In the case of a man, one part of ability is one part of happiness. In the case of a woman, one part of looks is one part of happiness.' (Lu Yang 1964:14). That is, in looking for a prospective mate, a woman looks primarily at a man's ability or earning power and a man looks at a woman's appearance. It was suggested in the educational materials that the obvious concern of women with marriage choice reflected the historical economic and social dependence of women on their marriage partners, a tradition which could be summed up in the constantly heard refrain 'Marry a man, marry a man, clothes to wear and food to eat'. This dependence was said to have no basis now that women entered social production and were economically independent, and it is certainly evident that the new ideology has influenced women to the extent that few continue to feel comfortable in the presence of those whose only attribute is their wealth.

The operation of a number of restrictions on marriage choice and the presence of clearly defined status groups according to political or socio-economic criteria suggest that there was not only a certain amount of hypergamy (upward mobility through marriage) but also a certain degree of homogamy, or marriage within status groups. One means by which status groups may enhance their distinctiveness is through the encouragement of endogamy, or in-group marriage. One of the most clearly bounded of status groups is to be found at the apex of the political status gradient, or those who were members of political organisations, and it would not be surprising to find that this group tried to maintain their social distance by placing restrictions upon those marrying out. There is no doubt that the Communist Party and especially the Youth League provided unique opportunities for regular social interaction among young people of similar political status in both the urban and especially the rural areas. These opportunities laid the foundations for a certain amount of organisational endogamy and there is some evidence that this trend was reinforced by the placing of restrictions upon those marrying out. For instance, two government organs in one locality had laid down the following stipulations:

(1) Prior approval of the organisation must be obtained before courting a woman and before betrothal and marriage.

(2) Marriage to a woman comrade who is neither a Party or Youth League member is prohibited.

(3) Marriage to a woman revolutionary cadre who comes from a landlord or rich peasant family is prohibited. (ZQ 24 May 1956)

An article published in a national newspaper the following year suggested that rules such as these, which had a purpose during the intense class struggles of land reform and collectivisation, were still widespread. The newspaper article went on to reprimand all Party and Youth League organisations who continued to operate such restrictions and rules on the grounds that once people were encouraged to marry within their own organisation that group was on its way to becoming a new class (RMRB 12 January 1957). Although these restrictions were directly counter to the principles of the new ideology, there was not only some endogamy to be observed among those particularly advantaged, but also the very categorisation of certain groups as 'the disadvantaged' caused some exploiting-class endogamy. At the same time, though, there has also been some attempt by them to improve their political status through establishing marriage alliances with cadres (ZF 1 November 1955; Meijer 1971:136).

It is difficult to document the degree of homogamy and hypergamy which has continued to characterise contemporary Chinese marriage patterns. The degree of stratification observable in Chinese society and the popular disapproving reaction towards heterogamy and its recommendation as a model for emulation certainly suggest a continuing preponderance of homogamy or assortative mating over heterogamy. In the absence of detailed data on homogamy it is possible, however, to outline the most common patterns of heterogamy and identify the forces favouring homogamy, or marriage within status groups, and those that work against homogamy and favour heterogamy, or marriage between status groups.

HETEROGAMOUS MARRIAGE

Heterogamous marriages usually involve wide disparities between the political and social status of marriage partners, and in China the maximisation of both political and social-economic status has been difficult to achieve for those at each end of the spectrum on each of the gradients of status. The absence of one was normally not enough to compensate for the other, and the further apart their locations on each of the continuums, the more difficult they were to combine. For instance, if those with maximum political status were low-salaried or if those who received high salaries had no political status, then tension or conflict often resulted. The most common social categories involved in heterogamous marriages were technical personnel, who usually ranked lower in political status than in social status, and peasants who ranked higher on the gradient of political status than in social status. An examination of the tension and conflict generated by heterogamous marriages explicitly reveals the norms and expectations which surround the choice of any marriage partner.

In this context two sets of correspondence in *Zhongguo Funu*, each of which lasted for several months in 1957–8 and 1963–4, provide very interesting case materials. The first was occasioned by a letter from a typist who had fallen in love with a chauffeur, but was thrown into a state of great conflict and anxiety as a result of the criticisms of her sister and her peers that they were not well-matched. According to the editors of the women's magazine the publication of this letter elicited more than 1000 replies from readers and over 700 of these were in favour of her marrying the driver (ZF 14 November 1959). Among the letters selected for publication were those which included a number of similar case-histories. These consisted of matches between a college-educated wife and a soldier educated at grade school, a technician and a worker, a teacher at elementary school and an automobile driver, a high-salaried (16th grade) wife and low-salaried (21st grade) husband (ZF 14 January 1960). In all cases, the woman had enjoyed a much higher social position than the husband and in each case she had experienced considerable anguish as the result of criticisms from colleagues and close relatives. The college-educated wife of the soldier husband withstood the negative reactions of her sister and schoolmates to the difference in their educational and occupational status, and with the support of the Party and Youth League she married the soldier (ZF 14 December 1959). This was in contrast to the bank official who, after listening to the criticisms and warnings of her friends and family, broke off her relationship with a book-keeper and married a college student instead (ZF 14 December 1959).

In 1963–4 *Zhongguo Funu* again invited correspondence on the subject of 'What to look for in choosing a spouse' and many readers took the opportunity to describe the types of opposition they had encountered in choosing a marriage partner of a lower social status than themselves. One woman, a doctor, described the attitudes of her relatives towards her fiancé whom, she said, was loyal to the revolutionary cause, but who had a minor government position and was low-paid. Her sister had fiercely opposed her marriage, and tried to caution her with the words, 'You are young, clever and have professional skills. You needn't worry about finding an ideal husband. What a foolish thing to marry such a man! His income is low and he isn't skilled in any field. What happiness will there be if you marry him?' She urged her to give him up right away and her husband made a point of introducing his friends to her. He gave her photographs of several colleagues, all assistant professors at his university, and tried to tempt her with their conditions of work and economic situations. She recalled how he had urged her to choose from among them and assured her that any future demand with regard to livelihood which she cared to raise would be met (ZF 1 July 1964).

One girl described in detail her unhappy dilemma. Her boyfriend was of good class origins, progressive in thought, hard working and simple in life-style. He had all the characteristics she could want, but for the fact that his job was ordinary and his wages low. Simultaneously she met a technician who earned a high salary although he was not very 'progressive in thought'. Influenced by the new ideological model she rejected the technician on the grounds that 'to rest love on the foundation of money was undesirable'. Her family and neighbours were dismayed by her choice. Some advised her, 'You still do not face reality even when you are not well off'. Still others called her a 'fool' by saying, 'You simply ask for it'. She described how reactions like these had begun to shake her resolve. 'While it is not right just to seek enjoyment in life in choosing a husband', she thought, 'is it not so that the problem of livelihood remains a problem of livelihood? After all, reality is reality and after getting married one will still have to organise family life.' She continued to struggle with her mixed thoughts: on the one hand it was not good to marry for money, on the other hand she wanted to have a secure financial foundation (ZF 1 September 1964). Some girls withstood the pressures and criticisms of their peers and kin and others gave in and chose again. One girl, a doctor, reported how she planned to marry a grade 3 factory worker, despite the advice of her friends and parents. They had warned her against marrying this man who 'was only a class three worker' and who 'was not well off'. She chose to disregard their opinions and to go ahead and marry him (ZQ 16 September 1963). Another girl, dissatisfied with the low rank and small salary of a Party member who was otherwise progressive politically and ideologically gave him up once she had the good fortune to be introduced to a cadre who was politically admirable and had a high grade and a high salary (ZF 1 August 1964).

These cases all involve some mediation of the discrepancies between socio-economic and political status, but perhaps the cases which illustrated the maximum discrepancies between political and social status occurred in heterogamous marriages in which one partner was a peasant residing in the countryside. Although poor and lower-middle-class peasants enjoyed a measure of political status, it could in no way make up for their position of low socio-economic status. In the ranking of occupations, peasants were placed on the lowest rung. Indeed, social mobility was viewed as an urban phenomenon and it was often said that life in the countryside had 'no future'; peasants had low salaries and their cultural level was usually lower than those of other occupations. So that for a peasant girl an offer of marriage in the city was often cause for congratulations and smacked of hypergamy. When one village girl was pressed by a young man to come to the city to be married, her mother was said to be extremely happy, and the women in the neighbourhood were heard to say, 'Hurry up and go with him. Enjoy yourself. Such a good son-in-law can't be found anywhere even if you look with a lantern' (Lu Yang 1964:12). Several reports in the media mentioned the reluctance of village girls to stay in the countryside if they had the opportunity to do otherwise. One report cites two current sayings which illustrated this trend: 'I shall marry a man whose hair is groomed, who wears leather shoes, and carries a watch; I shall not marry one whose head is clean-shaven, who handles a hoe and works with a pick', and 'my prospective husband is to be either a worker, a cadre or a schoolmaster, I'd rather die than marry one who works on a farm' (HZX 15 December 1956).

In the correspondence on marriage in the Hunan newspapers, some girls wrote that, despite official moves to elevate the political and social status of peasants, they had their reasons for not wanting to marry them. 'Farming', they said, 'meant labour, hard living, no future and peasants had no "education".' One girl left no room for doubt as to her opinions. 'Farming', she concluded, 'was dark and dirty and without a future' (NCNA 2 July 1957). Others expressed their opposition to such a fate less directly. One girl wrote to *Zhongguo Qingnian* in 1962 describing the predicament in which she found herself owing to the fact that her boyfriend was returning to his village to participate in agricultural production. He proposed that they both return together and make arrangements for their wedding, but she was afraid that both her father and elder brother would oppose the match because of the distance between the two villages. 'If I go with my boyfriend', she writes, 'will it not amount to ingratitude to my parents and to my elder brother and sister-in-law who have brought me up? But if I break off relations with my boyfriend for this reason, will others not say I am imbued with bourgeois ideas and look down upon peasants?' She went on to describe how she felt very miserable and troubled in the face of such a quandary. The reply rather astutely asked her if it could be that she was seizing on her parents' and elder brother's reluctance to see her get married in a faraway place as an excuse for rejecting a future in rural areas (ZQ 17 July 1962).

Marriage of an urban girl to a peasant brought the maximum disapprobation. The parents of a senior middle school graduate, who was attracted to a teacher at an agricultural middle school and who was prepared to settle down in the countryside for life, were strongly opposed to their daughter's marriage plans. They said to their daughter time and again that there was no 'prospect' for her if she got married and went to live in the countryside. 'Since you have over ten years of schooling', they said, 'how can you marry a teacher of an agricultural middle school resident in the countryside?' To show the measure of their disapproval, they insisted that if she was to proceed with these arrangements she must return to them a sum of 3000 yuan to defray the expenses of her upbringing. At the same time they embarked on a search for a suitable husband for her in the city (ZQ 27 Noember 1962). Another girl correspondent was friendly with a peasant who had graduated from senior middle school and was 'progressive' in thought. But when the relationship became known to her mother, she was very surprised, saying, 'What are you looking for in a peasant? If you don't listen to your parents' words, you will suffer very soon. Don't ever try to marry him.' Her mother asked her neighbours and relatives to support her and to tell the girl that since she was a middle school student, she could still 'find a good prospect in a high position and make her mother satisfied'. 'If you are in love with that poor fellow, you won't do credit to your relatives.' The girl fought back with the idea that one who labours well, comes from a poor family and did his work well was to be admired in the new society (ZF 1 May 1964).

A young couple already married feared very much for the future of their relationship when the girl was recruited to the Teachers' Training College in the city. There she was teased about the status discrepancies in their match and she began to have doubts about her marriage, until her branch of the Youth League began to counter these influences by maximising her husband's political status. The Youth League emphasised the contribution of the peasantry to the history of the revolution and the value of their labour to present-day society, thus causing her to think again (ZQ 16 September 1963). In another case where the couple were already married the husband was sent to the countryside to do pig-raising work. As a result his marriage was put at risk. His removal to the countryside and his new occupation was much to the chagrin of his mother-in-law, who vented her displeasure on the young man. 'I intended that my daughter should marry a great man. But now she has married a pig-raiser. What a disgrace!' Despite political persuasion to the contrary, the girl soon began to feel that her life would indeed be intolerable if she had to stay in the countryside with a 'filthy and tired pig-raiser' for a husband (ZQ 16 September 1963). In all these cases it was the girl who was thought to be marrying or to have married beneath her status.

Residential propinquity has served to circumscribe the number of marriage alliances crossing the rural–urban divide, but the low social status and obstacles to intermarriage with peasants has been brought into sharp relief by the recurrent government policy to encourage young urban school graduates to migrate from the cities to the countryside and settle permanently. Since 1957 there has been a policy to encourage educated Chinese youths or urban school graduates and others to migrate and settle in the countryside and work on the communes or on State Farms in the countryside or in isolated border regions. These educated youths are collectively referred to as *xiaxiang* youth (Gardner 1971; White 1974). The term derives from the name of the movement to send youth 'up the mountains and down to the countryside' (*shangshan xiaxiang*). It is an attempt to effect large-scale and permanent migration for educated youth,* and they are expected to 'strike roots' in the rural areas. As a sign of their intention or determination to settle in the rural villages for life, each *xiaxiang* youth is encouraged to establish a family and settle down permanently (*anjia*

* This movement is not to be confused with the *xiafang* movement, or system of downward transfer, which required that all the personnel of government and Party, armed services, enterprises and industries, students as well as teachers, spend at least one month a year at a lower or basic level of their respective units, or in rural villages where they participate in manual labour.

luohu). There is evidence to suggest that the problem of marriage is one of the obstacles to their integration into peasant society and is the cause of much dissatisfaction and disaffection among these young people, a few of whom have found their way to Hong Kong (Lelyveld 1974; RMRB 30 January 1971). Not only did they fear that marriage in the countryside would 'root them there permanently', but the new migration patterns brought young urban-educated youth into close association with the peasants. Examples of their intermarriage have been given maximum publicity over the years and their experience draws attention to the discrepancy in the political and social status of the peasants.

One case of intermarriage was written up in the newspapers in 1957, the first year of large-scale migration of this type. A young girl student became friendly with a boy from a poor peasant family who was a Youth League member and enjoyed a certain measure of popularity in the village. But before she made up her mind to marry him she agonised over whether or not her schoolmates would laugh at her and whether it might not be better therefore to find a cadre or a worker who 'were more suitable matches for middle school graduates'. She eventually decided to go ahead and marry the peasant and the wedding was much applauded for breaking down traditional social class barriers and for marking a reversal of the trend of village girls to move to the city on marriage. It was said at the time that village girls should cease to look down on peasants and follow the new trend initiated by this marriage. Another girl student in the same village was already said to have followed her example and fallen for the Secretary of the Youth League Branch (SRB 29 December 1957). Two decades later in 1974 a similar case was cited in which a *xiaxiang* girl teacher of the commune middle school was married to a peasant boy. This marriage aroused similar conflicting reactions. It was hailed by some as a revolutionary act, 'taking the road of integration with peasants and workers', but it was also ridiculed by others who thought that a university student should marry another university student and not a peasant in the countryside (SWB 14 February 1974). This was also the experience of another teacher, who found that the comment 'it is ridiculous for a Beijing-born college graduate to marry a peasant' was a common reaction to her plans for marriage. Her father, who was among those who voiced some disapproval, asked of her: 'What future will you have if you marry a peasant and live in the countryside all your life?' A fellow-teacher called it a 'scandal'. The girl concerned thought that these comments showed that people still thought college graduates should only marry workers and cadres. She surmised that it was because peasants were still associated with the idea of 'dirty' manual labour (*ibid.*).

Most of the cases cited in the media concern *xiaxiang* girls and peasant husbands. From a number of cases, it seems that educated girls did find it easier to make interclass marriages and were themselves considered to be an asset to a peasant family. In one of the above examples a groom's mother had reacted to the news of her new daughter-in-law by telling others in high spirits that she had 'never dreamed her peasant son could find a middle school student' (SRB 29 December 1957). It is noticeable, too, that in the case studies the girls chose future husbands who maximised both political and social status within the confines of the village. They chose peasants high in political status who were members of the Youth League or Party and who were renowned for their physical labour. In rural terms they had as much 'future' as could be expected, and certainly this was so in comparison to the girls' fellow migrants, the *xiaxiang* boys. It was much more difficult for an inexperienced *xiaxiang* boy to earn as much as a peasant boy who was long experienced in agriculture (White 1974:504). Also, custom often demanded marriage expenditure which the *xiaxiang* boy could not afford, and he on his own was much disadvantaged in his ability to provide for a wife compared to a peasant boy and his household. In comparison then, some peasant boys often seemed to combine the maximum political and social status within the village, but they were always carefully chosen. As one *xiaxiang* girl said on the occasion of her friend's wedding to a peasant boy, 'I'm positive about looking for a peasant boy,' but she also went on to say that 'it might take longer to find a suitable one' (SRB 29 December 1957).

The data presented above, and many similar cases, strongly support the proposition that both political and social status influence choice of marriage partner and that this was so whether the younger or the older generation initiated the negotiations. In both urban and rural social fields the preferential mate was defined in the expectations of immediate reference groups as someone who combined both

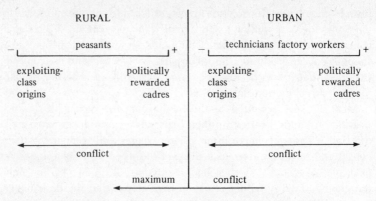

Fig. 3. Choice of mate: political and social status gradient

socio-economic and political status. Where there were discrepancies in the status systems, tension and conflict often resulted and the most likely social categories to be involved can be located diagrammatically; see fig. 3. A study of heterogamous marriage patterns reveals that in every case the marriage negotiations were initiated by the younger generation and that each set of criteria, political and socio-economic, had a basis of support. The tension and conflict which such marriages generated reveals more than any other data base the competitive norms and expectations which surround the choice of marriage partner. Those who adopted the recommended criteria and selected a marriage partner without regard for socio-economic attributes had to withstand the criticisms of their immediate reference groups of friends, relatives and neighbours. Those who defied the common norms of homogamy turned to the Party, Youth League and other political organisations for support. Certainly before the Cultural Revolution, the norms of homogamy predominated over heterogamy, but the principle of homogamy and the importance of the socio-economic status system in the choice of marriage partner was criticised during the Cultural Revolution. For instance, the adaptation of the new ideology underlying choice of marriage partner in favour of a syncretic model incorporating both political and socio-economic status, as recommended by Lu Yang in *The Correct Handling of Love, Marriage and Family Problems* (1964), came under attack. At the same time, there were criticisms of the new stratification patterns based on the political status assumed by Party, political cadres, Youth League members, the presumed association of social origin and political consciousness and the new differentials in wealth and educational opportunities which had emerged since 1949. If and how these criticisms have influenced choice of marriage partners has yet to be determined.

6

THE CEREMONIAL OF MARRIAGE

According to Ching dynasty law and custom, a marriage was invalid and without legal effect unless it was the occasion of public celebration and recognition (Chiu 1966:4). No law had prescribed any compulsory forms or procedures to be followed in the performance of marriage ceremonies, but the customs and rules of propriety handed down from generation to generation were characterised by a lengthy and elaborate sequence of ceremonies and prestations which provided for the separation of the bride from her natal home and her integration into her husband's household. There was some geographical variation in the ritual detail and only those with wealth and status could follow the ceremonial sequences in their totality, but all marriage ceremonies were occasions of some public celebration* and reflected the fact that the marriage contract had been negotiated between heads of households and not between the individual parties. The new ideology replaced the elaborate series of prestations and ceremonial forms (*jiehun yishi*) by a simple registration ceremony at which the marriage as contracted by the individual parties obtained the legal recognition of the political authority or the State.

The Marriage Law of 1950 marked the first occasion on which the State had intervened in the recognition of marriage, and Article 6, the last in chapter 2 of the Marriage Law, provided for the validation of the marriage contract through registration:

In order to contract a marriage, both the men and the women should register in person with the people's government of the district or township in which

* One variation of arranged marriage sought to avoid the ceremonial expenses of marriage altogether. This was the *tang yang xi* (daughter-in-law raised from childhood) (A. Wolf 1968:864) or *siaosiv* (little daughter-in-law) (Fei 1939:53) system whereby the small daughter-in-law was adopted into the household of the groom at the time of betrothal. It was not a common practice and was mainly adopted by poorer families, for whom one of the advantages was the reduction in expenditure occasioned by the absence of marriage gifts and elaborate ceremony.

they reside. If the proposed marriage is found to be in conformity with the provisions of this law, the local people's government should, without delay, issue marriage certificates.

Both parties were thus instructed to proceed in person to the local street office in towns, or the brigade or commune office in the rural areas, with the relevant documents showing name, age, marital status and occupation. There they were acquainted with the legal conditions of marriage and provided with a marriage certificate. This marriage certificate furnished conclusive proof of marriage and the couple were henceforth recognised as husband and wife in the name of the law and their rights and interests protected. There is no provision in the 1950 law for a further ceremony, and whether or not a marriage ceremony is held after registration is said in the educational materials to be very much up to the bride and groom themselves. A booklet published in 1964 reminded readers that it is unnecessary to have any kind of marriage ceremony after registration has taken place. Once the marriage certificate is issued, it obtains the legal recognition of the State, and any further ceremonial, in either its traditional elaborate or more simplified forms, does not further legitimise the marriage in the eyes of the political authority. At the same time it also recognised that because it was customary to perform some kind of ceremony, there may still be some necessity to allow for formal social recognition in addition to the new political recognition (Lu Yang 1964:35).

The government recommended that any social recognition of marriage take the form of a simplified ceremony in which the couple proclaim themselves to be man and wife in the presence of their friends and family, perhaps at an evening party at which light refreshments were served. The new model disregarded the customary practices of choosing auspicious days (*huangdao jiri*), the traditional sequence of rites of separation from the bride's natal family and integration into her husband's family, the transfer of the dowry (*jiazhuang*) and the celebration of the marriage feast (*bai jiuxi*), at which selected guests were invited to attend and proffer their gifts. What is advocated is a curtailment of the traditional ritual, with the elimination of symbols which took their meanings from the superstitions and extended kin relations of the old society, and a reduction of marriage expenses to end the financial dependence of the young people on their parents. The educational materials in support of the new model assumed that the advantages of economy and simplicity would be self-evident, once the repercussions of the expenses and the significance of many of the symbolic gestures was explained and understood. Yet in China today the celebration of marriage commonly invokes some form of social as well as political recognition.

The form that the political recognition takes, or the registration of marriage, is standardised throughout China, and it is normally the preliminary to some form of ceremonial inviting social recognition of the partnership. It is this latter form of recognition which is often referred to as the marriage itself. In one case recorded in 1963, a young couple, having completed their registration on the afternoon of Chinese New Year's Eve and obtained their marriage certificates, returned at once to one another's home to tell their parents that they 'planned to get *married* the following day' (my italics – ZF 1 June 1963). The form which the social recognition took ranged from the simplified ceremony in which the couple proclaim themselves to be husband and wife in the presence of their friends and kin at an evening tea-party, to a more elaborate form which retains many of the traditional customs. Where the ceremonial takes a more elaborate form it may include the use of the bridal sedan chair, the transfer of the dowry, the ritual integration of the bride into the husband's family and the marriage feast.

THE BRIDAL SEDAN CHAIR

A significant feature of the traditional ceremonial had been the use of the bridal sedan chair customarily hired by the groom's parents to transport the bride to their home. Only an inferior form of marriage contracted in such a way as to avoid the expenses of bringing up a daughter or the cost of a marriage ceremony was associated with its absence, and the practice of sending the bridal sedan chair seems to have been one of the more tenacious of the procedures which characterised the traditional marriage ceremonial. In rural areas and as late as 1974 its use was reported in the media (SWB 21 March 1974). In the case studies, the use of the sedan chair is seen to be a common cause of conflict both between the generations within the family and between the kin of the parties to the negotiations. Those who supported the custom based their claims on the fact that it was still a sign or symbol of a 'right and proper marriage', just as it had always invited public recognition that the ceremonial was being properly conducted (*mingmei zhengzhu*). In this respect its absence was to be interpreted as a cause for loss of status or 'face' (*timian*). The mother of a son who refused to be married with the sedan chair followed by a parade of the dowry was very angry that the bride did not even 'have the decency to arrive properly'. She said that she was aware of the advantage of the new ways and all the arguments against the continuation of this old practice, but nevertheless 'what sort of day was it when they lost face on this, the greatest day of one's life?' (PC 16 June 1949).

Fifteen years later, in the mid-1960s, young couples still came under considerable pressure from their parents to duly celebrate their marriage. In one case, the parents stated that 'as we had a bumper harvest this year we should make the wedding presentable and give our daughter away in the right manner, so that everybody involved can take pride in the event'. The 'right manner' included the use of the sedan chair and, in their argument with the younger generation, the parents had much local support. 'People get married only once in a lifetime, it is natural that she should sit in the sedan chair!' The young couple were aware that it was an old custom not encouraged by the new ideology, but listening to local opinion they had become perplexed and uncertain what to do. Under their influence the prospective bride began to feel that if she didn't sit in the sedan chair, people could cite an old saying that without the sedan chair 'goods delivered were just not presentable'. Indeed, it took some convincing to persuade her otherwise (ZQ 30 January 1964). The two most commonly cited reasons for its continuing use seem to centre on the desire to distinguish the occasion from all others by giving it due importance and to avoid arousing gossip and talk. As one mother said to her daughter, 'getting married is something that happens once in a lifetime. It should not be taken lightly. You had better take a sedan chair' (ZQ 16 January 1966). When a prospective groom suggested to his bride that they arrange an alternative form of transport to the sedan chair, she responded, 'when other people get married, the bride either sits in a sedan chair or rides a horse and if I walk to your door, people will talk' (ZQ 19 November 1964).

In the past, the use of the bridal sedan chair symbolised the control of the marriage negotiations by the older generation. It played a significant part in the rites of separation by expressing the resistance of the bride to leaving her own home, and it also highlighted the fact that she had been carried to her husband's home at the behest of his parents (M. Yang 1945:113). Young people, and especially brides, may have colluded in its persistence precisely because it absolved them from a certain amount of responsibility should tension and conflict result from their introduction into the new household. In the past it has been suggested that, at the same time as the daughter-in-law was establishing a relationship with her new husband and obtaining a foothold within the family, the mother-in-law was also making concerted efforts to maintain the special relationship with her son which she had worked so hard to establish as a means of manipulating control of the affairs of the household, and as a guarantee for her security in her old age (M. Wolf 1972:35–6). On occasions of complaint or disagreement, the daughter-in-law could always claim that she had been brought to their door by the sedan chair.

That brides were still wary of losing this defence was illustrated by the following case study, in which the groom persuaded his bride to dispense with the chair on the grounds that they were getting married of their own free will. Their marriage had not been arranged by their parents and therefore she need not now have this defence, for 'women had straightened their backs and both mother and daughter-in-law were now masters of their house' (ZQ 19 November 1964). In the same year an educational booklet suggested that one of the reasons why the sedan chair was still used could be due to the fact that its abolition gave any mother-in-law the excuse to admonish 'You came to this house on your own two feet', meaning that she had of her own free will walked into that household (Lu Yang 1964:34). There is no doubt that where the sedan chair has persisted, it has been in rural areas where marriages are more likely to have been initiated by the older generation and where patrilocal marriage was the norm. Where the sedan chair was dispensed with, and there are no cases cited of its use in urban areas, the bride either walked to the bridegroom's house accompanied by her friends or by the groom himself, or sometimes she took a pedicab. Where registration was made on the same day, the couple often met at the registration office and then walked from the place of registration to their future home for further celebrations.

THE DOWRY

In traditional times the sedan chair was usually accompanied by a procession of porters carrying the items which made up the dowry. A dowry, defined as the property given to daughters to take with them into marriage, customarily formed one of the series of prestations between the kin of the groom and the kin of the bride (Goody and Tambiah 1973). In anthropological literature, the dowry has variously been interpreted as primarily a form of pre-mortem inheritance to the bride and within the complex of women's property rights (Goody and Tambiah 1973:1, 17), or as primarily a visible symbol reflecting on the wealth and status of the bride's kin. In China, anthropologists have argued that it was the symbolic attributes of dowry rather than the female claims on property which guided the provision of the dowry in traditional times (Freedman 1966; McCreery 1976). For example, Freedman claims that while the endowment of the bride might cause a considerable economic drain on her family's resources, they provided it

not because the girl has any specific economic claims on them (she is not a member of the property-owing unit) but because their own status is at stake; a bride-giving family must, in order to assert itself against the family to which it has lost a woman, send her off in the greatest manner they can afford. And it is no accident, therefore, that dowry and trousseau are put on open display; they are not private benefactions to the girl but a public demonstration of the means and standing of her natal family. (Freedman 1966:55)

The daughters of the wealthy, then, could expect to be sent off with a substantial dowry in the form of jewelry, clothes, household furnishings and cash. The wealthier the family, the more likely the dowry provided by the girl's household would more than match the gifts made by the groom's family at the time of betrothal. Among the peasants and the artisan classes, the dowry was often less than the amount received in betrothal gifts, for it might form the fund out of which brides were procured for the sons of the family. However, the stigma attached to this practice and the community gossip which it aroused caused families to provide for their daughters if they possibly could in order to escape talk of marriage by purchase (*maimai hunyin*) (M. Yang 1945:108).

The goods which now accompany the bride to her new home are not necessarily referred to as dowry (*jiazhuang*), but simply as gifts or presents made by the families and friends of the bride and groom. In rural areas, however, these gifts retain certain characteristics which identify them in effect as the traditional dowry. They are provided by the kin of the bride on the grounds that their absence would draw adverse attention to the bride's household, and they provide the foundations for the conjugal fund. In the 1950s, one girl's father intended to sell some of his stores of rice in order to furnish his daughter with a dowry. He calculated that he would buy her four suits of clothes, two of serge and two of calico, some pieces of furniture, some pots and bowls, mirrors, face powder, soap cases and the like. When his daughter questioned his intentions, he defended the custom, saying that 'since you were old enough to work, you've done a great deal for the family. I as your father must be seen to do you justice' (PC 16 June 1949). In another case in the mid-1960s, the bride's family began to sell the fat pigs raised by the family. It was forecast that they would probably fetch from 70 to 80 yuan each, which was to be used to buy their daughter a dowry consisting of a dressing-table and trunks, a wardrobe and some cosmetics for her personal use. When the daughter remonstrated she was informed that this was a matter of prime importance in her life. 'How can your wedding be conducted in the manner you have in mind? If we don't spend some money and provide you with some form of dowry, will not other people laugh at us?' (ZQ 16 January 1966). In cases citing the persistence of the practice, the overwhelming argument cited in defence of the dowry was its representation of, and its contribution to, the status and social standing of the bride's family.

GUANGDONG PROVINCE, 1977

In rural areas in Guangdong province in 1977, in every family which I interviewed, the bride and groom had been provided with gifts by their parents and brothers and sisters. These gifts were always composed of the furnishings for their rooms set aside for the use of the conjugal couple. They included a bed, bed clothes, a wardrobe, chest, often a desk and chair and a clock, other substantial items such as a bicycle, sewing-machine, a fan and personal articles of clothing. The amount which the bride's family contributed to the new fund varied substantially between the rural counties of Guangdong and the rural suburbs of Guangzhou. In one county 40 km away from Guangzhou, the groom's parents said that they had contributed from 900 to 1000 yuan to both the furnishings and the celebrations, in comparison to the bride's family, whose expenses ranged from 150 to 300 yuan. Two of the groom's families there specifically stated that they would, or had, spent less on their daughters at the time of marriage because they had needed or would need all their funds to pay for their sons' marriages. In other suburban communes nearer to Guangzhou, the expenses incurred by both families were more evenly matched and ranged from 300 to 400 yuan for each family. The bride's family provided much of the moveable property and the groom's family contributed to the latter and provided for the banquet and celebrations occasioned by the wedding itself. In one case, for example, the bride contributed a bicycle, and much of the furniture, while the groom's family had bought the bed, some other furniture and the banquet. In another case, the groom's family had contributed the wardrobe, bed and the banquet while the bride's family had contributed a bicycle, a chest and a desk and chairs. Many of the more substantial items such as a bicycle, sewing-machine and fan were not in the couple's room but were placed in the sitting-room for the common use of the kin of the groom. They were normally identified as the young couple's property and would be taken by them in the event of the division of the household.

In every family I visited where there had been a marriage within the last five years or so, the furnishings of the room which the young couple inhabited were a great source of pride. They were without doubt the most elaborately furnished rooms of the household and served as a constant reminder of the total amounts afforded by the kin of the bride and the groom at the time of the marriage. Each family could quite precisely remember how much was spent and the details of the contributions made by each family. For the kin of the bride there may have been some conflict between the funds that were lost to them and the desire not to lose status, and where there was competition for son's and daughter's marriages, the daughter was seen to have less claim on the familial funds. Normally, however, the marriages were spaced sufficiently to allow accumulation for the marriage expenses of each member of the family. For several families, the ability to accumulate in order to meet marriage expenses at all was a privilege which was once only enjoyed by a few, and now they were only too pleased to provide gifts for all sons and daughters. One widow with two daughters in their early twenties was already saving for their marriages although neither of them had made any plans for marriage in the near future.

In urban areas the room of the newly or recently married couple was equally a source of pride, but this reflected on the resourcefulness and thrift of the young couple rather than on the contributions afforded by their families. Usually the young couple had saved up for their marriage themselves and used their individual savings to provide for the furnishings. In one family, the bride and groom had used their joint savings to buy some furnishings and clothes, and in another family that I interviewed they had bought a sewing-machine, a bed, a cupboard and bed coverings. In addition each couple had received small gifts in kind and in cash from their kin, friends and fellow-workers. In urban areas the amount used to cover these expenses and the celebrations themselves ranged from about 300 to 600 yuan.

Compared to other customs, such as the practice of the betrothal gift, the bridal sedan or wedding feasts, the continued transfer of gifts with all the connotations of the traditional dowry seems to have given less cause for concern on the part of the political authorities. In the new ideology there is no mention of the dowry, and in the educational materials the marriages of role models are either marked by its absence or it is presented as an outmoded custom which is offered by the parents of the bride but rejected by the bride herself. Interestingly, however, praise has also been bestowed on families who retain the form of the dowry, but invest it with a new political and revolutionary significance. In one case a girl was praised for accepting a dowry offered by her parents which was composed of revolutionary ideas and farm tools (ZQ 16 January 1966). Another girl described in the media how she walked unescorted to her husband's home and took with her 'four volumes of the *Selected Works of Mao Tse-tung*, two bamboo baskets, a spade and a pick' (RMRB 24 January 1972). The parents of one bride were praised for their adoption of the new ways and were selected as models for emulation. They had pondered for quite a long time on the question of a dowry for their daughter and after due consultation they finally came up with the idea of giving her their farm tools, a hoe, a sickle, a pick and a rake. The tools were awards which they had won and they hoped that the constant sight and use of tools engraved with the words 'award', 'increase production and practise economy' and 'practise industry and thrift in housekeeping' would remind their daughter and son-in-law of the hopes and expectations of the older generation (ZQ 24 April 1962).

The attention given to the new contents of the dowry and their selection for emulation is in great contrast to the adverse comment aroused by the reduction of the betrothal gift to a 'warm pleasantry'. It may be that, in comparison with the betrothal gifts which is the first in a series of prestations, it is viewed as a counter-prestation and by concentrating efforts in breaking the cycle at its point of initiation, it is assumed that the dowry will automatically disappear with the abolition of the betrothal gift. On the whole, though, it seems that it has been invested and is still invested with less economic or symbolic significance than the betrothal gift. It can't be construed as payment for the bride as can the betrothal gift, it expresses and achieves status for the wife-givers and it is instrumental in providing the necessary furnishings for the room set aside for the couple and the basis of their conjugal fund.

THE CEREMONIAL OF MARRIAGE

The celebrations inviting social recognition of the marriage of the bride and groom were marked by ceremonials which varied from those which were simple and in accord with the new recommendations to the more elaborate, which involved a selection of rituals inherited from the traditional forms. The new and simple ceremonials emphasised the role of the bride and groom as individuals in a new partnership of equals, which was in marked contrast to the traditional ceremonials at which supernatural sanctions had been imported to stabilise the union and integrate the bride into her rightful place in the groom's descent group and immediate household. Many of the celebrations, and especially those in the cities, followed closely the forms recommended in the educational materials. In these new ceremonial forms, the young people normally stand side by side in the room of the bridegroom's house or in a room in the factory, which has been specially decorated for the occasion with auspicious symbols including the characters for 'happiness' and 'long life', congratulatory scrolls and couplets presented by friends and relatives and numerous flowers. Red, the traditional lucky colour to be worn at weddings, seems to still predominate in the decorations. In a place of honour hangs the portrait of Mao Zedong, in front of which the couple either proclaimed themselves man and wife (WC 1 June 1953) or, in some cases, were described as bowing to the portrait three times (ZQ 19 November 1964). The bowing is reminiscent of obeisance to the ancestors or the gods of heaven and earth, but now the portrait of Mao Zedong (Mao Tse-tung), much like that of Zhongshan (Sun Yat-sen) before 1949, symbolises political rather than religious recognition. The political respects are said to symbolise the commitment of the couple, beyond their immediate households and kin groups, to the local and national communities. The new ceremony is symbolic of the fact that now marriage should represent interpersonal relations between an individual man and woman who are as a part of the community and new society as they are members of kin groups. At a ceremony described to me by an informant in Guangzhou in 1977, the individual bride and groom made short speeches to each other in front of the assembled guests of kin, friends and fellow-workers. In these they pledged to give mutual support to each other in production, livelihood, study and the household. By these means the individuals were encouraged to participate directly in the ceremony, which invested the conjugal role with more significance than merely the relation of the couple to their kin, and especially to the bridegroom's parents. Many of the new ceremonials, however, though they might approximate the desired new forms, also retain some allusions to the traditional supernatural sanctions and hierarchical familial relations.

The general secularisation of the ceremonial outlined in the new ideology has obviously reduced the sacred character of the ritual, although a number of supernatural sanctions have continued to stabilise the union and guarantee good fortune. Traditionally the day of the celebration of marriage had been selected by a ritual specialist for its auspicious qualities (*huangdao jiri*). Days which were generally recognised to be specially fortunate included the third, sixth and ninth days of a ten-day cycle or the second, fifth and eighth days. There is evidence to suggest that this custom is still practised in the 1960s and 1970s. When the chairwoman of a rural women's association in Shandong province visited one commune, she was there for only two hours before four young couples had come in for marriage registration. The commune secretary told her that by the Chinese calendar it was the second day of the second month, or the double two, and it was often chosen as a day for marriage (CR 1 July 1962). The first step in one woman's preparations for her twenty-year-old son's wedding in 1965 was to consult a geomancer about the choice of an auspicious date for conducting the wedding. The geomancer specified the sixth day of the ninth moon (lunar calendar) as a 'lucky day' (NFRB 25 January 1965). The only case study found so far in which there is a conscious rejection of this custom was recorded in 1972, when a leader of the local Youth League intentionally chose the seventh day of the first month of the lunar year because it was a day not traditionally designated to be auspicious (RMRB 24 January 1972). In rural Guangdong the 'lucky' season for marriages was reported to be around the Chinese New Year or Spring Festival. The selection of the marriage date traditionally marked the beginning of the preparations for the marriage ceremony itself.

Seldom now do the young couple marry 'in the presence of the gods', nor are they 'introduced to the ancestors' at the altar. At the behest of the gods they used to be symbolically knitted together with invisible red and green threads which were believed to bind them together for life. The couple had traditionally been introduced to the ancestors at the altar in order to stress their role in the continuation of the line of descent, and the constant references to fertility reflected the main injunction that it was the purpose of their union to provide descendants. According to the new educational materials, such injunctions were considered to be no longer relevant in contemporary China where marriage was to be by self-determination and stable through choice. In the case studies it is a rare young couple who now worship heaven or earth, the gods or the ancestors, or who even come under parental pressure to do so. There are one or two occasions recorded in the case studies. In 1964 a young couple were described as 'walking to the *altar* in spanking new outfits' (my italics – RMRB 28 June 1964). In one case study a couple described how they had come under pressure to bow to the gods of heaven and earth (ZQ 30 January 1964), and another young couple in describing their 'modern new-style wedding' explicitly stated that 'we did not worship our ancestors and the Gods of Heaven and Earth', which may suggest that they wished to differentiate their marriage either from the traditional form or from those of others of their acquaintance (NFRB 18 January 1965).

There are seldom any reference to the multiple symbols of fertility which punctuated the old-style ceremony, although given the value placed on the birth of children, it would be surprising if there were no informal good wishes and references to the birth of future children at some point during the celebrations. Traditionally this first phase of the rites of integration, or the introduction of the couple to the ancestors to stress their role in the continuation of the descent group, would be followed by a second ritual sequence which established the relation of the couple to the living kin and emphasised the couple's subordinate place in the hierarchy of family relationships. The couple bowed to each person according to their place in the family genealogy, and the bride ritually served tea to her husband's parents to initiate her into her future role of servitude. Only one case study makes reference to any continuation of these rites. One couple 'paid respect to their elders by bowing three times to each in turn' (ZQ 19 November 1964).

The old-style ceremony had often been accompanied by a certain amount of ribaldry and teasing of the bride,* an ordeal through which, now unveiled, she was supposed to remain quite still and serene. The new ceremony is usually accompanied by many speeches, much story telling and good-humoured conversation. Apparently many of the stories, true or purporting to be true, relate to the lives of the particular couple or the storyteller and are meant to amuse and/or instruct. In nearly all the accounts of new-style weddings, a local cadre or leader made a speech listing the advantages of free-choice marriage and of a joyful and frugal wedding. At many, the young couple themselves were asked to describe how they met or to recount any amusing episode in the history of their attachment. At one new-style wedding, the guests reportedly chanted, 'Let the bride tell us how she found her man and how she was wooed' (PC 16 June 1949), and one young man reported that the guests had asked him to tell them the story of his 'falling in love with his bride' (ZF 1 October 1963). If there was a history of romance, this request could take the form of much teasing and jesting with the couple, and it has been known for them to be asked to perform physical feats and give evidence of their affection for each other. One guest at a wedding held in 1965

* Freedman has noted that during the 'teasing of the bride' two rules of propriety may be broken: the rule that the seniors must not behave informally with juniors, and the rule that bars the expression of sexuality in the house. Senior men and women might come into the room to fling idle remarks at the young couple. Old and young might make pointed remarks on the bride's appearance. Bawdy rhymes were often recited and the couple were required on the pain of forfeits to perform ridiculous manoeuvres and repeat tongue-twisters (1967:20).

described how the guests teased the bride and groom by asking them to cross together a wooden plank laid across two chairs, to share the same piece of candy and so on. He thought the whole scene was essentially a revival of the former practice of 'teasing the bride' and referred to this new-style wedding as trying to fill new bottles with old wine (NFRB 25 January 1965).

THE MARRIAGE FEAST

Perhaps the most tenacious of the old customs was the association of weddings with a feast or banquet (*bai jiuxi*) put on by the groom's family for kin, friends and neighbours. The provision and size of the traditional marriage feast was both a ceremonial obligation to be met by all those who could possibly afford it and a visible symbol of the wealth and status of the groom's family. It had thus represented a relatively heavy expenditure for rich and poor alike.* The government has recommended that registration be followed by a tea-party that provides light refreshments for the guests in the form of candies, cakes and pastries, which both invites social recognition, yet is also both simple and frugal. It marks and differentiates the occasion for kin yet is less exclusive in its selection of guests. Compared to the traditional marriage feast or banquet, which provided the opportunity to reinforce ties of kinship solidarity by demanding their corporate presence and the exchange of gifts, the guest list of the informal tea-party is not associated with traditional kin obligations or the exchange of gifts, and friends and neighbours of both the bride and groom could also partake of refreshments and offer their best wishes. It is less of a financial drain on the resources of the household and the collective productive unit. In one case a simple tea-party was cited as costing 2.80 yuan (ZQ 19 November 1964), and another as 7.0 yuan (RMRB 28 June 1964). In one village, there had been thirty-six funerals and twenty-five weddings held between mid-August 1963 and June 1964, and it was

* In Peking the cost of a group of weddings was found to vary from 1.5 to 9.0 times the monthly family income, but for one-half of them the expenditure was from 4.0 to 4.5 times a month's income (Gamble 1933: 199). In rural areas where the average income ranged from $185 to $247, a rough estimate of the wedding expenses for the groom's family ranged from $200 for a wealthy family, $100 for a middle-class family and $50 for a poorer family (Gamble 1954: 383). The wealthy of the towns and countryside might spend thousands of dollars to mark the occasion of a son's or daugher's wedding.

estimated that the brigade had saved over 5,000 catties of food grain, more than 7,000 yuan and 1,000 working days (for both men and animals) by observing these occasions in the new frugal style (*ibid.*).

The case studies suggest that an evening tea-party has become a common means of inviting social recognition from kin, neighbours and friends and it has come to characterise the ceremonials of marriage in many areas of China and especially in the urban social field. One family that I interviewed in Guangzhou had combined both the simple form for friends and fellow-workers with a more elaborate banquet for kin. In the morning they had met with their friends and fellow-workers in their newly decorated rooms and after the meeting they had provided light refreshments for them. Later in the evening, they had held a small dinner-party for close kin of the families, which included the members of the groom's household, his elder brother and sister-in-law and the bride's brothers and sisters (her parents were dead), and the dinner had cost quite a considerable amount of money.

While the large feast may have disappeared as an integral part of the social recognition and celebration of marriage in the urban areas, the provision of the large marriage feast in some rural areas has proved to be one of the more tenacious of the traditional marriage customs. In one village, inhabitants were heard to ask, 'What does a wedding look like if a feast is not held?' (NFRB 18 January 1965). In 1965 one villager estimated that holding a feast with from twenty to thirty tables was the custom, and a feast with from eight to ten tables which could cost 200–300 yuan was the minimum number to maintain the reputation of the household and 'prevent others laughing' (*ibid.*). There were constant complaints in the media that the cost of these feasts not only exhausted the savings of individual households, but siphoned-off the individual surplus into consumption rather than into reinvestment in production (RMRB 28 June 1964). Certainly, ways of meeting these large expenses would have to be planned in the private sector over a period of time. I found that families in Guangdong were saving for marriage expenses even though no marriages were planned or anticipated in the immediate future. In due course livestock would have to be raised and food prepared for the occasion. The media has cited evidence that some families still went into debt by borrowing from kin and friends in order to meet the expenses, and as a result some families were left in financial difficulties which affected the whole household (RMRB 28 June 1964; ZQ 19 November 1964).

But despite the cost of the feast many families have continued to invite their kin and friends and neighbours to partake of a feast or dinner.

In Guangdong in 1977 nearly every family I spoke to mentioned the expense of the wedding feast or banquet. One family said that they had answered the call of the government to spend little and be frugal, so they had held a feast composed of only a few tables for close relatives which had cost about 200 yuan! Of all the grooms' families interviewed, a substantial proportion of the average 400 yuan they had spent on the marriage had been apportioned to the provision of the feast for relatives and friends of both the bride and the groom. Sometimes the relations of the groom seem to have continued to make up the majority of the guests; in traditional times the marriage was almost always celebrated at the groom's household, to which the kin of the bride were not invited. The anthropologist William Geddes analysed the guest lists of two weddings held in Kaihsienkung in the mid-1950s. At one wedding there were eleven guests; two relatives and nine friends of the groom, but no relatives of the bride were invited, even though the maternal kin of the groom's mother were present. At the wedding, twenty persons were present. Ten were friends of the bridegroom, six were relatives of his including maternal relatives, and four were friends of the bride, all of whom came from her village. In both cases the relatives of the groom formed the predominant category of kin, but they were outnumbered by the numbers of friends (Geddes 1963:30). In Guangdong in 1977, families spoke of the attendance of a mixture of close relatives of the bride and groom and friends of the young couple. The inclusion of the kin of the bride and peer groups of the young people themselves indicates a readjustment in affinal relationships and the new importance assigned to the younger generation.

The marriage feast was one of a series of reciprocal and ceremonial obligations between kin and friends, and each guest was still expected to offer a gift, the amount of which was normally determined by the proximity of the relative or friend (Geddes 1963:25). For the groom's family the proffered gifts were expected to partly, or in exceptional cases wholly, offset the costs of the feast, and for the kin it was a matter of honour to offer the gifts as 'tokens of human feelings'. A popular saying illustrated that even if a relative has no money he has an obligation to go into debt or even sell the cooking-pot to meet this obligation: 'Expression of human feeings is as urgent as repaying a loan and the cooking-pot has to be carried on the head to be sold' (ZQ 19 November 1964). Villagers often proved to be reluctant to break the circle of ceremonial obligations. In one particular case study published in 1964, the groom described the procedures that the arrangement of his impending marriage had set in motion. Relatives and friends began to call on the family to learn of the wedding date in order that they might prepare the wedding presents. All of them were certain that they were to attend a wedding feast, and, in anticipation, some of them borrowed money while others withdrew a portion of their savings from the credit cooperative. One cousin who was short of money borrowed 45 yuan from the credit cooperative, and another relative sold his suckling pig for 18 yuan to be used for 'gift-packets'. Although the prospective groom told them repeatedly that no dinner-party would be given, they just would not believe him. A large dinner had always been given on the occasion of a marriage and relatives and friends of the family required to offer their gifts (*ibid.*). Another case was reported in the same year in which the cadres and workers of a commune factory, on hearing that a fellow-worker was to give a wedding feast, went to choose gifts to take with them. Some chose bottles of wine, chickens and other kinds of food, and others presented red gift-packets of money. Talking about the custom later, many of the workers in the factory defended it on the grounds that 'when a kinsman or friend gets married, it would be impolite and people would talk if we did not give any presents and did not attend a feast' (RMRB 20 November 1972). It was not unknown for the receipt of presents to be a factor that encouraged the giving of wedding feasts, and there are a few references in the early 1960s to cases where hosts in positions of authority actually made a profit (Chen and Ridley 1969:109).

Above all, though, the persistence of the feast was due to its traditional function as a status symbol in the local community and its appropriation by the socially mobile to advertise their new status. There is no doubt that for many peasants, the feast provided an opportunity to display newly found subsistence, security and surplus gained since 1949. The parents of one groom who planned to make their son's wedding impressive said, 'We lived in a straw hut by the river when we were young. Conditions now have improved. Now that the eldest of our three sons is getting married, we have to make the wedding impressive and celebrate in a style appropriate to that of a household which has achieved self-sufficiency' (ZQ 24 April 1962).

As the single most important occasion other than funerals, the elder villagers have displayed a remarkable capacity to remember the details of every wedding banquet within a generation.

The following case study suggests that a reputation dented by the previous absence of celebration had not been righted before the marriages of the next generation. One young groom, who was determined to conduct his wedding frugally, found his parents more adamant than most in their insistence that they must give a big feast of twenty-five tables to entertain their relatives and friends. They had already planned for the occasion and raised two head of fat pigs and from twenty to thirty chickens and ducks to 'conduct a presentable and well-attended wedding for their son'. His father said to him that 'there is only one marriage in a man's lifetime and it is therefore worthwhile to be wasteful just for one. I should know!' When he himself had come to the village to be married, he had given a small wedding party due to lack of money. Local gossip in the village described him as 'miserly', 'lacking in generosity' and he was accused of having 'brought disrepute to the family'. The gossip was not quietened until he had borrowed 35 pieces of silver from the landlord for an additional small dinner of several tables. Now he felt the family was living well with their own supplies of food; pigs, chickens and ducks. They had practically everything they wanted and could now afford to give a large feast. But even without their present prosperity he thought they would have had to borrow to give a big wedding banquet, for they could 'no longer stand the ridicule of other people that our family is miserly and not generous' (ZQ 19 November 1964).

Elaborate feasts had long been associated with households in positions of authority in the village, such as those of landlords or government officials, and some of those in new positions of authority in the village thought that they likewise should appropriate the old symbols of status. The feast had always provided an opportunity for the rich and powerful to differentiate themselves from the rest of the community. As one of the most important ritual occasions for indulging in conspicuous consumption, a marriage had supplied a unique occasion to advertise wealth and status. The Lienchang documents for the early 1960s suggest that the problem of extravagant feasting, even at a time of general food shortage, was more likely to be found among the cadres than among the other villagers. One case was cited where a brigade leader had arranged a feast of thirty-four tables when his daughter was married, and another was reported to have held a feast of eighteen tables (Chen and Ridley 1969:107, 192). There have been several other cases where cadres have been criticised in the media for 'investing in pomp and holding grand feasts' in order to attract the esteem of others (e.g. NFRB 18 January 1965; 25 January 1965).

In nearly every case study, those persons who still followed the old customs were well aware of the newly recommended forms and their economic advantages. For example, after attendance at a simple evening tea-party to celebrate with the bride and groom, one guest commented 'if that little is spent and that much [pleasure] is got in return, this surely is a good way of celebrating a marriage' (RMRB 28 June 1964). But despite the economic advantages of the new forms and a consciousness of the new social and familial relations which they symbolised, some of the old customs remained influential in determining the forms which marriage ceremonials took, particularly in the rural areas. An examination of the common ceremonial forms in contemporary China does begin to allow for a continuum to be drawn up between the more elaborate and the new and simpler ceremonial forms which also coincides with a progression from the rural to the urban social field. Where the parents controlled the negotiations, from their initiation to their conclusion, the ceremony inviting social recognition was likely to be more elaborate in form and to incorporate old customs. Where the couple controlled the negotiations, the ceremonial was more likely to take a simpler form. The survival of traditional customs frequently occasioned conflict between the generations or between the kin of the bride and groom, and, as on other occasions, each party to the conflict could call on either the sanctions at the disposal of kin and neighbours or those at the command of political associations to support their point of view.

7

THE 'MODERNISATION' OF MARRIAGE AND KINSHIP STRUCTURES

In the negotiation of marriage, four main types were distinguished according to the patterns of control and authority which they exhibited. They ranged from type (1), in which the negotiations, from their initiation to their conclusion, were entirely monopolised by the older generation or parents, to type (4), where the controls were exclusively operated by the parties to the negotiations. Between these two poles, a variety of immediate models combined elements characteristic of both pre-existing marriage customs and concessions to the new ideology of marriage introduced in 1950. Throughout the negotiations of marriage there was a close correlation between the form which the initial negotiations took and the procedures characterising pre-marital rituals, choice of marriage partner, age of marriage and ritual and ceremonial forms.

Where the older generation initiated the negotiations, the preliminary procedures were much more likely to take the form of betrothal, whereas if the younger generation personally took over the initiation of the negotiations, courtship, albeit often at a low level of institutionalisation, became the dominant pre-marital form. The majority of pre-marital rituals included the modalities of both betrothal and courtship, for each was commonly modified to provide for the mechanisms of consent or shared controls by parents and parties. Despite constant campaigns by the government to raise the age of marriage, it was still likely to be nearer the legal end of the 'appropriate' age spectrum in the rural areas, where the older generation initiate the negotiations. In the choice of a marriage partner, whether by the older or young generation, the customary norms of homogamy have predominated over the recommended ones of heterogamy. It seemed as if the principles of homogamy and hypergamy, defined in terms of both socio-economic and political status, enjoyed wide support in Chinese society, at least before the

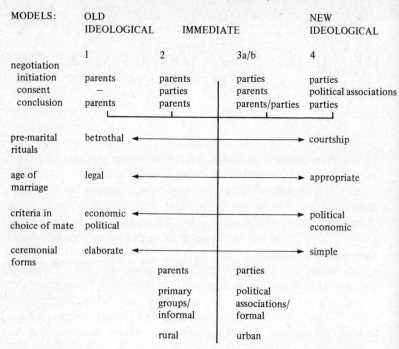

MODELS:	OLD IDEOLOGICAL 1	IMMEDIATE 2	3a/b	NEW IDEOLOGICAL 4
negotiation				
initiation	parents	parents	parties	parties
consent	–	parties	parents	political associations
conclusion	parents	parents	parents/parties	parties
pre-marital rituals	betrothal ←		→	courtship
age of marriage	legal ←		→	appropriate
criteria in choice of mate	economic political ←		→	political economic
ceremonial forms	elaborate ←		→	simple
		parents	parties	
		primary groups/ informal	political associations/ formal	
		rural	urban	

Fig. 4. Patterns in the negotiation of marriage: the People's Republic of China

Cultural Revolution. The case studies incorporating heterogamous marriages, especially those negotiated between partners of differing socio-economic and urban and rural backgrounds, indicate, however, that where the younger generation initiated the marriage negotiations themselves, there was at least the possibility of a heterogamous marriage. Equally, where the negotiations were initiated by the older generation they were likely to exhibit a more elaborate series of prestations and ceremonial forms than the negotiations initiated by the younger generation.

The correlation between the controls of the negotiations and the procedures followed at each stage of the negotiations can be summed up as follows: where mates are primarily acquired by parents or persons other than the parties, there is more likely to be a betrothal, a lower age of marriage, a homogamous or hypergamous marriage and elaborate ceremonial forms. Conversely, where the negotiations are conducted by the couple themselves, there is more likely to be a period of courtship, a higher age of marriage, simpler ceremonial forms, and there is at least the possibility of a heterogamous marriage. The models with all their ramifications can thus be placed on a continuum according to the degree of parental and parties' participation in the negotiations. In evaluating the relative weight of the control and authority of each, the main dividing line on the continuum as drawn up in fig. 4 coincides with the point at which the parties take over the initiation of the negotiations. All the available evidence assembled in the last few chapters suggests that this point tends to roughly coincide with the division into rural and urban social fields and the transition in dominance from the informal to the formal arbitration of socio-political control. In the absence of certain types of data it has not been possible to correlate marriage patterns with the distribution and maintenance of power by individuals and groups of various compositions at national, lineage or village levels, but it has been possible to identify two arenas of competition for *control* of the marriage patterns. The younger generation has competed with the older generation for the control of the negotiation of marriage, and primary or kin groups have competed with political associations for the control of marriage patterns. The greater adherence to the traditional ideological model in the rural social field has required the concurrence of both parents and parties in the maintenance of traditional patterns of controls. The greater adherence to new forms in the urban social field required that the younger generation take control of the negotiations. In the implicit or explicit bargaining process between the younger and older generations the sanctions at the disposal of each will determine the form which the marriage patterns take.

The most common of the contemporary marriage patterns, models (2)and (3), combined elements characteristic of both the traditional and new ideological models and derived from patterns of social behaviour evolved in the last two decades to mediate the competition between the old and new ideological models. Thus the projected line of social change proposed and introduced into China by the government in 1950 can be contrasted with the actual lines which social change has taken in the past two decades (see fig. 5). The variety of marriage patterns identified in this study, then, do not yet reflect the unqualified dominance of the new ideological model in China today, and the question is, are we observing a transitional process or

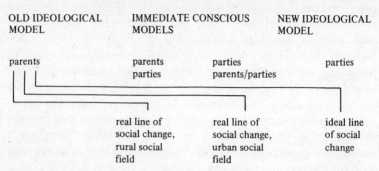

Fig. 5. Ideal and real lines of social change for the negotiation of marriage

a progression from one form to another? Do the economic and ideological pre-conditions exists in Chinese society and encourage the institutionalisation of the new ideological model of 'free choice'? Previous studies have assumed that social change in marriage and kinship structures in the People's Republic of China is proceeding and that they are on the way to being 'modernised', and that this process has parallels with that which has taken place in Republican China and Taiwan. In each of these social fields scientists have argued that it is the new socio-economic factors or the process of industrialisation or 'modernisation' which has primarily encouraged changes in marriage patterns and family types.

REPUBLICAN CHINA

Scholars of Republican China have argued that changes in marriage patterns in the People's Republic pre-date the promulgation of the new Marriage Law, and that changes after 1949 merely reflect a continuation of the effects of the process of industrialisation or 'modernisation' which they observed to be taking place before 1949. The process they observed and their analysis of social structures in Republican China convinced anthropologists such as Lang (1946), Levy (1949) and C. K. Yang (1959) that it was the new socio-economic factors, or the process of urbanisation and industrialisation, which had primarily brought about the practise of new marriage patterns and the establishment of the nuclear family as alternative forms of social behaviour in the cities. The new forms of marriage had their origins in the new ideologies and new economic relations introduced China in the early twentieth century. The cause of free choice and romantic love was taken up as an expression of 'freedom', 'individualism', 'self-fulfilment' and 'equality of the sexes' and became a platform of popular appeal among students in the years immediately prior to the May 4 Movement in 1919. Then the new periodic press contrasted procedures in mate selection in China with those in Europe and North America and encouraged the younger generation to free themselves from the authority and controls of the older generation. The ensuing campaigns rejecting the old family system came to centre on the right of an individual to choose his or her own marriage partner free from parental interference. Free choice of marriage partner became a symbol of wider social rebellion. At the same time, the influx of foreign capital and investment of Chinese capital in trade and industry had created new employment opportunities in the main urban centres. The increasing numbers of factories needed an expanding workforce, and the widespread establishment of schools in both rural and urban areas allowed numbers of boys and girls to undertake further education and move into the clerical, business and professional occupations that were expanding in the cities. By the late 1930s it was estimated that in some areas of China there was hardly a household in both rural and urban areas which did not have sons and daughters working in the cities (Lang 1946:159). According to the studies of Republican society, it was this mobility and the new forms of economic support as an alternative to that of the parental household, rather than the new ideology of 'free choice', which had allowed for and even encouraged the practise of free-choice marriage.

The new ideology of free-choice marriage had been vaguely formulated in terms of abstract ideals, and although the new Family Law of 1931 provided legal recognition for free-choice marriage conditional upon parental approval, a major limitation of the new law was that it did not require the marriage contract to be signed by bride or groom; it was not actively enforced, few had access to legal institutions and even more remained ignorant of the law's very existence (Fei 1939:81-2). The overwhelming impression conveyed by the autobiographies and letters of the period, and it was confirmed by sociological enquiries, was the lack of any established behavioural patterns which could be followed by those who rejected the traditional model. The fact that from the initiation to the conclusion of the marriage negotiations there were no precedents for young people to follow, because in their immediate circles the new patterns 'seemed to be unprecedented', elicited a great deal of anxiety and uncertainty among the younger generation. One student who, after much agonising, worked out a plan to break off her betrothal prior to her marriage to a partner of her own choice had to puzzle out 'who should marry us? How should we be married? Who was to give me away? Or should we even have a wedding? (Chao 1970:77, 191).* The sociologist Chin Ai-li concluded from her study of letters published in the media in the late 1940s that for those adopting new forms of marriage there was a recognisable vacuum in standards. It was not merely a problem of choice between alternative forms of behaviour so much as uncertainty about what were to be the options permitted. The 'emancipated young men and women', she says, 'are faced with new unfamiliar situations for which there are no established patterns and no agreed-upon cues, with which to judge or interpret other people's behaviour. This problem extends to the very question of how to find friends of the opposite sex as well as how to behave once acquaintance is made' (China 1948:4). Those who adoped the new form in the face of opposition were made vulnerable by the very novelty and vagueness surrounding its definition. It was fear of gossip or loss of dignity, and lack of sympathy and support within the immediate face-to-face informal circles, which frequently contributed to capitulation, despair and even suicide among the young (Burgess and Locke 1945:52; Witke 1967:138). For others it was more the fear of losing their monthly allowance which deterred them from adopting the new forms. Many were like the young man who badly wanted to break off his betrothal, but dared not because he was economically dependent on his father.

My father is a good friend of her father. If I should break the engagement, my father would be very angry. Most probably he would stop my allowance and refuse to pay any tuition for me. In that case I could not study in the school. I do not know what I should do. I have thought about my problem so much that I am sick of it. (Burgess and Locke 1945:52)

* In the absence of an institutionalised alternative, one young girl resorted to the unusual tactics of creating chaos in the large household while the horoscopes of her sister and her parentally chosen mate sat on the family altar. In this way she and her sister hoped that the apparent signs of 'bad luck' would impress upon the household the inauspicious nature of the proposed match (Wong and Cressy 1953:131).

It was the new socio-economic conditions, which provided both new forms of economic support and encouraged migration, that proved to be necessary for, and even encouraged the practise of, the new marriage patterns. Time and again those who married according to one of the new forms had escaped from their home environment by means of a scholarship or employment and therefore were away from the efficacy of both economic sanctions and pressures of local public opinion. This form of escape was made increasingly possible by the development and expansion of industry and manufacturing which had opened up new venues of employment and demanded a highly mobile labour force. This had encouraged the migration of large numbers of young people to the cities, which allowed for the establishment of independent and separate households on marriage (Freedman 1966:44ff). The new and alternate forms of economic support considerably weakened the sanctions at the disposal of the older generation. In the community studies it is made clear that it was those who were mobile, beyond the reaches of the sanctions of kin and local community, who had adopted the new models in practice. In West Town, those who had broken their betrothals sought refuge in nearby towns (Hsu 1948:91-3). In Taitou village, when the young men migrated to jobs in the cities and divorced their village wives, the bitter criticism of their action was largely ineffectual because the 'real culprits' had placed themselves out of reach and beyond the ties of the old community and the family rules (M. Yang 1945:117). In a survey undertaken in a factory in a provincial town in the 1930s, most of the women workers interviewed said that they had taken jobs in order to escape from intolerable family situations and that they intended to return to their homes once the conflict was resolved to their satisfaction (T'ien 1944).

The migration and dispersal of members of households reached a high point in the 1940s with the anti-Japanese and civil war, the increasing demand for industrial labour and the deteriorating agrarian conditions due to famine, drought and invasion. Where household members dispersed, the possibility of the household head conducting the negotiations on behalf of the young, or the consultation by the young of the older generations, was reduced, and free choice by default was frequently forced on the individual. Marion Levy, writing in the late 1940s, noted that it was often the case that the mobile young lost contact with their families for long periods of time if not completely, and that even young people who adhered to the traditional ideological model in principle found that they were forced into a situation in which they had to make new decisions and search for new rationales for their behaviour (1949:298). Levy terms this new phenomenon 'individualism by default' as opposed to 'individualism by ideal', and he concluded from his observations that, though the mobile young had adsorbed a certain amount of 'individualism by ideal' as the result of contact with new ideals, 'individualism by default' would seem to have been a more effective and widespread solvent of the traditional model than 'individualism by ideal' (*ibid.*). These observations led Levy to argue that the changes introduced in the economic substructure of the family have been a primary factor in introducing new forms of behaviour (1949:318), C. K. Yang, while giving more weight to the new ideological factors than Levy, also concludes that the social changes visible in marriage in the Republic of China were not either self-conscious or the result of a specifically defined conceptual form of marriage and the family. Rather, he says, 'socio-economic environmental pressure became the major factor in altering the basic economic position of the family and in forcing a change in the family economic structure' and with it, in marriage forms (C. K. Yang 1959:136). On the basis of their research both Levy and Yang forecast an acceleration of this process of social change under the new Communist government.

In 1948 Levy had anticipated that the greater development of industry and urbanisation programmes would undoubtedly lead to new forms of marriage and the establishment of neolocal post-marital residence patterns. He argued that the patterns of the Republican period, which combined elements of the traditional patterns and elements of the patterns associated with urban industrial society, could only be temporary social phenomena. He thought industrialisation had already modified the traditional patterns sufficiently to suppose further change in a similar direction. 'The odds are', he suggested, 'that this new pattern will be simply the conjugal family unit of the West rather than a patchwork of parts from the one and the other' (Levy 1949:364–5). C. K. Yang anticipated that the spontaneous processes of the economic and social changes already well established in the Republican period would continue, but be amplified by the coordinated and conscious planning of an organised political power (1959:19–20). The predictions of these scholars were corroborated by fieldworkers who took their data from the comparable and more accessible social field of Taiwan.

TAIWAN

Despite the fact that there has been no new ideological model similar to that operating in the People's Republic of China introduced into Taiwan, the marriage patterns in both social fields show remarkable parallels in their form. Both Taiwan and the People's Republic of China shared the same traditional ideological model, and in rural Taiwan today, arranged marriage is still to be found, although here too it is very much on the decline (Tang 1973:152–4; Schak 1973:203; Arcay *et al.* 1968:7; M. Yang 1962:70). In the most common form of marriage negotiations in Taiwan, the traditional form has been modified to include a 'formal meeting' of potential spouses and allow for their consent to the match. This adaptation is what is normally meant by 'modern marriage' in the rural areas (Diamond 1969:53; Bessac 1965:24–5). Parental authority combined with the consent of the parties was popular with the older generation, for it enabled them to continue to control the selection of a spouse and yet to be relieved of the total responsibility for arranging the match (M. Wolf 1972:102; Gallin 1966:206; Bessac 1965:24–5). Few parents were prepared to allow the marriage negotiations to become the exclusive responsibility of the young, for the importance of marriage for 'family continuity' required that marriage still remain within their control (Gallin 1967:5; Pasternark 1972:66). At the same time they also thought that in present-day Taiwan arranged marriage was much more likely to end in the dissolution of the household, and their acceptance of the new modifications was like an insurance policy taken out in the interests of buttressing familial solidity and stabilising and preserving family unity (Gallin 1967:6–7). The new form allowed the younger generation to exercise a negative sanction and any further initiative on their part in the negotiations would have presupposed at least some form of contact, dating or courtship patterns, and these institutional pre-conditions were lacking in rural Taiwan and were not yet fully established patterns of social behaviour even in the cities (Gallin 1966:202; March and O'Hara 1961:6; Diamond 1969:41).

The most recent innovation to be introduced into the procedures of marriage in Taiwan was the choice of marriage partners by the younger generation themselves. The principle of 'freedom of choice' had gained currency in the urban areas and especially in the capital, Taibei, among the middle classes. According to fieldworkers the new form was by no means universally practised in the cities and it has barely penetrated the rural areas (Bessac 1965:24–5; M. Wolf 1972:101; Marsh and O'Hara 1961:5). Where the young couple do choose their own partners, the marriage negotiations may still be formally negotiated by the heads of households, who continue to employ a go-between or some other third party to arrange a formal engagement and the exchange of gifts. Some parents were willing to let the young persons make the initial choice and then would check it out for themselves through friends, relatives or a formal go-between before embarking on the traditional ceremonial sequences as if the marriage had been arranged. According to one woman quoted by a fieldworker: 'The best thing is to let the boy and girl make their choice, and then have a go-between to discuss the engagement with both sets of parents, arrange what gifts are to be exchanged. Then, on the wedding day, you invite relatives and friends to the ceremony, and have a big celebration' (Diamond 1969:55). Young people already familiar with each other would go through the formalities of giving their consent or a traditionally arranged marriage as if they were total strangers. Several field studies refer to this camouflage or facade adopted by families to suggest that marriages were conforming to the traditional ideological model in order that the families involved may maintain 'face' or retain a certain aura of respectability (Diamond 1969:55; Schak 1973:213; Bessac 1965:24–5).

Although the variety of marriage patterns in Taiwan show re-markable similarities to those characteristic of the People's Republic of China, there is one important difference. The absence of a new ideological model has meant that changes in the marriage patterns in Taiwan are not only viewed as undesirable modifications of arranged marriage to be obscured if at all possible by its ritual and ceremonial forms, but arranged marriage is the only yardstick against which to measure any change. The only competition on the ideological level for arranged marriage originates in the foreign media, or in the foreign movie versions of romantic love and courtship imported into Taiwan, and as 'alien, direct and brazen' versions of the phenomenon these do not readily constitute acceptable models for most Chinese (Schak 1973:170). Most scholars have not only concluded that the ideological impetus for change is weak in Taiwan, but that any change in the norms of family life and traditional patterns of authority have been actively discouraged. Family legislation, which follows closely the form of the 1931 Family Law and allowed for both arranged marriage or consent by the parties to a match negotiated by the parents, has not so far been used to implement changes that would undermine traditional customs (M. Cohen 1976:82). In the media, traditional values and patterns of authority are upheld and those who attempt to introduce and institutionalise changes or try to oppose the old forms in any way are severely disadvantaged as a result. Morality tales portraying situations of conflict between the generations over the right to choose a spouse conclude in favour of the older generation, and promise tragedy to those who ignore the traditional patterns of obligation and authority which mark parent–child relations.

Anthropologists of Taiwan generally attribute the modifications of arranged marriage to socio-economic factors which have caused the increasing independence of the individual from the peasant household and the household from the rural village or community. In more and more farm households, members of the younger generation have taken advantage of the new employment opportunities which provide them with a source of economic independence and either necessitate permanent or temporary migration or at least daily commuting to the cities. The authority of the older generation in the household is now threatened by the fact that the younger generation is no longer economically dependent on the family estate. Indeed they are more likely to contribute a necessary cash component to the family income. As a result they have acquired a new bargaining position with which to resist the traditional authority of the parents to control marriage negotiations. Sons and daughters have proved less willing to return to their villages and marry a spouse they have had no part in selecting, let alone one they have never seen. Those who choose their own mates and marry in the face of sustained parental opposition risk a break with their families, a permanent move away from the village and a reduction of the family income.

The reduction in both the number of persons employed in agriculture and the proportion of farm income derived from agricultural sources has meant that the household has become less dependent on agriculture and more reliant on other sources of income; and that household ties now extend far beyond the immediate village environs to the urban centres. The elaboration of these networks, caused by the incorporation of the previously cohesive village into a broader economy, with the consequent weakening of village organisation and solidarity, has been identified as one of the most significant social changes occurring in Taiwan (Gallin 1967). The fact that the household no longer finds it necessary or advantageous to focus on the interrelationships within the village, which in turn no longer possesses the means to meet its major needs, has reduced the sanctions at the disposal of the older generation and the kin and neighbourhood group in the event of conflict. Parents in the rural social field themselves have admitted that since the conditions of their social environment are now so different, it may be better to voluntarily relinquish their monopoly of the controls and modify the traditional marriage negotiations, which still gives them some measure of authority but also allows for participation by the younger generation (Gallin 1967:5).

ANALOGIES WITH THE PEOPLE'S REPUBLIC OF CHINA

In Taiwan, then, the studies of anthropologists would suggest that economic changes have primarily enforced adaptations to the traditional ideological model of arranged marriage. The independence of the individual from the rural household and the household from the village are identified as the significant social changes in rural Taiwan and these are directly attributed to the current economic policies of industrialisation and urbanisation. As for Republican China, there has been a tendency among the anthropologists of Taiwan to draw parallels between their own experience and findings in this province and social change in the People's Republic. Perhaps the anthropologist who has stretched these parallels to their limits is Bernard Gallin. He concluded that although there were qualitative and quantitative differences between various areas in the People's Republic of China, there was no doubt in his mind that by observing and analysing the nature of social change in Taiwan, anthropologists could derive some insights into social developments taking place in the People's Republic. For, he says, 'many of the changes taking place both in Taiwan and in the People's Republic of China are primarily due to the same cause – the encroachment of urbanisation on a traditional agrarian culture whether enforced by the Japanese, Nationalist [Republican] China or the Communists' (1966:4). He suggests that it is part of the Communist policy of social development to break down the large kinship groups in order to accelerate the process of urbanisation. He therefore attributes the supposed breakdown of the traditional village and kinship and family relations in the People's Republic, not to the introduction of communism and its ideological attack on such traditional Chinese concepts as large family and kinship groups, but to 'such developments as socio-economic factors and improved communications which increasingly draw the rural areas into closer contact and relationship with the changing urban and industrial forms of life', as it is in Taiwan (Gallin 1966:281).

The significance of socio-economic factors in introducing new marriage patterns has also been a feature of the previous studies of marriage and kinship in the People's Republic of China. Writing in 1958, with the advantage of several years of direct and indirect observation since 1950, C. K. Yang thought that the direction of social change under the Communist Party contained no new substance (1959:18). In the early 1960s William Goode analysed the links between the process of industrialisation and family patterns in China and concluded that the acceleration of industrial development and urbanisation in the People's Republic would continue and would lead to the greater exercise of free-choice marriage and the establishment of some type of conjugal family (1963:270). He based his conclusion as much on an important component of 'modernisation theory', which links economic development and family type, as on the study of marriage patterns in contemporary China itself. Although he attacked the conventional formula that industrialisation undermined the extended family, he continued to view the individualisation and isolation of the nuclear or conjugal family as the most fundamental of the social changes associated with industrialisation or 'modernisation'. He did substitute the broader ideological and economic processes of 'modernisation' for industrialisation, but he nevertheless continued to assume a universal 'fit' between industrialisation and the small-family system. As the demand for a mobile and qualified labour force increases, so does the presence of free-choice marriage and the conjugal household. Moreover, he argued that this is a universal phenomenon and in China, as in other countries, economic and ideological factors were uniformly working to move familial structures in the direction of the conjugal form (1963:320).

THE PEOPLE'S REPUBLIC OF CHINA

In taking either Taiwan or Republican China as empirical analogies and 'modernisation theory' as a conceptual framework, previous studies have correlated certain characteristics of the marriage negotiations which are common to all three social fields and attributed them to common socio-economic causes. The material presented in the next two chapters questions the analogies drawn from the comparative social fields of Republican China and Taiwan. A more detailed correlation of marriage patterns with both social and economic relations within the household and between the household and primary kin or neighbourhood groups in the People's Republic of China suggests that there, the economic policies in rural areas have had precisely the opposite effects on the socio-economic patterns of rural social life: they have reinforced the interdependence of the individual on the household, restricted mobility and solidified kin and village ties. In China there are very real economic reasons why the old forms of marriage should persist and continue to dominate social behaviour in rural areas. Primarily these have to do with the structure and function of the household or domestic group and the nature of primary groups in rural areas. The next two chapters seek to examine two related questions: what factors encourage the older generation, especially in the rural areas, to keep the initiative in marriage negotiations and withhold their consent to the marriage should they lose this initiative, and secondly why should young people, especially in the rural areas, allow their parents the right to initiate their marriage negotiations or, if they acquire this initiative themselves, feel parental consent to be necessary to the conclusion of the marriage negotiations? The answers to these questions mainly have to do with the structure and function of the household or domestic group and the nature of primary groups in rural areas. This book puts forward two hypotheses. First, a qualitative examination of the data suggests that the degree of parental participation in, or the continuing influence of the old ideological model on, the negotiations of marriage, is directly correlated to the structure and function of the household. Secondly, that the degree of parental participation in, or influence of the old ideological model on, the negotiations of marriage, varies directly with the degree to which households are encapsulated by overlapping primary groups or influenced by informal socio-political controls. The potential or real opposition between successive generations for the control of marriage negotiations operates first within the internal structure of the domestic group.

8

MARRIAGE AND THE DOMESTIC GROUP

This chapter sets out to assess the degree to which the household contributes to the maintenance of customary patterns of marriage in rural areas. It examines the extent to which the current concept of the household acts as part of the ideology and becomes itself an instrument of dominance and control over the younger generation through the relations of dependence established within its boundaries. In strengthening the marital bond as opposed to all other kin bonds, the new ideology attempts to redefine marriage to form an institution symbolising the relations between two individuals or equal partners and not that between two households or kin groups. However, marriage is not simply defined as the 'social form of the union between two sexes'. At the same time its purpose is described as providing the foundation of the 'basic social cell of society' or the domestic group (ZQ 16 December 1956). The form which the domestic group takes has wide repercussions for the institution of marriage, and it can be argued that the boundaries and structure of the domestic group and the socio-economic functions assigned to it in contemporary rural China are such that the two aims combined in this definition of marriage – as a relationship between two freely chosen and equal individuals of the opposite sex and as the foundation of the domestic group – stand opposed to one another. That is, the form which the domestic group takes in rural areas has encouraged the older generation to retain their controls over the negotiations of marriage.

In contemporary China the domestic group is defined as 'mainly a unit of life in which the husband and wife share their married life together, rear and educate their children and care for their elder near relatives together' (PR 13 March 1964). The implications of this definition for the structure of the domestic group are far from clear, for the new ideology seems to have left vague the projected forms which the residential group or family formation should take. Virilocal

142

marriage, or the recruitment of wives to the domestic group in which the husband resided prior to marriage, was widely practised in traditional China and nowhere are new rules of post-marital residence explicitly stated. Rather, the domestic group or household is said 'to stem from the marital bond for either it functions to establish a new household completely or it perpetuates an old household for a further generation' (Lu Yang 1964:7). On the one hand the strengthening of the marital bond above all other familial bonds might suggest the establishment of a conjugal household, and in the educational materials advocating the rise in the age of marriage, marriage is almost by definition seen to require the establishment of an independent economic base for the livelihood of the couple and their children. The allocation of new housing to young couples in the urban areas, where there was no acute shortage of supply, seems to assume the establishment of a neolocal household rather than the incorporation of the new marriage partners into the larger economic unit of the joint family. Indeed, anthropologists who have studied the family, domestic group or household in contemporary China have argued that there has been a rise in the number of households of the conjugal type (Goode 1963).

On the other hand the recent recommendation that uxorilocal marriage (the recruitment of the groom into the bride's household) should exist alongside virilocal marriage assumes that a joint or extended household will remain the norm. During the campaign to criticise Confucius and Lin Piao (1973–5), the population was encouraged to emulate those Party committee members who had promoted uxorilocal marriage as a normal form of post-marital residence. Apparently these Party committee members supported any groom who chose to settle in his wife's family after marriage on the grounds that then the birth of daughters could be as advantageous to the future of the rural household as the birth of boys. Parents of daughters need no longer fear for their future, for the new custom broke with the traditional idea that only wives could be recruited into the household on marriage (SWB 30 January 1975; 11 February 1975). The establishment of these new residential patterns was designed to break with the old virilocal post-marital residential patterns, but in this case neither the old nor the new prescriptions advocated neolocal marriage. Certainly in both rural and urban areas, both the older and the younger generations have been advised to care for each other and redefine their relationships in order to reduce areas of tension within the household, however it is defined (Marriage Law 1950 (see Croll 1974); ZQ 1 December 1956). Indeed it seems as if the current concept of the household or domestic group forms one of the underdeveloped areas of the new ideology.

The new definition of the household also omits any references to its property base or the socio-economic functions which have characterised the traditional domestic group in China and which underlie the usual anthropological definitions of the domestic group. Anthropological definitions usually identify the domestic group as the 'housekeeping unit organised to provide the material and cultural resources needed to maintain and bring up its members' (Fortes 1971:8), 'the dwelling unit, the reproductive unit and the economic unit' (Goody 1972:106) and the 'residential unit, the unit of production, consumption and reproduction' (Sahlins 1974:76–100). In comparison to its policy on residential patterns, however, the government in China is clear in its aim to reduce the socio-economic functions of the domestic group. In the 1950s a number of policies were designed and introduced in China to collectivise the means of production and remove the property basis of the domestic group. In urban areas the establishment of joint State–private enterprises, craft and other productive cooperatives and neighbourhood factories were all introduced to replace the domestic group as the unit of production. In rural areas, policies were designed to gradually collectivise the land, and to collectively organise production and many subsidiary occupations (see Perkins 1969; Schran 1969). With the establishment of communes, the production brigade and the production team became the effective owners of the means of production, and formed the basic units of accounting, planning and distribution of incomes. In both rural and urban areas it was anticipated that the establishment of collective consumer services such as common dining facilities, child care, laundry, food processing and others would mean that a large part of consumption would eventually take place outside the individual household.

Social scientists abroad foresaw the implications of these policies for the structure and functions of the domestic group in China. They suggested that by taking out the last vestiges of private land-ownership and management, the commune had destroyed the estate or economic basis of the joint family (M. Cohen 1976:231) or the traditional peasant family (Lethbridge 1962:380). The payment of individual wages, collectivisation of land and the collective organisation of production were all interpreted as weakening the controls of the older generation over the marriage negotiations of the young (C. Yang 1959:39ff; Goode 1963:301–2, 313). However, despite the new definition of the domestic group and the policies designed to reduce its economic basis, the evidence suggests that the traditional structure of rural households may have been maintained or even elaborated, and that it is these same characteristics which both encourage the older generation to control the marriage negotiations, and which place certain resources and sanctions at their disposal.

THE HOUSEHOLD

In both rural and urban areas the basic unit of domestic organisation is the household (*hu*), which was defined in my fieldwork as the group of kin relations distinguished by a common budget and single kitchen. It may or may not coincide with the family (*jia* or *jiating*), which seems to have been a relative term used as variously in the past as in the present (Osgood 1963:355–6). In my interviews, the term *jia* (or family) was often used to refer to the members of a particular household, or it might refer to members of the household plus those related by blood who were not identified as present members of the household, such as married sons and daughters who had their own separate households, or unmarried sons and daughters who were temporarily resident elsewhere. Members of a household did not always share a common residence and in Jiang village the members of several households were dispersed by housing arrangements (see fig. 6).

There has been some debate concerning the size of the individual household before 1949. Although the Chinese household was initially characterised abroad as one that included representatives of several generations deriving from one patriline and as many male siblings as possible plus their spouses and children, the work of anthropologists in the twentieth century suggested that the nuclear two-generational type was the more common pattern (Hsu 1943; Fei 1946). It seems as if the average number of persons constituting a peasant household may not in fact have changed very much. Taeuber has analysed a hitherto unpublished 1929 survey of 38,256 farm families in 22 provinces of China and found that the average family size then was

Table 12. *Average size of household: Guangdong 1977*

Locality	No. of persons	No. of households	Average size of household
Jiang village	147	27	5.44
No. 11 production team	250	55	4.54
Huadong commune	63,200	13,400	4.71
Yue village	585	145	4.03
Renhe commune	73,532	15,568	4.70
Haomei village	480	110	4.40
Dali commune	68,000	15,900	4.30

5.2 persons (1970:71), and her figures are corroborated by others who placed the average family size before 1949 within the range of from 4 to 6 persons (C. Yang 1959:7). In Guangdong province the figures collected during my interviews are similar; see table 12. However, the similarities in average size may mask the range in the size of households and the variations in any one household at different points in its developmental cycle and their differences within the rural and urban social fields.

In rural areas post-marital residence is still generally patrilocal. Marriage immediately occasions the expansion of the domestic group and the establishment of stem and joint families, although it eventually also precipitates fission (*fenjia*) and its concomitant economic partition. Normally, however, the latter takes place some time after marriage and it very much depends on factors internal to the domestic group. If the husband is the only son, then division is rarely likely to take place at all, whereas if he has brothers, and if he is the eldest, he will be more likely to separate than if he is the younger son. Moreover, the division may not take place until several children have been born to the married couple. In Jiang village in Guangdong this was very much the pattern.

In Jiang village, where I interviewed members of every household, post-marital residence patterns continued to take the patrilocal form and the formation of conjugal households was coincident with house-hold division rather than with marriage. Conjugal households were rarely established before the birth of the third child or the occasion of the second son's marriage. The most common explanation given

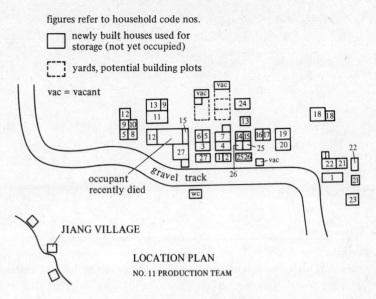

figures refer to household code nos.

☐ newly built houses used for storage (not yet occupied)

┌─┐ yards, potential building plots
└─┘

vac = vacant

occupant recently died

JIANG VILLAGE

LOCATION PLAN

NO. 11 PRODUCTION TEAM

Fig. 6. Household plan: Jiang village

for family division was the present size of the household, which was often expressed in terms of the number of tables required for eating, and division often seems to have coincided with an increase to more than one table. At any time in the rural social field there were households which were of the conjugal, stem or joint form depending on their stage in the developmental cycle. In Jiang village there were, in April 1977, 79 male and 68 female residents distributed between 27 households. Current residential arrangements, as illustrated in fig. 6, reveal that members of a household did not always share a common residence, and that 12 out of the 27 households had more than one house. In the village the average size of the household was 5·44 persons, and their sizes ranged from 9 persons to 3 persons (see table 13).

At the time of the interviews there were 17 conjugal families and 10 stem families but no joint family households (see table 14). Although with the imminent marriage of a second son, one household was about to take the joint form. Several of the households had been joint family structures in the recent past, but family division had caused their break up into conjugal and stem households. This pattern

Table 13. *Range in household size: Jiang village*

Number of persons	Number of households
9	1
8	1
7	4
6	7
5	7
4	4
3	3
	27

corresponds to Levy's claims that in traditional China new families were most commonly formed through the *famille souche* pattern of division, which creates conjugal families and maintains stem families (1949:55–6). Both Lang (1946:15–16) and Levy (1949:55) have noted that in traditional China it may have been quite common for stem families to maintain themselves for many years. They pointed out that poverty and poor health care may have left many families with only one son surviving to maturity in each generation. Now, however, it seems likely that the improvements in diet, health and welfare services have lengthened the life-span in the last twenty-five years and increased the number of surviving sons. In Jiang village an average of 2.5 sons had survived for each mother over the age of 40, when child-bearing could reasonably be expected to have ceased.

It was particularly noticeable that in all three villages visited a high value was attached to the number of sons. When members of the household were presented or listed by the senior representative of the household, the sons were enumerated before the daughters and daughters-in-law regardless of age order. In families with several sons there was a degree of confidence and investment in the future of the domestic group that was not characteristic of families with one son and many daughters. The former households gave the impression of planning and saving for future expansion and development, when all the sons would marry and recruit wives and later separate into their own households nearby. There is a close correlation between the number of sons per household and the households which had built new and additional houses.

Table 14. *Household composition: Jiang village*

Household code no.	No. of persons	Structure		Residence	
		Conjugal	Stem	Concentrated	Dispersed
1	7		+		+
2	5	+		+	
3	6		+		+
4	6		+	+	
5	8		+		+
6	4	+		+	
7	6	+		+	
8	6		+	+	
9	7	+			+
10	4	+		+	
11	5	+		+	
12	6	+			+
13	3	+		+	
14	5	+		+	
15	5		+		+
16	4	+		+	
17	3	+		+	
18	5	+			+
19	7		+	+	
20	6		+	+	
21	9		+		+
22	4	+			+
23	5		+	+	
24	3		+	+	
25	7	+			+
26	5	+			+
27	6	+			+

The following summary shows the number of households of a particular structure and form of residence. Figures in parentheses show the average numbers of persons in households of a particular structure or residential form.

Structure of household	Type of residence	
	Concentrated	Dispersed
Conjugal	10 (4.5)	7 (5.7)
Stem	5 (5.4)	5 (7.0)

Of the seven households which had recently built a new house, six had three or more sons who were reaching marriageable age. While opportunities for migration to the cities remain very limited, it would appear that demographic factors may have contributed to a new vertical and horizontal proliferation of the generations, in close proximity if not within the same household.

In contrast, in urban areas post-marital residential patterns are generally neolocal, with the formation of conjugal-type households on marriage. In principle, housing is allocated by municipal authorities on a neolocal basis, although where there is a housing shortage, as there has been in many of the larger cities, young couples may live temporarily with the parents of one of the spouses, usually the groom's. But even in this situation, there is the implicit assumption that common residence will be of a limited duration until separate housing can be provided. At a later date, however, a widowed parent of either spouse may move in with their son or daughter and the household will move from the conjugal to the stem form. Although residential arrangements in rural and urban areas may ultimately take the same forms, it seems as if the developmental cycle in the domestic group may pass through different sequences in rural and urban areas. In the rural areas the maintenance or elaboration of the traditional structures can be attributed to socio-economic factors specific to the rural household.

THE HOUSEHOLD ESTATE

The *jia* estate has been defined as that body of holdings, such as lands, residences, household effects, farm tools and livestock, to which the process of family division is applicable (M. Cohen 1976:59). Anthropologists who have studied the forms that the domestic group took in traditional China have argued that the key factor in the maintenance of the joint or complex form has been the existence of an estate sufficient in size to meet the claims of its members (Freedman 1958:30; M. Cohen 1976:231). This had been taken as the crucial characteristic distinguishing the forms which the domestic group traditionally took for different social classes, chiefly the gentry and the peasantry (Fei 1946). Its abolition has thus been taken to be the main factor responsible for destroying the economic base of the joint or complex family form in China today. But it can be argued that initially, the economic policies which the Chinese government introduced at the same time as it implemented the new Marriage Law, at first maintained or even strengthened the property base of the peasant family.

At the time of land reform the government supervised the redistribution of land on an equal basis to individual households. The government had initially forecast that only land reform could lay the social and economic foundations for the implementation of the new Marriage Law by giving all members of the domestic group, and especially women and the young, access to ownership of the means of production and a new bargaining power. Several articles in the media suggested that the redistribution of land and an equal inheritance law would create the objective conditions of free-choice marriage by providing the basis for economic independence and independence of choice for the younger generation. They argued that without the destruction of the economic basis for filial obedience, the Marriage Law itself would not have been practicable among the rural population (PC 1 June 1951; 1 March 1953).

But it can also be argued that the redistribution of land not only did not abolish the land component of the estate, but it actually strengthened the property base of the small peasant productive unit, especially for the rural peasant household hitherto landless, and therefore it contributed to the authority of the head of the household. Land reform strengthened the land component of the *jia* estate, and its exploitation maximised the functionality of the domestic group as a unit of production, and with it the sanctions at the disposal of the household head rather than the resources at the command of the younger generation. Within the domestic group individual claims to the land often remained more potential than real, and often the beneficiaries held land in name only, for the younger generation, especially the women, had little experience in organising agricultural production (Davin 1976:116; Croll 1978). The fact that women could then bring a share of land to their marriage, or that the household might be allocated a further share of land on the marriage of one of its sons, only served to strengthen the resolve of the head of the domestic group to consolidate its property base through the timely negotiation of marriage of one of the sons. Although the case studies reveal no direct correlation between the redistribution of land and the marriage forms, the tremendous hostility with which the Marriage Law was initially greeted has been well documented (see chapter 9), and it may be that in the early 1950s these new economic forces did not encourage and even actively discouraged the older generation from relinquishing their monopoly of marriage negotiations. However, this situation was short-lived, as the Communist Party soon attempted to abolish the land component of the estate.

The Chinese Communist Party had identified private property as the primary foundation of the domestic group, and the collectivisation of agricultural land became a priority of the government from the mid-1950s. Policies were introduced to transfer the ownership of the land from the direct control of the individual domestic group to the collective. The establishment of rural cooperatives and communes had the opposite effect of land reform and did reduce the land component of the individual *jia* estate and the economic basis of the individual household. However, the residual land component and certain other socio-economic factors specific to the rural household still continue to underlie its economy and encourage the older generation to control the negotiations of marriage.

THE RESOURCES OF THE HOUSEHOLD

The economic organisation of China demands that the rural household continue to mobilise its resources in order to find solutions to two organisational problems, namely production and the transformation of materials for consumption. Despite a number of policies to reduce the socio-economic functions of the rural household, it is still a unit of production (although greatly reduced in scope), and because community services are very unevenly distributed in rural areas it is also the primary unit of consumption. The economy of the domestic group no longer relies on the exploitation of the *jia* lands or estate, but on the paid and unpaid labour of each member of the group. Within the household, the principal divisions of labour are sexual and generational, and in the rural areas access to and organisation of women's labour is necessary for each household in order to combine the three sectors of the economy: the income-earning contribution from the public or collective sectors of the economy, the sideline activities of the private sector of the economy and the non-economic earning contribution within the domestic sphere.

In the collective sphere of the economy, the welfare of the family relies very much on the ratio of wage-earners to dependants within

Table 15. *Ratio of wage-earners to household members: Jiang village*

Household code no.	No. of persons	No. of earners	Ratio of earners to total	Structure of household
1	7	4	0.57	S[1]
2	5	2	0.40	C[2]
3	6	4	0.67	S
4	6	2	0.33	C
5	8	5	0.63	S
6	4	2	0.50	C
7	6	2	0.33	C
8	6	3	0.50	S
9	7	4	0.57	C
10	4	2	0.50	C
11	5	4	0.80	C
12	6	2	0.33	C
13	3	3	1.00	C
14	5	2	0.40	C
15	5	2	0.40	S
16	4	2	0.50	C
17	3	1	0.33	C
18	5	2	0.40	C
19	7	5	0.71	S
20	6	3	0.50	S
21	9	7	0.78	S
22	4	3	0.75	C
23	5	3	0.60	S
24	3	2	0.67	S
25	7	5	0.71	C
26	5	2	0.40	C
27	6	2	0.33	C
	147	80	0.54	

Ratio of wage-earners to total population 0.54.
Ratio of wage-earners to total population in stem households 0.61.
Ratio of wage-earners to total population in conjugal households 0.49.
[1] Stem.
[2] Conjugal.

the household. The households of Jiang village ranged from those in which members of the domestic group were all wage-earners to those in which there were only two wage-earners to four wage-dependants (see table 15). The recruitment of a daughter-in-law immediately added another wage-earner to the domestic group, for women often

Table 16. *Occupations of men and women in the labour force: Jiang village*

	Men	Women	Total
Agricultural production team	26	38	64
Other occupations outside team	13	1	14
Barefoot doctor	1	–	1
	40	39	79

formed a high proportion of the local agricultural labour force. In Jiang village, for example, all but one of the women worked in agriculture in the production team; see table 16. In the production team of which Jiang village was part, thirty of the women members from the village were wives who had been recruited into the village and ten were daughters who had yet to marry out. Except for a few older women who worked part-time, all the women worked a full day, although they worked 24 days compared to men's 26 days per month. Although the types of work which women undertake in the collective may differ and they may be less well rewarded, each is a major contributor to the household budget.

In the private sector, the household is still an important unit of production. This sector includes private plots which comprise 4–5 per cent of the total area of collectively owned land, which is allocated on a *per capita* basis. The food crops which are grown on these plots are often tended by the women of the household and they provide most of the vegetables for consumption by household members and their livestock. In addition to growing crops, the private sector includes activities such as pig- and chicken-raising and the gathering of fuel, which are traditionally defined as women's tasks. These make up both important food resources and cash contributions to the household economy. Domestic labour involving the transformation of produce for consumption, such as grinding corn, preserving vegetables, sewing, cooking and child care is an important female contribution to the household economy that reduces the costs of household maintenance. Although there were important attempts in the middle and late 1950s to establish community dining-rooms and communal nurseries for child care in order to reduce the functions of the individual household and its labour requirements, these were not always uniformly established or maintained with equal success. In the rural areas most of the community dining-rooms did not survive the Great Leap Forward, and although nurseries for child care have met with more success, it is my own impression and that of others that these are usually for children from three years upwards and are by no means universally established in rural villages (Sidal 1972:84–5). Despite later attempts in the 1970s to redefine the division of labour within the household,* much of the domestic labour, such as washing, mending, cooking and child minding is still regarded as women's work. At particular stages in a woman's life-cycle her labour tends to be distributed in favour of the domestic and private sector. It is a common occurrence at the recruitment of a new daughter-in-law (or wage-earner in the collective sector) to retire an older woman from the collective sector to manage the side occupations of the private sector. She will then undertake domestic labour and child care with the help of members of the younger generation.

The maintenance of the domestic group as an economic unit primarily relies on the distribution of labour resources between the three sectors of the economy, the interdependence of the generations and the recruitment and 'self-exploitation' of peasant women. Chayanov has argued that the aim of the domestic group as a unit of production is household consumption, and thus peasant production is not exploitative of others, but it is rather based on a certain degree of invisible labour which he terms 'self-exploitation' (1966:xvi). The domestic group in China today is a much-reduced unit of production compared to other peasant societies, but a certain degree of invisible labour or 'self-exploitation' remains necessary to its maintenance. The 'self-exploitation' of the family labour in the peasantry fundamentally exploits women's labour, especially that of the older generation. The demands of the economy of the domestic group also contribute to the economic interdependence of the generations within the household.

* To reduce the sexual division of labour and to accommodate domestic labour, men have been encouraged to undertake an equal share of the housework. Numerous role models have been published in the media of men who previously indulged in patriarchal attitudes and dismissed housework as women's work, but who, with the encouragement of trades union and women's groups, have discarded these attitudes and now undertake their share (CR 1 June 1975). This policy seems to have had some results in the urban areas and among the younger generation, but in 1973 articles began appearing in the media suggesting that the division of labour within the household and especially in rural areas has altered little, both because of 'limited material conditions and the influence of male supremacy' (*Hongqi* 1 December 1973).

In the absence of State pensions in rural areas, the elders are dependent on the wage labour of the young, while the young are dependent on the older generation for their unpaid labour in the domestic and private sectors of the economy. In comparison to rural areas, the economic interdependence of the generations and the private and domestic demands on women's labour are much reduced in urban areas. There is a State pension scheme for the retired, and the production, transformation and consumption of food, clothing and housing make fewer demands on the labour resources of the urban household. There are many more child care services, public or enterprise dining-rooms and a better provision of community services.

It is the demands of the rural economy on the household as a unit of production and consumption that have encouraged its expansion in numbers, at least for certain periods in its developmental cycle. Indeed, the joint phase of the developmental cycle may serve as a unique opportunity for the household to make use of its extended labour resources to specialise or diversify the economy of the domestic group and to accumulate wealth immediately prior to division. In any society where labour forms the major part of the total means of production and where control over labour is the major source of social differentiation, the recruitment and reproduction of labour itself is in constant demand. Where the individual and private hiring of agricultural labour is prohibited by law, as it is within the People's Republic of China, then marriage becomes the major, if not the only means of the reproduction and direct recruitment of labour.

THE RECRUITMENT OF WOMEN

One of the most common explanations or rationalisations given by the parents in initiating marriage negotiations was that cited in terms of the recruitment of additional labour, usually a woman's, to maintain the household as an economic unit. In Liuling village where Myrdal did his second study in the late 1960s, there was little opposition to one twenty-year-old girl's marriage and the recruitment of a son-in-law, because her father was in ill health and she was the only wage-earner. The village leaders defended their agreement to the match on the grounds that in these circumstances it would not have been right to suggest that they postpone their marriage in line with current educational programmes in the village (Myrdal and Kessle

1973:111). In the 1970s in Upper Felicity village, one set of parents, at the time of initiating the negotiations for the elder of several children, said that they were negotiating the marriage early as they would be glad of a daughter-in-law's help (J. Chen 1973:80). This rationale is particularly explicit in cases where the father or mother has died and left many young family members. In these circumstances, the elder son might well be urged to marry in order that a daughter-in-law might contribute wages or maintain and service the household. One medical student in just such a situation wrote to *Zhongguo Qingnian* for advice. His mother had died leaving his father, himself and a younger brother and sister. On his return home during winter vacation, his father indicated to him that they were greatly in need of a housewife in the family as cooking and cleaning 'gave them a great headache'. To have someone manage the household, his father asked him to take a wife as a solution to the problem. Friends and relatives supported the father in his request, and the son in a quandary turned to local political associations for help in finding a way out of his dilemma. The political associations supported him in his refusal and suggested that the other members of the household themselves share and undertake the domestic chores (ZQ 12 February 1963). It may be that the parents of daughters, and particularly widows, feeling their future security in a patrilocal marriage system to be doubly vulnerable, initiated negotiations for a matrilocal marriage to ensure the recruitment of an individual agreeable to uxorilocal residence. Certainly some households with a low ratio of wage-earners to dependant sons and daughters opted for a reverse solution and married their young daughters out, thus immediately reducing the number of wage-dependants. In two cases quoted in *Zhongguo Funu*, parents initiated marriage negotiations with a wealthy family who would be able to meet the cost of their daughter's education and her living expenses in order to lighten their present 'family burden' (1 May 1964; 1 February 1966).

That girls of marriageable age were prized for their labour power is illustrated by the value placed on their labour by the payment of the betrothal gift. In chapter 3 the most common explanation given for its persistence was that it took the form of compensation to the girl's family for the expenses of her upbringing and loss of her labour. Many parents stated that after years of raising a daughter they ought to be able to get something, if not a handsome sum, in exchange. Those who thought the amount of the betrothal gift too small complained that they were getting a small return for raising and bringing up a daughter. One indignant parent objected to such small returns on the grounds that they would have received more for the exchange of a pig. In rural households parents of daughters still expected to be compensated for the expenses associated with raising a daughter and the loss of labour they suffered subsequent to her marriage.

The economic pressures in favour of the early biological reproduction of the labour force was an important factor favouring the early initiation of marriage procedures by the older generation in rural areas. Although it is usually couched in terms of their personal satisfaction at the birth of a grandson and the folk-sayings 'to find a wife for one's son early enables one to live in comfort early', it is clear that practical considerations underlie these sentiments. One correspondent to *Gongren Ribao* suggested that, although he was only twenty-three years of age, there were advantages in him getting married now. Not only could he and his wife work, but his parents who were still in their early fifties could also continue in agricultural work. Moreover, by the time his parents retired, his own children would be nearing the age of entry into the labour force. He thought that there certainly was some truth in the folk-saying: 'Plant seedlings early and you will harvest a rice crop early; have a daugher-in-law early and you will enjoy happiness early' (GRB 11 September 1962). The advantages, if not the necessity, to reproduce labour at an early age is nowhere more explicitly stated than in a discussion reported by Parish between peasants and a young educated youth who, in line with the new ideology, recommended that they got married at a later date. The peasants hurriedly retorted that he just did not understand their problem. If they waited to marry until they were thirty years old, then when they were fifty years old their first son would scarcely have become an able-bodied labourer, and if they got sick or ill in the meantime, or if for some reason there was no adult to support the household, then its members would just sink into poverty (1975:618). For economic reasons alone they felt they had to encourage the members of their household to marry at or as near the legal age as possible.

In rural areas the opportunities offered by the negotiation of marriage to maximise the socio-economic resources of the household have not only encouraged the parents to retain their authority and controls, but the structure and functions of the domestic group have also placed sanctions at the disposal of the older generation which are not available to their urban counterparts.

PARENTAL SANCTIONS

The economy of the household in the rural areas is largely organised along collective lines which provided the older generation with certain sanctions. McAleavy has noted that in the past the general rule was that the fruits of the labour of all family members, whether they worked at home on the family land or earned money from jobs outside the home, had to be put in the common fund from which the family supported itself and which on partition was divided among those so entitled (1955:545). In rural areas today the household budget is reckoned collectively. The individual incomes in kind and in cash are pooled and added to the income from the private sector. In one household in Jiang village where there were seven persons made up of five wage-earners and two dependants, the grandmother and a young grandson, they received an average of 72 jin of food grain per month per person in one year. The main source of cash income had been that distributed to them by the production team according to the number of work points they had earned. This totalled 700 yuan, including the earnings of the son who worked in the commune shop. In addition, the household received 120 yuan by selling an average of two pigs each year. They grew all their own vegetables and much of the meat came from the allowances given in lieu of the two pigs and their fifteen chickens and hens. In this household, as for other peasant families, not only was the income inclusively tallied, but also their expenditures were reckoned collectively. The main items of expenditures were housing, clothing, consumer items such as bicycles, sewing-machines, radios, fans and wristwatches and the expenses associated with marriage. Each household had one common savings account out of which these expenses were met.

The organisation of the household economy on these collective lines meant that although they contributed to the common fund, the young were ultimately dependent on the household to meet the expenses engendered by marriage. These were reckoned as one of the collective expenses of the household. The importance of this source of support for individuals of the younger generation is confirmed by the difficulties

Table 17. *Urban household accounts: a sample from Guangzhou city*

	Factory housing			Housing estate			
No. of persons	8	4	5	5	8	3	6
No. of wage-earners	6	2	5	3	7	2	3
No. of wage-dependants	2	2	–	2	1	1	3
Total income (yuan)	272	150	203	144	317	90	140
Per capita expenditure per month (yuan)	20	22	29	20	15	14	15

which *xiaxiang* boys in rural areas experience in negotiating a marriage. They are not only disadvantaged in that they were normally inexperienced agricultural workers earnings lower wages than the experienced peasant lad (White 1974:504), but unlike the peasant boys they did not have the good fortune to share in the resources of their households. *Xiaxiang* boys did not have access to the supportive network that provided opportunities to distribute labour between the various sectors of the economy or to accumulate capital in order to meet the customary marriage expenses and provide housing.

In contrast, in urban areas the income and the expenses of the household are reckoned on an individual basis. The monthly expenditures of the household are calculated and divided among each wage-earning member. For example, in several households where members were interviewed by me in the city of Guangzhou, the monthly expenditure of the household was reckoned on a *per capita* basis per month (see table 17), with all members contributing periodically to the purchase of some consumer item. The remainder of each individual's income is at his or her disposal, and for young people one of the main expenses to be saved for is their own marriage. The young couples I interviewed in urban areas had met their own marriage expenses out of their individual savings, and the unmarried daughters who had no definite plans for marriage were greatly teased about the fact that they were already saving up for their own marriages. The furnishings of the rooms of newly married couples reflected their independence and individual thrift rather than the relative contributions of their natal households and their dependence, as would be the case in rural areas.

Although the collectivisation of land has removed the land com-

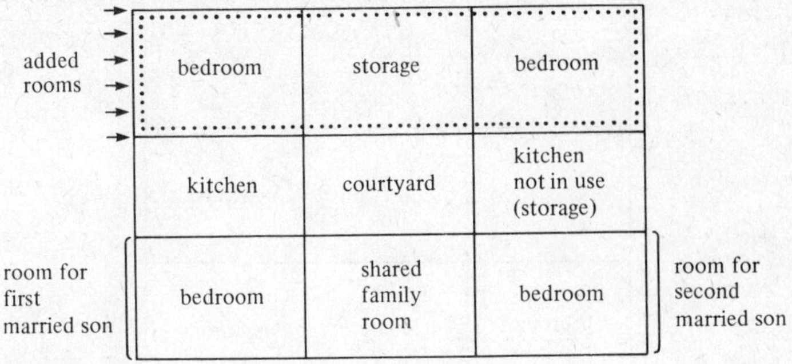

added rooms →	bedroom	storage	bedroom
	kitchen	courtyard	kitchen not in use (storage)
room for first married son	bedroom	shared family room	bedroom

room for second married son

Fig. 7. House plan: Jiang village. Residential pattern before division (2 married sons)

ponent of the *jia* estate in rural areas, the estate still includes residences, household effects, farm tools and small numbers of livestock. The Sixty Articles governing communes state that peasants shall own their own tools and house, have the right to buy, sell or rent their house and, according to the laws of inheritance, to pass it on to their children. Out of this estate the older generation is expected to make provision for the members of the younger generation and their spouses on marriage. In the rural areas where virilocal marriage is the norm, young couples are almost entirely reliant for the provision of housing on the resources of the groom's household or, in the event of uxorilocal marriage, on the bride's household. Normally it is the groom's household which rearranges the residential arrangements of the domestic group to make provision for the newly married couple. Alternatively, they might use household savings to renovate an old wing or to build a new one. Eventually the older generation may provide a new house to enable their son (or sons) to establish a household nearby. The exact procedure followed probably varies according to the wealth of the individual household, the numbers of its members and the pressures on land for housing in the local village or community.

A survey of the household rearrangement and divisions at and after marriage in Jiang village reveals the reliance of the younger generation on the older for the provision of housing. In one household the elder son had been provided with a room for the couple's exclusive use at the time of his marriage, and the second son, who was about to be

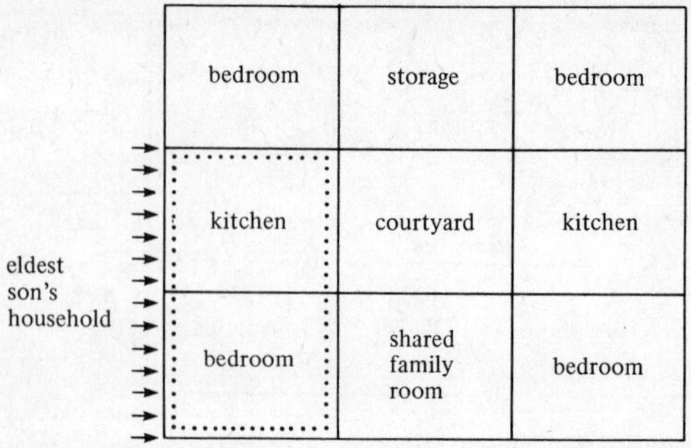

bedroom	storage	bedroom
kitchen	courtyard	kitchen
bedroom	shared family room	bedroom

eldest son's household →

Fig. 8. House plan: Jiang village. Residential pattern after division (1 married son)

married, was also to be allotted a room. Before both sons were married, the household had anticipated such expansion and had therefore built additional rooms to the original suite of rooms (see fig. 7).

In another family where there was more than one married son and several other sons and daughters, the household had similarly built additional rooms and the eldest son had been allotted a room at the time of his marriage. After the birth of his third child in 1976, there had been a household division. Now he had his own separate household comprising a bedroom and a kitchen, and he continued to share the large central family room (see fig. 8). In addition to the division of the household residence, there had also been division of household effects and family savings. For instance, the household had previously owned three bicycles and one had been given to the eldest son. After the family savings had been divided, he had used some of his portion to purchase a second cycle for his wife.

In a third family, two married sons were originally provided with rooms within the existing household, but instead of adding rooms, the household had built a new house at the time of the eldest son's marriage in anticipation of further expansion and eventual household division. This had taken place in 1975 when the original house was divided between the parents and their two unmarried sons, and the second married son and his family (see fig. 9). The eldest son had

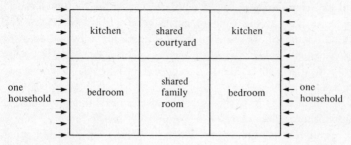

Fig. 9. House plan: Jiang village. Division of single suite of housing

moved into the new house (see households 16, 17 and 18 on plan of Jiang village – fig. 6).

The reliance of the younger generation on the older for the provision of housing is less likely in urban areas where post-marital residence is largely neolocal. Although a young couple may move in temporarily with either of their parents when there is a housing shortage in some of the larger cities, it is a temporary expedient based on the understanding that as soon as housing is allocated to them they will establish their own separate household. Housing is not usually privately owned or part of the *jia* estate in urban areas, rather it is owned by the municipal authorities or occupational enterprises and allocated to young couples for their life-span.

FAMILY FORM AND MARRIAGE

The contrasting socio-economic functions of the household in rural and urban areas can be said to have given rise to a new dual familial form in contemporary China. The main differences in residential patterns are no longer that between social classes as formerly, but between the urban and rural social fields. The structure of the household in each can be correlated directly to their respective socio-economic functions. In urban areas where there is a minimal, if non-existent, private sector of the economy, and where there are institutionalised State and community provisions for retirement and for servicing and sharing in the maintenance of the household, the functionality of the household as a socio-economic unit lessens. It is less a unit of production and consumption than its rural counterpart and the residential patterns tend towards those of the nuclear or conjugal type at the time of marriage. In rural areas where the individual household is still called on to maximise its resources in order to perform a number of socio-economic functions, marriage is generally virilocal. Each form has had repercussions for the negotiation of marriage.

In rural areas it is the interests of the individual household in maximising its labour resources, especially in the reproduction and recruitment of labour power, which has encouraged the old generation to maintain control of the marriage negotiations of the younger generation. What emerges in the rural and urban social fields is a direct correlation between the household composition, the economic interdependence of its members and the degree of parental participation in the procedures of mate selection. In urban areas where post-marital residence is more likely to be neolocal, where the household coexists alongside community institutions, and where the functionality of the household is minimised and it is less a unit of production and consumption, then parental control is weaker. In rural areas where post-marital residence is more likely to be virilocal, where the household is more of a unit of production and consumption demanding the recruitment and reproduction of labour, and where community institutions are less developed, then the interests in the negotiation of marriage and the sanctions at the disposal of the older generation are greater. Far from decelerating the degree of familial control over marriage, it may be that the very structure and functions of the patrilocal domestic group has worked against the implementation of free-choice marriage in rural China.

9

MARRIAGE AND PRIMARY GROUPS

The traditional balance of power between the older and the younger generations within the domestic group could only be maintained as long as it was supported by both the formal and informal arbitration of socio-political control. The existence of the Marriage Law introducing a different ideology of marriage, combined with new political associations active in its support and government intervention in its favour, presented an alternative to the established power relations of the informal social field, and in turn brought these into competition with new sources of political authority. Traditionally, the government had supported the authority of the elders over kin members and, as an old colloquial saying had made clear, 'Even an upright magistrate does not intervene in domestic affairs' (Smith 1902:292). Now, family affairs, which included the marriage negotiations of the younger generation, were incorporated into a law which was specifically designed to provide 'a powerful weapon for the younger generation in their struggle against the old marriage and family systems' (KMRB 27 February 1957; PR 13 March 1964). Once an individual, defying the elders' authority, could look to resources outside the family institutions for support, then the power of the elders was at risk, and to provide the requisite conditions political authorities and associations were exhorted to break with the custom of non-interference and non-intervention and to concern themselves with marriage and the internal affairs of the domestic group. As one article stressed, 'the attitude of perceiving the masses' problems of marriage and family as small matters in life, as personal problems of individual commune members is incorrect...marriage and domestic affairs are indeed serious problems of collective concern, and cadres should be concerned with them' (ZF 1 January 1966). It was impressed upon these cadres by the government that 'only their support, guidance and intervention could demonstrate that their concern and responsibility is more encompassing than that of relatives and friends or those who were traditionally concerned with domestic affairs' (*Village Reader* 1963:11). The intervention of the government in support of the Marriage Law brought the government and political institutions into direct conflict with primary groups. In nearly every case of conflict, parents in rural and urban areas mobilised kin and neighbours in support of their traditional controls of mate selection, while the younger generation turned to government cadres, the Party, the Youth League or the Women's Federation for support. The patterns of marriage, then, were likely to reflect the dominant socio-political influences and the resources and sanctions which each could exercise at any point in time or in any one location.

In both rural and urban areas the introduction of the new ideology of marriage threatened the traditional influence and dominance of the primary groups. Primary groups have been defined anthropologically as those characterised by face-to-face, permanent, affective, non-instrumental and diffused interpersonal relations (Litwak and Szelenyi 1969:465). The three types of social relations normally identified as primary groups include kinship ties beyond the immediate household, neighbours and friends. Kinship structures may be distinguished by the semi-permanent biological or legal ties between households, and neighbours are characterised by the geographical proximity of members and consequent face-to-face contacts. In contrast, friendship may rest on affectivity alone and structurally constitutes the weakest of these bonds. It has neither the permanence of the kinship link nor the face-to-face contact characterising the neighbourhood. There has been little attention given to the structure and function of primary groups in contemporary China, chiefly because previous analyses have operated on the common assumption that the very form which the political and economic development of the People's Republic takes rests on the decline and eventual disappearance of such groups.*

It has usually been presumed that the development of a new form of political authority in China required social conditions which were antithetical to the maintenance of the primary group, and that political organisations and associations were more effective than primary groups in achieving the goals of social development. In an

---

* Exceptionally, Norma Diamond has recently drawn attention to the fact that the household in many rural production teams and brigades remains embedded in a network of male kinsmen (1975:27).

article on new types of interpersonal relations, Ezra Vogel suggests that comradeship, or ties based on common political affiliation, has superceded those based on kinship, the neighbourhood and friendship (1965:46). After the establishment of communes, Lethbridge has argued, the extension of Party control right down to village level has meant that compared to the government and the Party, family and kin can offer only the most fragile of support for the individual (1962:381–3). Some scholars have drawn out the implications of these assumptions for control of the negotiations of marriage. Lethbridge concluded that the greater Party control made possible by the commune structure has allowed for the finer scrutiny of the marriage contract and has helped to guarantee the free choice of marriage partners (1962:383). C. K. Yang also suggests that the establishment of Party controls has weakened kinship and family ties and released the young from their control, thereby encouraging the development of free-choice marriage (1959:36). At study of marriage patterns in contemporary China, however, suggests that in the rural social field the influence of kin and neighbours are still forces to be reckoned with and that they have continued to compete with political associations and authorities for local socio-political control.

THE INFLUENCE OF KIN AND NEIGHBOURS

At every stage of the neogitations of marriage the older generation was likely to have the support of their kin and neighbours, and in the case studies it was their influence which the younger generation found particularly difficult to counter. Young people who were attracted to each other found it difficult to disregard the local gossip (*xianhua*) and meet each other openly. In interviews conducted by a Swedish observer in Liuling village, Shaanxi province, in the mid-1950s, it was evident that, though not all the inhabitants maintained traditional attitudes and felt uneasy at the thought of women laughing and joking with men, most continued to think it indecent, immoral and shocking that young people should talk with each other (Myrdal 1967:291). In the 1960s there were cases where kin and neighbours were of the opinion that nothing good could come of the free association of the sexes and they actively intervened in defence of their family reputations (ZQ 27 October 1964; 16 April 1966). One report said of the influence of kin and neighbours that 'they criticise [the younger generation] in order to cause shame, and brand them as "improper" or conspire so that they lose their reputation' (Lu Yang 1964:17–18). In 1971 in a village in Henan it was still the case that a girl who was seen talking to boys and making friends would soon be considered 'too easy' or 'loose' in her relations with the opposite sex (J. Chen 1973:77). In this atmosphere of rumour and gossip, individuals of the younger generation, if they did meet and attract one another, were often afraid to express their affections openly to each other in public. They feared the censure of local public opinion. In order to adhere to the new ideology of late marriage, young people who had decided to delay their own marriage had to withstand constant pressure from kin and neighbours. Several correspondents to the media wrote that from their own experience and observations, it was all right to accept late marriage in theory, but when it came to putting it into practice it was very difficult to withstand the pressure of others, particularly parents, kin and friends. In one letter the correspondents said that they had discussed the question of raising the age of marriage at length and concluded that 'though the policy of late marriage theoretically rested on sound foundations, in actual practice, it could not find ready acceptance, for a number of persons around them will often chide them, put pressure on them, or jeer at them and express pity as if they had done something wrong' (GRB 18 September 1962). Another correspondent warned against treating the problem of social pressure lightly because the public opinion it has formed often exerts a fairly strong pressure in favour of 'early' marriage (GRB 27 September 1962).

The ritual and ceremonial forms associated with marriage were all identified with the maintenance of individual and family status in the community. The betrothal symbolised the ability of the older generation to maintain their authority and controls within the domestic group and thus to maintain their status among kin and neighbours. Free-choice marriage was seen to cause loss of face or to tarnish local reputations. The main criterion for the acceptance or the rejection of a betrothal gift was whether the household would maintain its standing in the village. 'If I decline to accept it, will it not reflect on *my family's social standing* and way of doing things in style?' (my italics – ZQ 19 November 1964). The arguments put forward in favour of the bridal sedan chair were couched in terms of the loss of status *vis-à-vis* kin and neighbours should the bride not be seen to be arriving in 'the proper manner or in style'. Likewise, the provision of the dowry provided the opportunity to gain or at least not to lose social status. In cases where the practice persisted, the overwhelming argument cited in its defence was its contribution to the status and social standing of the bride's family. 'If we don't spend some money and provide you with some form of dowry, *will not other people laugh at us?*' (my italics – ZQ 16 January 1966). But perhaps the most important social obligation by which reputations could be lost or gained lay in the provision of the marriage feast. It was required to be of a certain standard in order to prevent loss of status and it was an opportunity to lay obligations and return obligations. In rural areas, households have proved reluctant to break the circle of obligations and invoke the gossip of their relatives and neighbours.

Frequent articles in the media have reflected the continuing concern of the government with the general problem of countering the influence of primary groups in reforming marriage patterns. One article on the ceremonials of marriage summed up its discussion of marital forms with the observation that

Although some people realise the importance of changing prevailing bad customs and practices, talk eloquently about the evil and harm of old feudal customs, or may have taken a firm stand at the beginning, they are often unable to withstand the trial at the crucial moment. They begin to waver and compromise by force of habit under the pressure of their parents who may have given them a good scolding, or under the influence of their relatives and friends who may have used persuasion to talk them into conforming with tradition and the trends of the times so that they may not be outcasts from their own circles. (NFRB 25 January 1965)

Some members of the older generation in Zhejiang province were interviewed in *Renmin Ribao* and asked for their observations on the new marriage system. They were of the opinion that although it might be a good arrangement all round, the traditions of marriage had passed from generation to generation and were too deeply entrenched to be undone overnight. They said that they themselves did not mind, but the problem was how to face their relatives and friends.

What if it sets the tongues of others wagging and makes your friends and relatives mad at you. You can't get away from being called things like 'cheapskate', 'petty devil', 'cool-blood animal'... People also may say things like 'You took gifts from others before. But now you give nothing in return.

You just take and not give.' How then can you hold your head up? (RMRB 28 June 1964)

So they concluded 'that they had better stick to the old standard', for they 'just could not take the pressures from relatives, neighbours and friends'.

It was comments like these that caused in editorial in *Renmin Ribao* to suggest that although people may recognise the reasons why the old customs should be dropped, the real obstacle to social change was the heavy pressure of public opinion brought to bear on each person. 'Like a massively closely woven net', it concluded that

old habits, and influences and social opinion limit and dictate people's thinking and action. Everyone seems to be acting not out of his own will or needs, but out of desperation for acceptance among relatives, neighbours and all. The same relatives and neighbours, meanwhile, dare not do anything not hitherto accepted by others, if just to avoid gossip. Thus everyone fears everyone else...this is so-called pressure of public or social opinion. (*ibid.*)

THE INFLUENCE OF POLITICAL ASSOCIATIONS

Set against the pressure of public or social opinion from kin and neighbours was the influence of the political authorities or associations in support of the new patterns of marriage. Yet there is evidence to suggest that the competition between the sanctions and support of primary groups and political associations has been somewhat uneven. Not only has the support system provided by primary groups continued, but the support which the political authorities have been exhorted to give to those exercising their new rights in marriage negotiations has not always been forthcoming. This was particularly so in the early 1950s when the law came into operation before the new ideology had a basis of power or authority sufficient to compete with that supporting the old forms. In the event of conflict, the mere citation of the terms of the Marriage Law was not enough and the formal basis of active political support for those adhering to the new law was often unreliable. In these early years there were numbers of suicides and murders among those who attempted to adopt the new patterns of marriage, especially among women who traditionally had rarely possessed a power base within the domestic group to compare with that of the elders.* The conventional interpretation of the events of this initial period of implementation of the Marriage Law has been that the cadres held the population in their grip and that their political authority enabled them to apply the provisions of the law without regard for the opinions and wishes of the local population. It was this forced implementation of the law which primarily caused the problems reported in the media (CNA 25 September 1953). But reports from the local investigations into the conditions of implementation undertaken at the time suggest otherwise. They reveal that it was much more likely that those who attempted to exercise free choice did not obtain the requisite support from cadres and political associations which they needed in order to implement the new rights.

In 1951 reports on the problems encountered in the campaign to reform marriage patterns began to place particular blame on the failure of local cadres or those in positions of political authority, village leaders and members of political associations such as the Youth League, Women's Federation and Peasants' Associations, to support those struggling against feudal marriage customs. Towards the end of 1951, *Renmin Ribao* openly admitted for the first time that the increase in the murders or suicides of women was not owing to conservative thought or feudal customs, but was owed in considerable part to the failure or disinclination of Party cadres and leaders to enforce the law and give support to individuals who wished to negotiate their own marriage free from the interference of third parties (RMRB 29 September 1951; 13 October 1951). On several occasions the national newspapers and periodicals described how those who resisted old customs lost heart or sometimes their lives as a result of the lack of public sympathy and political support. A column was set aside in *Renmin Ribao* to report on the implementation of the Marriage Law and to draw attention to the irregularities committed by local

---

* For example, a report from the Central-South Democratic Women's Federation estimated that in the year ending 30 August 1951 there had been a total of 10,000 deaths as the result of the introduction of the Marriage Law. They cited some local statistics in evidence (ZJ 30 August 1951).

Area	Date	Women's lives lost
Changsha Special District	May–August 1950	98 (68 suicide)
Huanghua Xian, Hubei	July–August 1950	14
Shangshui Xian, Hunan	3 months 1950	90
Ningyuan Xian, Hunan	2 months 1950	17 (all suicide)

authorities. One case reported in *Women of New China* (see Chen Hsu 1952) concerned a young girl who had been promised in marriage by her parents, who had also exacted a gift of a measure of rice. The girl, however, wished to marry a neighbouring lad of her own acquaintance and she therefore applied to the People's Court for permission to terminate the betrothal negotiated by her parents. The court upheld the betrothal, as did another court at a higher administrative level. Three months before the arranged marriage was due to take place, the girl again approached the court for a second decision. In the face of further procrastination by the courts, and becoming increasingly desperate about her own approaching fate, the girl threw herself into a well in the court compound and died (WC 1 October 1951). There were numbers of cases published in the media all supporting the accusation that cadres interfered in the freedom of marriage either by forcibly separating couples who wished to negotiate a free-choice marriage or by forcibly arranging marriages between the young people themselves (ZJ 30 August 1951).

Many reports in the early 1950s began to identify the negligence of local cadres as the 'greatest stumbling block' to the implementation of the Marriage Law (RMRB 29 September 1951; WC 1 October 1951). They were accused of adhering to the old customs by conniving with local village elders to support the old marriage system. They either openly tolerated the old forms or adopted an attitude of indifference to complaints from those wishing to adopt the new patterns, and they even punished those who wished to defy parental interference in marriage negotiations. In some cases the offending young people were expelled from the Youth League or other political associations (NCNA 29 October 1951). According to these same reports the cadres were motivated to oppose the introduction of the new forms of marriage by any of several factors. Apparently some feared that the disappearance of traditional customs would create a vacuum in morals or 'all confusion under Heaven' and certain social disorder, in which sexual relations would become as easy as sipping the proverbial glass of water. Individual cadres feared that their own authority as head of the domestic group would be threatened; they thought that marriage had never been, and never should be, a matter of state policy and interference. Thus, it was their belief that the policy to reform marriage was of low priority, or a distraction from the real affairs and priorities of the State, such as land reform. Others thought that it was but a temporary fad of the new government and that it would pass just as 'a large clap of thunder is followed by small drops of rain'. Custom would surely win out in the end and it was no use fighting it. Some shelved it in the belief that their communities were not yet ready for that kind of reform (RMRB 20 March 1953). Numbers of government circulars and directives were published which were full of reproofs for the large numbers of judiciary organs, cadres and Party members who had failed to give their full support to those abiding by the new provisions of the law (RMRB 19 March 1953). Through the media, the government attempted to directly inform young people that they had its support and should not under any circumstances take the law into their own hands or resort to suicide (NCNA 31 January 1953; 25 February 1953).

Complaints that young people failed to find support from the political authorities and associations declined notably after the early 1950s, although a few cases have appeared in the media after the first decade of Communist rule. In 1962, for example, an adopted daughter-in-law appealed for help via the media when the personnel of the government department concerned had refused to uphold the Marriage Law (NFRB 5 July 1962). Over the years there have been a number of articles addressed to the members of the Party, the Youth League and the Women's Federation calling on them to pay more attention to the Marriage Law and to support young people who resisted arranged marriages. There is evidence to suggest that their continued reluctance was less the result of disagreement with or disinclination to support the principles of the Marriage Law, than the fact that marriage reform is generally perceived to be a low-priority policy, and of less importance than many others to the welfare of the community. Moreover, members of the party, the Youth League and the Woman's Federation are at one and the same time members of local primary groups in rural areas, and many feared that any action on their part would be interpreted as a preoccupation with or interference in the private or personal sphere of marriage relations (ZQ 1 April 1955; TKP 12 September 1964).

These inhibitions displayed by the political associations suggest that there is still a tendency to divided the private or domestic from the public or political sphere of activities, and place the former in the control of the primary as opposed to the political groups. This separation may be encouraged by the differing degrees of importance attached to the institution of marriage by its own definitions. Although marriage is defined as important for both the individual and society, it is placed in a position secondary to 'revolutionary activities' or 'socialist construction', thus implying that it lies outside these boundaries. In the debates entitled 'What is the correct view of marriage?', 'Is marriage a matter of minor or major importance?' or 'Is marriage really an important matter or a small matter?', marriage is accorded an importance as a fresh stage in the life-cycle of the individual, but relegated to a secondary position in establishing social priorities: 'Compared with revolutionary work, marriage and love is really a small matter' (ZQ 14 September 1962); 'An individual must try and place love in a secondary position to the revolution in one's life' (ZQ 1 April 1955); 'Compared with the undertakings we have been called upon to do, marriage after all takes second place' (ZQ 2 February 1963). Although the educational materials, after stressing the secondary placing of marriage in relation to the importance of the revolution or socialist construction, went on to say that it was a question deserving of serious concern by the individual (GRB 22 November 1962; Lu Yang 1964:11–12), in the last resort it was always associated with the secondary, individual, private and domestic domain as opposed to the primary, social, public and political domain (ZQ 30 August 1956; RMRB 15 November 1956).

PRIMARY GROUPS IN RURAL CHINA

If the continuing influence of the primary groups and the inhibitions displayed by the political associations have contributed to the nation-wide and uneven competition between the generations and the primary and political groups, the variety in marriage patterns demonstrates that the competition may have been even more weighted in the favour of primary groups in rural areas. Within the village the primary groups provided greater competition for the influence of political associations. It is noticeable that the basic-level cadres or representatives of political authority in rural villages have often been blamed by the Chinese government for the failure of certain policies (Baum and Teiwes 1968:13). But it may be, if the study of marriage is any indication, that it is not so much the weakness of basic-level cadres, as the strength of the overlapping primary groups which should be held responsible for the slow implementation of some government policies. Indeed, the form which the marriage patterns take can be directly linked to the differences in the immediate social environment of individuals and households, and in particular to the structures and functions of the primary groups. That is, where primary groups overlap and encapsulate the individual and the household, they may be more likely to provide a single reference group and unidirectional social pressures which support the controls and the authority of the older generation. It can be argued that in rural areas in China, primary groups, far from being weakened, have not only continued to overlap to form a single concrete and close-knit group, but that the interrelationships within these groups have been formalised and institutionalised by the new demographic and economic policies. It is this structural feature of rural society which has suggested the second hypothesis explaining the variety of marriage patterns in the People's Republic of China: that the degree to which the old form predominates over the new, and therefore the extent to which parental participation characterises marriage patterns, varies with the degree to which primary groups overlap.

An important general feature of social structure is the way in which primary groups are connected with the territorial arrangement of persons. In China there has been no large-scale rearrangement of the territorial distribution of rural persons, and rural areas continued to be characterised by discretely bounded villages which vary in size from a few dozen to a few hundred households. These villages now have a new definition and function, and, since the establishment of the communes from 1957, they tend to coincide with the organisational level of either the production team or the production brigade. Production teams may consist of from 30 to 150 households, and most scholars have concluded that their boundaries may coincide with the territorial village. Conversely, and depending on its original size, the village may either combine with neighbouring villages to form a production team or itself be divided into production teams. However it has been organisationally redefined, the spatial continuity of the village remains. Apart from the exchange of women in marriage, there is now little permanent movement between production brigades, teams or villages, and this very important demographic factor encourages a high level of involvement in primary groups.

I observed that in contrasting the social conditions of the past with the present, several leaders of Huadong commune and members of individual households in Jiang village made unsolicited references to the necessary dispersal of members of kin groups in the previous generations because of natural calamities and emigration to the cities and to South-east Asia. One of the commune leaders quoted an old local folksong:

> The peasantry here on the land is very poor,
> Every village links each other into a river,
> The natural calamities has not its end,
> And people are obliged to leave their native land forever.

This dispersal of kin groups was contrasted with present social conditions in which men need not leave their birthplace. This means that it is in the context of a territorially bounded group of the production team or village that primary groups are most likely to overlap and have their most continuous influence on individuals and households. Within the discretely bounded village, neighbours may be kin and friends at one and the same time.

The proportion of kinship ties to other relations in the village may vary from those characteristic of the southern provinces, such as Guangdong and Fujian, where single-surnamed village members comprise a single lineage (*zu*), to the multi-surnamed villages of the northern provinces. In the past the southern provinces were dominated by lineages or large localised kin groups whose boundaries often coincided with those of the village. Freedman (1966) examined their historical forms in some detail, and evidence from other scholars suggests that lineage-based settlements continue to characterise villages in the southern provinces (J. Chen 1973; Diamond 1975).

JIANG VILLAGE

In the three villages which make up a production team in Guangdong, my survey of the households revealed that they all had the surname of Jiang, and that they probably composed a fragment of a higher-order lineage. Within the village each household was asked to identify its nearest kin. Without exception close kin (*jinqin*) were identified as brothers who had established separate households, father's brothers and father's brother's sons, and a line was drawn between them and father's father's brothers and their sons who were either designated 'distant kin' or not cited at all. Only one household had no close kin

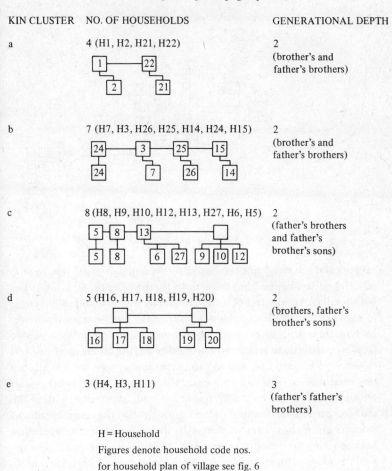

KIN CLUSTER	NO. OF HOUSEHOLDS	GENERATIONAL DEPTH
a	4 (H1, H2, H21, H22)	2 (brother's and father's brothers)
b	7 (H7, H3, H26, H25, H14, H24, H15)	2 (brother's and father's brothers)
c	8 (H8, H9, H10, H12, H13, H27, H6, H5)	2 (father's brothers and father's brother's sons)
d	5 (H16, H17, H18, H19, H20)	2 (brothers, father's brother's sons)
e	3 (H4, H3, H11)	3 (father's father's brothers)

H = Household

Figures denote household code nos.

for household plan of village see fig. 6

Fig. 10. Kinship organisation: Jiang village

in the village, and they were recent settlers driven by crowded housing conditions from the nearest neighbouring village where they had numerous kin, all again with the same surname Jiang. Jiang village itself is characterised by geographically concentrated clusters of agnatic kin who are either groups of ego's brothers or father's brothers. They are identified in figs. 10 and 11.

Instead of provinces like Guangdong and Fujian constituting

177

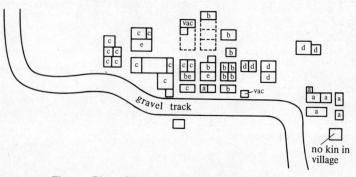

a b c d e   households belonging to different kin groups

vac = vacant

Fig. 11. Plan of kinship organisation: Jiang village

exceptional cases of lineage-based settlements, it may not be too far-fetched to suggest that over time the proportion of kinship ties within villages in the rest of rural China may increase and might come to approximate the forms characteristic of the southern provinces. At present, though, it can certainly be assumed that the same demographic factors contribute to relations of proximity having all the intensity and closeness of kinship ties, and to this extent it may well be that kinship ties continue to directly influence the patterning of other social relations based on common residence and affectivity within the village. Structural features which provide for the overlapping of primary groups have been reinforced by the extent to which cooperation between the households is required to provide and maintain the welfare of the rural household, and encourage a high degree of intimacy or frequency of contact between kin and neighbours.

A wide variety of functions that used to be performed by the household are now undertaken by the village as part of, or the whole of, a unit of production, distribution and accounting. As Harris (1976) has argued, social scientists have generally tended to isolate the household and even conceptualise it as a mode of production by minimising the links between households, or by seeing links or exchanges between households as analytically unimportant to the underlying structure of the present form (Chayanov 1966; Sahlins 1974). In the past, fieldwork in villages of rural China, and Ramon

Myers' study of north China villages (1970) have amply demonstrated that cooperation between peasant households was a widespread practice. Labour, instruments of production and loans of produce and cash were exchanged between households. In rural China today this exchange of goods and services between households has been institutionalised and magnified by the process of collectivisation. By this process all kinds of exchanges have moved from an informal and an *ad hoc* basis to one that is now institutionalised and prescribed on the basis of a common neighbourhood. The inhabitants of the villages are required to work together and to cooperate on an unprecedented level of exchange of goods and services. The production teams and brigades are now units of production, the owners of the means of production and the dominant units for the recruitment and organis-ation of labour within its boundaries. Members of these units not only work in close proximity, but the ordering of the exchange and cooperation are reinforced by the new ideology which encourages the individual household to place a high value on the exchange of goods and services within the collective. They are actively exhorted to solve common problems and to mobilise common resources to improve the level of their services through cooperation. The structure and functions of primary groups in rural society has had the effect of maintaining, if not of solidifying, the bonds between the individual inhabitant and the primary group.

MEASURES OF SOLIDARITY WITHIN PRIMARY GROUPS

The solidarity of primary groups in rural areas may be measured by the degree to which the individual household is prepared to defy the norms of the primary groups, the extent to which ritual and ceremonial forms symbolise their solidarity and the success of the government in imposing class divisions within the primary groups. In a social field where there is a greater cleavage between the common practices and the new ideology, an individual or household may have the choice of either conforming to the ideology at the risk of losing status in the local community, or rejecting the ideology and conforming to the practices of the community in exchange for their acceptance and a certain amount of status. The case studies suggest that in the rural areas individuals of both generations found defiance of the norms of the local community the most difficult obstacle to overcome in the establishment of the newly recommended marriage patterns. All except those who had access to the extended networks of the Youth League or Party beyond the confines of the face-to-face community preferred to defer to, rather than take on, the local community.

In rural areas the case studies have suggested that the cohesion of the primary groups rests to a large degree on the maintenance of ceremonial and ritual forms, and the previous chapters have demonstrated that village inhabitants were time and again markedly reluctant to break the circle of reciprocal obligations and prestations within the ritual and ceremonial of marriage. Also, there is some evidence that it has been much more difficult to establish horizontal or class links within primary groups and especially within those based on lineage or kin. Where villages have been dominated by a single lineage it seems as if the establishment of active poor and lower-middle-class peasant associations may have been more difficult. At the time of land reform, the most potent period of class struggle in rural areas, there was evidence that landlords exploited kin ties and certainly in one single-lineage village, the procedures of land reform had to be repeated fifteen years later during the Cultural Revolution because the kin ties had been such that little of the landlords' property had been redistributed the first time round (J. Chen 1973:137–8). Educational materials have certainly emphasised the need to draw particular attention to class differences within lineages (ZQ 26 October 1963; RMRB 23 November 1964).

It is the structure and function of the overlapping primary groups in rural areas which have enabled them to maintain a certain measure of solidarity and to remain the primary or single most important reference group for the household in rural China. There seems to have been no important change in the types and unidirectional nature of social pressure from primary groups, and there are now fewer avenues of escape from their influence through channels such as migration. Moreover, the new economic policies have contributed to the maintenance of the sanctions traditionally imposed by the primary group. Through the sanctions at their disposal, the older generation have maintained their control of the norms of the local community which has enabled them to modify the new ideology in their own interests. One of the chief means by which the older generation have worked to maintain their controls of the negotiations of marriage has been by maintaining the norms of segregation within the local community.

Indeed, the primary group has been singularly successful at retaining these norms of segregation within the rural villages.

The form which the negotiation of marriage takes can be directly linked to the number of opportunities for social interaction among young people of marriageable age, and in rural areas today opportunities for meeting and mating are suitably circumscribed by the maintenance of the traditional norms of segregation. The evidence cited in chapters 2 and 3 suggests that it was the lack of other opportunities and the amount of rumour and gossip surrounding pre-marital ritual forms which encouraged young people to concur in the dominance of parental authority and controls. Moreover, the socio-economic relations between the households of the local community may have reinforced the bonds of solidarity within the household, for strains and divisions in the individual domestic domain must be kept at a certain level so as not to interfere with the welfare of the community. It would seem that the norms favouring parental participation in marriage procedures had a greater structural significance where interpersonal relations were dominated by overlapping primary groups whose influences were effectively unidirectional. The extent to which an individual remains wholly encapsulated within traditionally effective networks must vary enormously over the rural social field, but it is in contrast to the urban social fields that they can be so characterised.

In comparison, urban areas are characterised less by singular territorially bounded groups than by many different communities that have as their common criteria participation in an occupation, class membership, shared interests or previous membership of other social systems, as well as those based common residence, kinship and friendship. This social field is characterised by the dispersal of primary groups, and, just as kin are less likely to be neighbours, so neighbours are less likely to be workmates and so on. Cities are organised into neighbourhoods which are subdivided into residential groups of from 150 to 500 households approximately. These are officially organised local government groups whose main activities include public health and political study, and the establishment of kindergartens, community workshops and one or two small-scale neighbourhood factories. Such activities, while they require a certain degree of cooperation between households, are nowhere near to constituting the units of production, distribution and accounting that are typical of rural neighbourhoods.

It is also a feature of the organisation of urban neighbourhoods that they mainly attract the allegiance of the retired or otherwise unemployed members of the community, rather than those whose work takes them outside the neighbourhood or into large factories or enterprises. Friends were more likely to be a mixture of peers from school days or workmates sharing the same occupations or neighbours. With some notable exceptions, urban areas are not characterised by the geographical concentration of those related by kinship ties. The absence of familial control of housing, and its allocation either by municipal authorities or occupational enterprises, together with the pressures on urban housing, has meant that the residences of family members have very much been governed by the availability of housing, and although there is much less known about kin relations in urban areas in the People's Republic of China, it seems that there is a certain amount of dispersal.

Certainly in Guangzhou, when I asked members of several households the whereabouts of kin, I was told that they were either living outside the immediate neighbourhood or factory housing complex but in the same city, or they were resident in the respondent's village of origin. Relatives located within the same city frequently visited each other on rest days and although urban inhabitants may have left their native villages up to fifty years ago, they still regularly visited their kin on special occasions and festivals. A notable exception in Guangzhou proved to be the former boat people, who were rehoused in a large estate along the banks of the Pearl River in 1965. In their case nearly all agnatic and affinal kin resided within the estate itself. There were a number of blocks of flats which housed 40,000 people, or 7900 households. The six households that I visited were all in the Bingjian neighbourhood, which comprised 58 two- to three-storeyed blocks with 11,000 persons or 2700 households. In these households the wives had all come from within the estate and almost all the affinal and agnatic kin either lived within the same household or in a different household in the same or a nearby block. In the urban areas generally, however, the separation of different communities has meant that there is a much greater choice for individual interaction with kin and neighbours.

The dispersal of primary groups suggests that there may be a wider range of reference groups, and individuals and households may have had a considerable range of options in selecting the group or category that they identified with. Indeed, the case studies confirm this supposition. They illustrate that peer groups in the urban areas were more autonomous and influential, and that young people from the urban areas are as likely to take the advice or follow the example of friends, peers, fellow-members of class or political associations as of kin or neighbours. They will even be influenced by abstract categories or role models. In urban areas it was much more likely that the individual or household would come into contact with a variety of behavioural patterns and meet with a range of choices in making their selection. The correspondence on the age of marriage, for example, illustrates that the options considered by a young person very much depended on the reference group with whom he or she primarily identified, and it was as likely to be fellow-workers in the factory as kin and neighbours. In this social field the new ideology of marriage, upheld by associations and organisations, met with less competition from the influence of primary groups. Young people found it less difficult to defy the dispersed authority of kin and neighbours, and the older generation and primary groups did not have the immediacy and monopoly of sanctions at the disposal of their rural counterparts.

Although there might be wide variations in social practices within rural areas, it is in comparison to the urban social field that the structure and function of the rural household can be said to encourage the older generation to defy the new ideology of free choice and to maintain their control of marriage procedures, and it is the structure and functions of the primary groups in rural areas which enable them to retain old social customs which maintain these controls. In the rural areas it can be argued that the new economic policies have also contributed to the strengthening or at least the maintenance of the forms which the household and primary groups have traditionally taken, and together they have worked against the implementation of the new ideology of marriage. The identification of these structures and economic policies as factors encouraging the persistence of old customs of marriage, rather than as forces encouraging social change in the marriage patterns, challenges the expectations aroused by scholars of the Republican period in China and the suppositions put forward by social scientists, who have assumed that the modernisation of marriage, the family and kinship structures in China is analogous to that in other social fields.

10

CONCLUSIONS

The nation-wide adoption of free-choice marriage patterns in contemporary China has been limited by a number of factors which have particularly affected rural areas. It has been argued in the last two chapters that the authority of the older generation and the degree to which they continue to exercise control over marriage negotiations can be directly correlated to (*a*) the structure and function of the household and (*b*) the degree to which households are encapsulated by overlapping primary groups. What has emerged from an examination of the domestic groups in both the rural and urban social fields is a direct correlation between household composition, the economic interdependence of its members and the degree of parental participation in the procedures of mate selection. Where, as in rural areas, the accumulation of resources of the domestic group encourages the coresidence and economic interdependence of its members, the older generation has worked to maintain its controls over the recruitment of new members. Where, as in urban areas, the household is less a unit of production and consumption, and community facilities are more likely to service the individual household, the younger generation is likely to have acquired a certain measure of control. Far from discouraging a degree of familial control over marriage, the new economic policies may have contributed to the maintenance of the structure and functions of the patrilocal domestic group, which has worked against the implementation of new marriage patterns in the rural social field.

The introduction of free-choice marriage has also brought the traditional influence and authority of the primary kin and neighbourhood groups into competition with that of the political associations. At every stage of the marriage negotiations the older generation usually had the support of kin and neighbours and it is their influence which the younger generation, even with the support of political associations, found difficult to counter. The degree to which they did so was discovered to vary with the immediate social environment of the interested individuals and households. Where primary groups of kin, neighbours and friends overlapped and encapsulated the individual, they were more likely to provide the dominant reference group and unidirectional social pressures in support of the older generation. Moreover, it can be argued that the primary groups, far from being weakened as a result of the establishment of new political associations, have not only continued to overlap in rural village settlements to form a simple concrete and close-knit group, but that the interrelationship within these groups has been formalised and institutionalised by the demographic and economic policies. The reduction in migration and the institutionalisation of economic ties within and between the villages by the reorganisation of the relations of production and the establishment of rural communes has had the effect of maintaining, if not solidifying, the bonds between the individual households and the primary kin and neighbourhood groups. It is the structure and function of the overlapping primary groups in rural areas which have enabled them to maintain a certain measure of solidarity, retain certain sanctions at their disposal and remain the primary or single most important reference group for the household in rural China. In comparison to the urban social field, it can be said that the structure and function of the rural household has *encouraged* the older generation to defy the new ideology and maintain their control of marriage procedures and it is the structure and function of primary groups in rural areas which has *enabled* them to retain these controls.

A more detailed comparison of marriage patterns and the structure of domestic and primary groups in contemporary China suggests that previous analogies drawn from the comparable social fields of China in the Republican period and post–1949 Taiwan may not be appropriate, and may even have been misleading. It also raises questions concerning the assumptions on which the policies designed to reform marriage within China have been based. The Chinese government has generally perceived change within the domestic domain to be either the derivative of or an automatic accompaniment to broader socio-economic and political policies. It has therefore primarily defined marriage reform in terms of effecting ideological change. At the very least it has assumed that economic and ideological agencies are working in a uniform direction of change that is progressively institutionalising free-choice marriage. Thus the government has tended to attribute the persistence of old forms of marriage to the 'conservatism' or 'backwardness' of the rural population in adopting new forms of social behaviour. Since the 1950s, then, they have correlated the amount of social change with the degree of exposure to, and education in, the new ideology, and the ability of political associations to counter the competing influence of kin, neighbours and friends. One article posed the problem in the following words:

We all have our own families, parents, brothers/sisters and relatives. While in our own society the growth of youth depends mainly on the education of the Party and the State, the ideological influence of families and friends also produces an important effect on this process. (ZQ 16 September 1963)

It is the attitudes of conservatism which characterise primary groups that have been repeatedly identified as the chief obstacle to social change in rural areas. There has been little attention devoted to the economic foundations for the persistence of the traditional customs and attitudes, and instead the campaign to reform marriage has concentrated on educating the primary groups in the meanings symbolised by the customs, and persuading and convincing them of the advantages of the new forms. In the role models and reference groups portrayed in the media, for example, the point at which change takes place is seen to coincide with the acceptance of the new norms by the primary groups. In a village in Fujian province, it was reported that when the idea of late marriage was first introduced, it was the older members of households and kin groups who had to be persuaded of its benefits. Customary gossip had it that those who waited to marry late were thought 'to be still stuck with the family, although their hair was turning grey' or that 'they were becoming inferior goods which nobody wanted'. Apparently as a result of education, the opponents of change eventually recognised that these sayings had lost their efficacy, and it was at that point that late marriage was said to have become the common practice in the village (RMRB 12 June 1973).

This explanation for the variety of marriage patterns can be valid only if it can be demonstrated that there are significant differentials in the degree to which various sub-groups have been exposed to the new ideology, and that those can be directly correlated with the retention of old forms of marriage. Indeed, it is not uncommon for social analysis to attribute the persistence of custom to the degree of 'culture contact' (Schapera 1966) or to familiarity with a new ideology (Geiger 1968). Where sub-groups may remain 'almost isolated from the communications networks' (Rossi and Bauer 1952–3:658), then a new ideology would understandably provide less competition for the strength of traditional socio-political attitudes. This explanation, however, does not hold for contemporary China, where it can be argued that the government has made a sustained effort to familiarise the population with the new ideology, and in nearly every case study recorded in the media, the correspondents, both rural and urban based, showed themselves to be conscious of the contents of the new ideology. There was an awareness that the initiatives in the negotiation of marriage should have passed to the younger generation, an understanding of the reasons why betrothal should be discarded, an appreciation of the new criteria for choice of marriage partner and a recognition of the advantages of raising the age of marriage and reducing the expenses and ceremonial associated with marriage. The correspondents might not necessarily agree with the new ideological model, and may even argue vehemently against it, but they were certainly aware of the changes which it advocated. If it can be demonstrated that the new ideology of marriage is reasonably familiar to people throughout the country, then the retention of old forms cannot be interpreted, as it is in China, as a mere manifestation of social conservatism or isolation from the communications networks. Rather, the presence of the new ideological model must be considered as one of the forces working for social change.

The introduction of the new ideology of free-choice marriage has formed one of the main vehicles by which the State has actively intervened and attempted to articulate major changes in the relations between the generations, the sexes and between domestic and kin groups. The new patterns of marriage, even the smaller adjustments in the negotiations to provide for the consent of the younger generation in the countryside, do represent some modification of these social relations. However, the effectiveness of the new ideology of marriage in redistributing the locus of power and authority within the domestic group has been limited in rural areas by the fact that socio-economic and demographic factors have encouraged the maintenance or even the elaboration of domestic and kin groups. That is, while economic policies have worked to *maintain* or even elaborate the traditional *structures* of the household and primary groups, the new ideology of marriage has primarily worked to *modify* social *relations* within and between these structures in rural areas. Sooner or later the form that these structures take must limit the possible redefinition of the relations bounded by those structures. It is the considerable degree of competition or tension between the aims of the new ideology of marriage and the effects of economic policies which have been responsible for some redefinition of the new ideological model of free-choice marriage, the crystallisation of a variety of marriage patterns in contemporary China and the slow pace of change or even the impasse which presently characterises reforms within the domestic domain in rural areas.

The substitution of free-choice marriage for arranged marriage has been identified as one of the most difficult social reforms to implement in the history of the People's Republic. A woman interviewed by an Australian journalist in the late 1950s said that in her village 'one of the most difficult things to break down was the system of arranged marriage' (Cusack 1958:54–5). In a national discussion of the problem in the 1960s, the 'development of new marriage and family relationships' was singled out as one of the most difficult of social reforms to be introduced since 1949 (RMRB 13 December 1963). Again, Jack Chen, who published an account of village life in China in the 1970s, observed that in Upper Felicity the nature of change in betrothal and marriage customs had been more subtle than in some other institutions. They were at

a half-way stage that reflects the present state of social relations and outlooks in the village. The old feudal forms and content of life are being shed...but the socialist order has not yet fully taken over. (Chen 1973:60)

The findings of this study have suggested that the patterns of marriage, which represent both a significant departure from previous marriage customs, a concession to the new ideology and, very importantly, an adjustment to contemporary economic policies, may not in fact be in a state of transition in rural areas. They also suggest that the extent to which 'free-choice' marriage will uniformly supercede the old procedures and symbols of marriage in the future will depend on government policies taking cognisance of the fact that patterns of marriage not only have consequences for social relations between the generations, the sexes and domestic or kin groups, but also that they are a consequence of social structures maintained by current economic policies.

ABBREVIATIONS

ACDWF	All-China Democratic Women's Federation
CNA	*China News Analysis*, Hong Kong
CR	*China Reconstructs*, Beijing (Peking)
GRB	*Gongren Ribao* (Workers' Daily), Beijing
HRB	*Hebei Ribao* (Hebei Daily), Tianjin (Tientsin)
HZX	*Huadong Zhengfu Xuebao* (East China Journal of Political Science and Law), Shanghai
KMRB	*Guangming Ribao* (Guangming Daily), Beijing
NCH	*North China Herald*, Shangahi
NCNA	*North China News Agency*, London
NFRB	*Nanfang Ribao* (Nanfang Daily), Guangzhou (Canton)
PC	*People's China*, Beijing
PR	*Peking Review*, Beijing
RMRB	*Renmin Ribao* (People's Daily), Beijing
SRB	*Shaanxi Ribao* (Shaanxi Daily), Taiyuan
SWB	*Survey of World Broadcasts*, Far East Section
TKP	*Ta Kungpao*, Beijing
WC	*Women of China*, Peking
XG	*Xin Guancha* (New Observer), Beijing
XyP	*Xuexi yu Pipan* (Study and Criticism), Shanghai
XR	*Xinwen Ribao* (New Magazine), Beijing
ZF	*Zhongguo Funu* (Chinese Women), Beijing
ZJ	*Changjiang Ribao* (Yangtze Daily), Hankou
ZQ	*Zhongguo Qingnian* (China Youth), Beijing
ZX	*Zhong Xuesheng* (Middle School Student), Beijing

BIBLIOGRAPHY

SOURCES IN CHINESE

Anhui People's Publishing House, 1964, Hunyin Fa Jiangjie (Talks on the Marriage Law), Anhui.

Chang Fan, 1952, *Lianai hunyin yu fufu shenghou* (Collection of Articles on Love and Marriage), Shanghai.

Changjiang Ribao (ZJ), *30 August 1951*: Committee of the Central-South Democratic Women's Federation, 'Preliminary investigation of the implementation of the Marriage Law in the Central-South Region'.

Cheng Dongyuan, 1937, *Zhongguo Funu Shenghuo Shi* (The History of Chinese Women), Shanghai, Commercial Press.

Cheng Guyuan, 1937, *Zhonnguo Hunyin Shi* (History of Chinese Marriage), Shanghai.

Gongren Ribao (GRB)

14 July 1962, 'I give up my plan for early marriage'.

28 July 1962, Tao Cheng, 'A talk with young friends about the question of marriage'.

18 August 1962, Wang Xiaolan (letter), 'Money and love'.

11 September 1962, A selection of letters on age of marriage.

18 September 1962, A selection of letters on age of marriage.

27 September 1962, A selection of letters on age of marriage. Chen Xiao, 'Men and women old enough should marry'.

5 October 1962, A selection of letters on age of marriage.

9 October 1962, A selection of letters on age of marriage.

16 October 1962, A selection of letters on age of marriage.

7 November 1962, Zhou Xinmin, 'On the encouragement of late marriage and the statutory age of marriage'.

15 November 1962, Wang Wenbin, 'A talk about the question of age of marriage from the physiological angle'.

22 November 1962, Kan Feng, 'Foresight and prudence is necessary in handling the question of marriage'.

6 May 1965, Letter, 'Does one lose one's class stand by marrying a person born of a family of exploiting class?'

7 November 1965, A selection of letters on problems of family class background.

Bibliography

Guangming Ribao (KMRB)
4 June 1955, 'Make a good job of the registration of marriage'.
14 January 1957, 'A word to the judicial personnel who deal with marriage disputes'.
27 February 1957, Wu Zhangzhen, 'The principle of "freedom of marriage" should not be abused'.
18 January 1969, 'A new custom in marrying off daughters'.
Hebei Ribao (HRB), *8 April 1959*, Chen Jianwei, 'The breaking down of the system of feudal patriarchy'. (Also in *Survey of China Mainland Press*, no. 2039:1).
Henan All-China Democratic Women's Federation (ACDWF), 1955, *Ruhe Zhengque dui dai lianai, hunyin wo jinting wenti* (On marriage, love and family problems), Zhengzhou.
Hong Yenlin, 1956, *Diaocha Yenjiu yu Gongzuo Zongjie* (Investigation and research and the evaluation of work), Peking, People's Press.
Hongqi (Red Flag), *1 December 1973*: Xia Ping, 'Work hard to train women cadres'.
Huadong Zhengfu Xuebao (HZX), *15 December 1956*, Tao Ji, 'In the handling of divorce cases, we must struggle against bourgeois ideology'. (Also in *Extracts China Mainland Magazine*, no. 65:5.)
Kirin Ribao (Kirin Daily), *10 January 1959*, Du Gefu, 'On the question of the family'. (Also in *Survey of China Mainland Press*, no. 1961:1.)
Lin Yuehua, 1936, 'An enquiry into the Chinese lineage village from the viewpoint of anthropology', *Shehui Xuexi* (Sociological World), vol. IX. (See Freedman 1963.)
Lu Yang, 1964, *Ruhe Zhengque duidai lianai, hunyin, jiating wenti* (The Correct Handling of Love, Marriage and Family Problems), Jinan, Shandong People's Publishing House.
Mai Huiting, 1935, *Zhongguo Jiating Gaibian Wenti* (Problems of the Chinese Family Reform), Shanghai.
Nanfang Ribao (NFRB)
13 February 1952, 'Marriage problems during land reform'.
6 April 1962, Li Buchen, 'The debate on wedding feasts'.
12 May 1962, Letter, 'Marriage by choice and arranged marriage'.
15 May 1962, Questions and answers on the age of marriage.
5 July 1962, 'The evils of forced marriage and violations of the Marriage Law'.
26 July 1962, Letter, 'Should I marry a girl of Yao nationality?'
6 October 1962, 'Troubles in negotiating a marriage'.
25 December 1964, 'A brief talk on presents as "expressions of goodwill"'.
25 December 1964, 'Are betrothal presents a means of showing gratitude to parents?'
18 January 1965, 'How I refused to observe the old customs for my wedding'.
25 January 1965, 'How should we conduct a wedding?'

8 March 1965, 'How to help those of bad class origin make progress'.

Pan Dunzhi, 1950, *Xin Hunyin fen Jiben Renshi* (Basic Knowledge about the New Marriage Law), Kowloon.

Pan Guantan (P'an Kuan-tan), 1931, *Zhongguo Zhi Jiating Wenti* (Chinese Family Problems), Shanghai.

Pan Yumei, 1932, 'Yige cong zhengdi Nongfu' (Village Women), *Shehui Xuexi* (Sociological World), vol. VI. (See Lang, O., 1946, *Chinese Family and Society*, New Haven, Yale University Press, p. 377.)

Qingnian Chubanshe (Youth Publishing House), 1953, *Lun Shehuizhui Shehui ti aijing, hunyin wo jiating* (On Love, Marriage and the Family in Socialist Society), Peking.

Radcliffe-Brown, A. R., 1936, 'Proposals for a sociological survey of village life in China', *Shehui Xuexi* (Sociological World), vol. IX.

Renmin Ribao (RMRB)

    29 September 1951, 'Government Administrative Council directive on the investigation of conditions relating to the implementation of the Marriage Law'.

    9 October 1951, Li Cheng, 'Strengthen the study of the Marriage Law by cadres at Qu and Xiang levels'.

    13 October 1951, Shiliang, 'Attend seriously to the thorough implementation of the Marriage Law'.

    4 July 1951, Shiliang, 'The Marriage Law'.

    19 March 1953, 'Cadres trained through country for Marriage Law publicity movement'.

    20 March 1953, Liu Jingfan, 'Purpose of the new campaign to publicise the new Marriage Law'.

    23 August 1956, Shu Wu, 'Man selects woman, woman selects man'.

    15 November 1956, 'Show concern for young people's happiness in love and marriage'.

    12 January 1957, 'Marriage of Party members need not be approved by Party'.

    9 March 1957, 'Some young people in Tientsin involved in hasty marriages and divorces'.

    17 January 1959, 'Promote the family life of democratic solidarity'.

    29 May 1959, Liu Donggao, 'Treat marriage seriously'.

    4 April 1962, Letter on age of marriage.

    13 December 1963, Yang Tawen and Liu Suping, 'On the reform of our country's system of marriage and family'.

    28 June 1964, Cheng Hong, 'Persuade parents and relatives to break old customs and influences'; 'Economics in wedding and funeral expenses'.

    23 November 1964, Letter, 'Which is closer, clan ties or class ties?'

    31 August 1969, 'Firmly destroying old habits by insisting on late marriage'.

    2 February 1970, Liu Zuoren, 'Destroy old customs, establish new practices'.

30 January 1971, 'Encourage late marriage in the cause of revolution'.

24 January 1972, 'Revolutionary youths must take the lead in changing old habits and customs'.

20 November 1972, 'Changing customs and traditions in marriage'.

22 January 1973, 'Destroy the old, establish the new'.

12 June 1973, 'Young women of Houwang village struggle to marry late'.

Shaanxi Ribao (SRB)

29 December 1957: Zhang Buxin and Yang Jing, 'Girls graduated from middle school marry peasants in Shaanxi'. (Also in *Survey of China Mainland Press*, no. 1720:27.)

8 March 1958, Shu Ping, 'A talk with young comrades on love and marriage'. (Also in *Survey of China Mainland Press*, no. 1769:29.)

Song Tingzhang, 1957, *Zenyang Zhengque duidai lianai Wenti* (A Correct Perspective in Matters of Love), Shenyang.

Ta Kungpao (TKP)

22 December 1956, Yu Ming, 'We must adopt a solemn attitude towards the problem of love and marriage'.

12 September 1964, 'How should young workers look at the question of love and marriage?'

Village Reader, 1963, *Zenyang zuohao hunyin dengji gongzuo* (How to Manage Marriage Registration Work Well), Peking, Civil Office, Ministry of the Interior.

Wenhuibao, 28 July 1968, 'Stem the evil wind of falling in love and getting married early among literary and art circles'. (Also in *Survey of China Mainland Press*, no. 4250:17.)

Xin Guancha (XG), *16 October 1955*, Xie Quezai, 'The way to make friends'. (Also in *Extracts China Mainland Magazines*, no. 18:58).

Xinwen Ribao (XR), *28 April 1957*, 'Demobbed military man poses as a Party member'. (Also in *Survey of China Mainland Press*, no. 1556:26.)

Xuexi yu Pipan (XyP), *10 January 1975*, Sun Luoying and Lu Lifen, 'On Confucian persecution of women in history'.

Zhong Xeusheng (ZX), *3 April 1956*, Ge Zhangyue, 'Do not start making love too early'. (Also in *Extracts China Mainland Magazine*, no. 41:23.)

Zhongguo Funu (ZF)

1 November 1955, Liu Luochun, 'Why our marital relationships become strained'.

1 April 1957, Kua Dilin, 'The best marriageable age from a physiological standpoint'.

16 April 1959, Letters on 'Who is to blame for the breakdown of marriage?'

1 May 1959, Wang Jing, 'How he invites further trouble'.

1 May 1959, Ye Huiyuan, 'Beauty is not the only criterion'.

14 November 1959, Editorial on marriage.

14 December 1959, Letters on choosing a spouse.

14 January 1960, Letters on choosing a spouse.

1 June 1962, 'Organise social forces, care for child education'.

1 February 1963, Letters on criteria for choice of spouse.

1 June 1963, Yuan Ziren, 'Yi Shizhuan gets married'.

1 September 1963, Letters on 'What do women live for?'

1 October 1963, Chen Meiyung, 'How I fought for freedom of marriage'.

1 October 1963, Liao Suhua, 'What is revolutionary women's true happiness?'

1 May 1964, 1 July 1964, 1 August 1964, 1 September 1964, Letters on 'What is the criterion in choosing a husband?'

1 October 1964, 'What attitude should a husband take towards his wife?'

1 January 1966, 'This is an important matter that cadres ought to take care of'.

1 February 1966, Ning Mingye, 'The Party supports me in my struggle for self-determination in marriage'; Liu Kuihua, 'Marriage by purchase really harms people'; 'If you don't want betrothal gifts, your thought is red'.

7 November 1966, A selection of articles on the problem of an exploiting-class family background.

Zhongguo Qingnian (ZQ)

4 January 1955, Lin Hua, 'It's right that this affair of blind love should be considered as closed'.

1 April 1955, Xu Mingjiang, 'Several problems concerning the education of youth in love and marriage'.

1 April 1955, Fang Chun, 'Let youth devote their energies to the great cause of socialist construction'.

16 November 1955, Zhou Kenxian, 'How I handle my love problem'.

16 November 1955, Yu Li, 'How to deal with the shortcomings of your husband'.

16 November 1955, Su Yuan (letter), 'Who is the superfluous third person?'

1 May 1956, Letters to the editor on courtship.

16 May 1956, 'Respect voluntariness in love life'.

24 May 1956, Letter, 'Why can't we get married?'

30 August 1956, Fang Yujing, 'Arranged marriage is a serious problem in rural areas in Shaanxi province'.

6 September 1956, Huong Lianhai, 'A survey of marriage among factory workers'.

6 September 1956, Editorial on age of marriage.

1 November 1956, 'Give correct guidance to the problems of rural youth in love and marriage'.

16 November 1956, Xu Hua, 'Do not make love to middle school students who are still young'.

1 December 1956, Editorial on 'Relations between the generations'.

16 December 1956, Feng Ding, 'Love and support of parents is still a necessary virtue in socialist society'.

16 October 1958, Letter, 'Is intermarriage between the Han and Hui youths permissable?'

1 January 1962, Gu Xiqing, 'Love and spending money'.

22 February 1962, 'The correct approach to marriage'.

22 February 1962, Guang Hai, 'Thrifty weddings are good'.

16 March 1962, Letters on the relationship of money to love.

12 April 1962, Ye Gongshao, 'What is the most suitable age of marriage?'

24 April 1962, 'New ways of handling new things'; 'What things should be emphasised in handling a wedding well?'

10 May 1962, Letters on age of marriage.

1 June 1962, Yang Xiu, 'Late marriage'.

7 July 1962, Letters on age of marriage.

17 July 1962, Letter on choice between a married life in the countryside and single life in the cities.

21 July 1962, Ye Gongshao, 'My views on the problem of marriage, love and children'.

21 August 1962, Bai Wen (letter) on the custom of 'Sworn brothers and sisters'.

14 September 1962, Yang Xiu, 'Adopt a careful attitude toward your matrimonial question'.

3 November 1962, Hui Xian (letter), 'Does sterility constitute justifiable grounds for divorce?'

27 November 1962, Letter, 'Is it possible to compromise with parents, who refuse to give consent to marriage?'

2 February 1963, Fu Lianchang, 'A talk with young comrades on the question of marriage'.

12 February 1963, Cheng Shuizhi, 'Is my objection to an arranged marriage unfilial?'

9 May 1963, Letters on age of marriage.

16 June 1963, Letters on courtship.

28 July 1963, 'How can family relations be handled properly?'

16 September 1963, Yang Xiu, 'Correctly deal with the ideological influences of families and relatives'.

16 September 1963, Yao Ligong, 'Fight against bourgeois thought in dealing with problems of love and marriage'.

1 October 1963, Yao Wenyuan, 'Should one live for revolution or for love?'

26 October 1963, Letter, 'Is it still necessary to keep clan registers?'

26 November 1963, Letter, 'Should I refuse to participate in an arranged marriage?'

30 January 1964, Shen Lianding, 'Arrange weddings frugally'.

16 May 1964, 'Revolutionary youths must take lead in establishing new customs'.

28 July 1964, Letter, 'Can one find an ideal mate when one is old?'

1 August 1964, Qian Yan, 'She insists on late marriage'.

27 October 1964, Qian Feng (letter), 'Will young men and women working together bring disrepute to the family?'

19 November 1964, 'Young people should take the lead in ending the practice of betrothal gifts'.

19 November 1964, Luo Donglin (letter), 'How I broke with outmoded rules and old customs in conducting my wedding'.

1 May 1965, Letter, 'How can problems of love and marriage be correctly treated by those of exploiting-class origins?'

16 October 1965, Letter on problems in marriage for those of exploiting-class origins.

16 January 1966, 'Changing undesirable wedding customs and practices'.

1 February 1966, Letter on problems of rejecting an arranged marriage.

16 April 1966, Guo Yingfang (letter), 'How should young women handle the rumour and gossip when they participate in club activities?'

Zhongyang Renmin Zhengfu (Central People's Government), 1950, *Hunyin Wenti Cankao Ziliao huibian* (First Collection of Materials on Marriage Problem), Peking.

Zhoumobao (Weekend News), Hong Kong, *18 October 1952*, Shi Lu, 'Chinese farm girls now prefer to marry workers'. (Also in *Survey of China Mainland Press*, no. 436:34.)

GENERAL SOURCES

Abbott, K. A., 1970, *Harmony and Individualism: Changing Chinese Psycho-Social Functioning in Taipei and San Francisco*, Asian Folklore and Social Life Monograph no. 12, Taipei, Orient Cultural Service.

Arcay, S. J., Brena, J. S. *et al.*, 1968, *The Family in Taiwan (Present Situation and Tendencies)*, Taiwan, Chinese Language Institute.

Ayscough, F. *Chinese Women Today and Yesterday*, 1938, London, Jonathan Cape.

Baker, H., 1968, *A Chinese Lineage Village: Sheung Shui*, London, Frank Cass.

Barber, B., 1957, *Social Stratification*, New York, Harcourt, Brace and World.

Barclay, G. W., 1954, *Colonial Development and Population in Taiwan*, New Jersey, Princeton University Press.

Barnes, J. A., 1951, *Marriage in a Changing Society: A Study in Structural Change Among the Fort Jameson Ngoni*, Capetown, Oxford University Press.

1971, *Three Styles in the Study of Kinship*, London, Tavistock Publications.

Baum, R. and Teiwes, F. C., 1968, *Ssu-Ching. The Socialist Education Movement of 1962–1966*, China Research Monographs, Berkeley, University of California Press.

Beauvoir, S. de, 1957, *La Longue Marche: essai sur la Chine*, Paris, Gallimard.

Bessac, F. B., 1965, 'Some social effects of land reform in a village in Taiwan plains', *Journal of the China Society*, vol. 4, pp. 15–24.

Blood, R. O., 1969, *Marriage*, New York, The Free Press.

Bibliography

Bossard, J., 1932, 'Residential propinquity as a factor in marriage selection', *American Journal of Sociology*, September, pp. 219–224.

Buck, J. L., 1930, *Chinese Farm Economy: a study of 2,866 farms in seventeen localities and seven provinces in China*, University of Nanking.

1937, *Land Utilization in China*, University of Nanking.

Burgess, E. W. and Locke, H. J., 1945, *The Family*, New York, American Book Co.

Chao, Buwei Yang, 1970, *Autobiography of a Chinese Woman*, Connecticut, Greenwood Press.

Chayanov, A. V., 1966, *Theory of Peasant Economy*, ed. Thorner, D. *et al.*, Homewood, Illinois.

Chen, C. S. and Ridley, C. P., 1969, *Rural People's Communes in Lienchiang*, Stanford, California, Hoover Institution Press.

Chen Hsu, 1952, 'How Wang Kuei-lan married the man of her choice', *Women in China Today*, no. 8, All-China Democratic Women's Federation, October.

Chen, J., 1973, *A Year in Upper Felicity*, London, Harrap.

Chen Pi-Chao, 1972, 'Overurbanisation, rustication of urban educated youths and politics of rural transformation', *Comparative Policies*, April, pp. 361–86.

Chiao, C. M., 1934, *Rural Population and Vital Statistics for Selected Areas in China 1929–1931*, Shanghai, Bureau of Foreign Trade.

Chin Ai-li, S., 1948, 'Some problems of Chinese youth in transition', *American Journal of Sociology*, vol. LIV, no. 1, July, pp. 1–9.

China News Analysis (CNA)

   25 September 1953, 'Marriage Law and family reform'.

   1 April 1955, 'family and women'.

   13 May 1955, 'marriage reform'.

China Reconstructs (CR)

   1 March 1953, Yang Yu, 'Three conditions'.

   1 April 1953, 'The Marriage Law'.

   1 September 1953, Fang Yen, 'Making the Marriage Law work'; Chin Chiao-yang, 'Overheard conversation'; William Hinton, 'Two ordinary girls'.

   1 January 1955, Film review, 'Marriage'.

   1 July 1955, Pai Hsi-yen, 'Talks in a workshop'.

   1 December 1956, Yu Lin, 'Story told at a wedding'.

   1 May 1957, Lo Pin-chi, 'Father and daughter'.

   1 July 1962, Lu Chen-hsiang, 'Marriage in the village yesterday and today'.

   1 November 1962, Chen Kuei-pei, 'A Tai wedding'.

   1 November 1964, Pai Hua, 'What the Hani girl said to me'.

   1 June 1975, 'Between husband and wife'.

Chiu, V., 1958, 'Marriage laws of the Ch'ing Dynasty, the Republic of China and Communist China', *Contemporary China*, vol. 4, pp. 64–72.

1966, *Marriage Laws and Customs of China*, Hong Kong, New Asia College, Chinese University,

Chow Tse-tung, 1960, *The May Fourth Movement*, California, Stanford University Press.

Cohen, A., 1970, 'The politics of marriage in changing Middle Eastern stratification systems' in Plotonicov, L. and Tuden, A. (eds), *Essays in Comparative Social Stratification*, Pittsburgh, University of Pennsylvania Press.

1974, *Two Dimensional Man: An Essay on the Anthropology of Power and Symbolism in Complex Society*, London, Routledge and Kegan Paul.

Cohen, M., 1976, *House United House Divided, The Chinese Family in Taiwan*, New York, University of Colombia Press.

Croll, E. J. 1974, *The Women's Movement in China: A Selection of Readings 1949–73*, London, ACEI.

1977, 'Chiang Village: a household survey', *China Quarterly*, December, pp. 786–814.

1978, *Feminism and Socialism in China*, London, Routledge and Kegan Paul.

Crook, D. and I., 1959, *Revolution in a Chinese Village: Ten Mile Inn*, London, Routledge and Kegan Paul.

1966, *The First Years of Yangyi Commune*, London, Routledge and Kegan Paul.

Current Background, 10 November 1951, 'Marriage in Communist China'.

Cusack, D., 1958, *Chinese Women Speak*, Sydney, Angus and Robertson.

Davin, D., 1976, *Woman-Work: Women and the Party in Revolutionary China*, Oxford, Clarendon Press.

1976, 'Free-choice marriage in China: the evolution of an ideal', in Barker, D. L. and Allen, S. (eds.), *Sexual Divisions and Society: Process and Change*, London, Tavistock Publications, pp. 224–45.

Dean, I., 1927, 'The women's movement in China', *The Chinese Recorder*, vol. LVIII, pp. 652–9.

Diamond, N., 1969, *Kun Shen, A Taiwan Village*, New York, Holt, Rinehart and Winston.

1973, 'The status of women in Taiwan', in Young, M. (ed.), *Women in China*, Michigan Papers in Chinese Studies No. 15, Ann Arbor, University of Michigan Press.

1975, 'Collectivisation, kinship and the status of women in rural China', *Bulletin of the Concerned Asian Scholars*, January–March, pp. 25–32.

Duncan, J. D., 1968, *Symbols in Society*, New York, Oxford University Press.

Durkheim, E., 1951, *Suicide*, Glencoe, Illinois, The Free Press.

1954, *The Elementary Forms of the Religious Life*, London, Allen and Unwin.

Eberhard, W., 1963, 'Auspicious marriages: a statistical study of a Chinese custom', *Sociologus*, vol. 13, pp. 49–55.

1967, 'Research in the Chinese family', in *Settlement and Social Change in Asia*, Collected Papers, vol. 1, Hong Kong University Press.

Eckstein, A., 1975, *China's Economic Development; the interplay of scarcity and ideology*, Ann Arbor, University of Michigan Press.

Engels, F., 1954, *Origins of the Family, Private Ownership and the State*, Moscow, People's Publishing House.

Evans-Pritchard, E. E., 1951, *Kinship and Marriage Among the Nuer*, Oxford, Clarendon Press.

Fei Hsiao-tung, 1939, *Peasant Life in China: A Field Study of Country Life in the Yangtze Valley*, London, Routledge and Kegan Paul.

    1946, 'Peasantry and gentry', *American Journal of Sociology*, vol. LII pp. 1–17.

Firth, R., 1971, *Elements of Social Organisation*, London, Tavistock Publications.

    1953, 'The study of values by social anthropologists', Marett Lecture, *Man*, vol. LIII, pp. 146–53.

Fortes, M., 1971, Introduction in Goody, J., *The Development Cycle in Domestic Groups*, Cambridge University Press.

Fox, R., 1967, *Kinship and Marriage*, Harmondsworth, Penguin Books Ltd.

Freedman, M., 1957, *Chinese Family and Marriage in Singapore*, London, Her Majesty's Stationary Office.

    1958, *Lineage Organisation in South-eastern China*, London, Athlone Press.

    1963, 'A Chinese phase in social anthropology', *British Journal of Sociology*, vol. 14, pp. 1–19.

    1964, 'What social science can do for Chinese studies', *Journal of Asian Studies*, vol. 23, pp. 523–9.

    1966, *Chinese Lineage and Society, Fukien and Kwangtung*, London, Athlone Press.

    1967, *Rites and Duties in Chinese Marriage*, London School of Economics Inaugural Lecture, London, Bell and Sons Ltd.

    1969, 'Why China?' Presidential address, *Proc. of the Royal Anthropological Institute of Great Britain and Ireland*, pp. 5–14.

Freeman, L. C., 1958, 'Marriage without love: mate selection in non-Western societies', in Winch, R. F. (ed.), *Mate Selection*, New York, Harper and Row.

Fried, M. H., 1953, *Fabric of Chinese Society: A Study of the Social Life of a Chinese County Seat*, New York, Praeger.

Fu, S. L., 1955, 'The new Marriage Law of the People's China', *Contemporary China*, vol. 1, pp. 115–38.

Gallin, B., 1963, 'Cousin marriage in China', *Ethnology*, vol. 2, pp. 104–8.

    1966, *Hsin Hsing, Taiwan: a Chinese village in change*, Berkeley, University of California Press.

    1967, 'Emerging individualism in changing rural Taiwan', *Journal of the China Society*, vol. 5, pp. 3–8.

Gamble, S. D., 1933, *How Chinese Families Live in Peiping*, New York, Funk and Wagnalls.

    1954, *Ting Hsien, a North China Rural Community*, California, Stanford University Press.

Bibliography

Gardner, J., 1971, 'Educated youth and rural–urban inequalities 1958–1966', in Lewis, J. (ed.), *The City in Communist China*, California, Stanford University Press, pp. 268–76.

Geddes, W., 1963, *Peasant Life in Communist China*, Monograph no. 6, Ithaca, New York, Society for Applied Anthropology.

Geiger, H. K., 1968, 'Changing political attitudes in totalitarian society: a case study of the role of the family', in Bell, N. W. and Vogel, E. F. (eds.), *A Modern Introduction to the Family*, New York, The Free Press, pp. 219–34.

Gennep, A. van, 1960, *The Rites of Passage*, London, Routledge and Kegan Paul.

Gluckman, M., 1956, *Custom and Conflict in Africa*, Oxford, Blackwell.

Goode, W. J., 1959, 'The theoretical importance of love', *American Sociological Review*, vol. 24, pp. 38–47.

1963, *World Revolution and Family Patterns*, New York, The Free Press.

1970, 'Family and mobility', in Tumin, M. (ed.), *Readings on Social Stratification*, New Jersey, Prentice Hall, pp. 322–32.

Goody, J., 1961, 'Religion and ritual: the definitional problem', *British Journal of Sociology*, vol. 12, pp. 142–64.

1969, 'Inheritance, property and marriage in Africa and Eurasia', *Sociology*, vol. 3, pp. 55–76.

1971, 'Class and marriage in Africa and Eurasia', *American Journal of Sociology*, vol. 76, pp. 585–603.

1972, 'The evolution of the family', in Laslett, P. (ed.), *Household and Family in Past Time*, Cambridge University Press, pp. 103–24.

Goody, J. R. and Tambiah, S. J., 1973, *Bridewealth and Dowry*, Cambridge University Press.

Greenblatt, S. L., 1968, 'Introduction', *Chinese Sociology and Anthropology*, Fall.

Habbakuk, H., 1955, 'Daniel Finch, second Earl of Nottingham, his house and estate', in Plumb, J. (ed.), *Studies in Social History*, London, Longmans.

Hahn, E., 1942, *The Soong Sisters*, London, Robert Hale Ltd.

Harris, O., 1976, 'Women's labour and the household', paper presented to British Sociological Association, in Scott, A. (ed.), *Relations of Production on the Periphery*, London, Routledge and Kegan Paul (forthcoming).

Hinton, W., 1966, *Fanshen, a documentary of Revolution in a Chinese Village*, New York, Random House.

Hollingshead, A. B., 1950, 'Cultural factors in the selection of marriage mates', *American Sociological Review*, vol. 15, pp. 619–27.

Hsia, C. H., 1963, 'Residual femininity: women in Chinese Communist fiction', *China Quarterly*, vol. 13, pp. 158–79.

Hsien Ping-Ying, 1943, *Autobiography of a Chinese Girl*, London, Allen and Unwin.

Hsu, F. L. K., 1940, 'Problem of incest tabu in a North China village', *American Anthropologist*, vol. 42, pp. 122–35.

1943, 'The myth of Chinese family size', *American Journal of Sociology*, no. XLVIII, pp. 555–62.

1948, *Under the Ancestors' Shadow: Chinese Culture and Personality*, New York, Columbia University Press.

Huang, Lucy Jen, 1962, 'Attitudes towards inter-class marriage', *China Quarterly*, vol. 12, pp. 183–90.

Hutchinson, P., 1924, *China's Real Revolution*, New York, Missionary Education Movement of the USA and Canada.

Jahoda, G., 1959, 'Love, marriage and social change: letters to the advice columns of a West African newspaper', *Africa*, vol. 29, pp. 177–90.

Johnson, E. and G., 1976, *Walking on Two Legs: Rural Development in South China*, Ottawa, International Development Research Council.

Joint Publications Research Service 7 January 1974, 'Fujian Women's Federation circular, Fuzhou radio', no. 256:11.

Kan, A., 1965, 'The marriage institution in present-day China', *The China Mainland Review*, December, pp. 1–11.

Keeson, W. (ed.), 1975, *Childhood in China*, New Haven, Yale University Press.

Kerckhoff, A. C., 1963–4, 'Patterns of homogamy and the field of eligibles', *Social Forces*, vol. 42, pp. 289–97.

Kluckhohn, C., 1945, 'The personal document in anthropological science', in Gottschalk, L. *et al.*, (eds.), *The Use of Personal Documents in History, Anthropology, and Sociology*, New York, Social Science Research Council.

Kulp, D. M., 1925, *Country Life in South China*, New York, Columbia University Press.

Lang, O., 1946, *Chinese Family and Society*, New Haven, Yale University Press.

Langness, L. L., 1965, *The Life History in Anthropological Science*, New York, Holt Rinehart and Winston.

Leach, E., 1968, 'Ritual', *International Encyclopaedia of Social Sciences*, ed. Sills, D. L., vol. 13, New York, The Macmillan Co. and The Free Press, pp. 520–6.

1970, *Political Systems of Highland Burma*, London, Athlone Press.

Lee, R. H., 1949, 'Research in the Chinese family', *American Journal of Sociology*, May, vol. LV pp. 497–504.

Legge, J., 1876, *The Shih Ching, The Book of Ancient Poetry*, London, Trubner and Co.

1895, *The Chinese Classics*, London, Oxford University Press.

Lelyveld, J., 1974, 'The Great Leap Farmward', *New York Times Magazine*, 28 July, p. 6 and *passim*.

Lethbridge, H., 1962, 'The communes in China', in Szczepanik, E. F. (ed.), *Economic and Social Problems of the Far East*, Hong Kong University Press.

Lévi-Strauss, C., 1953, 'Social structure', in Kroeber, A. L. (ed.), *Anthropology Today*, Illinois, University of Chicago Press, pp. 524–53.

1968, *Structural Anthropology*, Harmondsworth, Penguin Books.

1969, *Elementary Structures of Kinship*, London, Eyre and Spottiswood.

Bibliography

Levy, M. J., 1949, *The Family Revolution in Modern China*, New York, Atheneum.

Lin Yueh-Hwa, 1948, *The Golden Wing*, London, Routledge and Kegan Paul.

Litwak, E. and Szelenyi, I., 1969, 'Primary group structures and their functions: kin, neighbours and friends', *American Sociological Review*, vol. 34, pp. 465–81.

Liu Hui-Chen Wang, 1959, *The Traditional Chinese Clan Rules*, New York, Locust Valley.

Lowrie, S. H., 1951, 'Dating theories and student responses', *American Sociological Review*, vol. 16, pp. 334–40.

McAleavy, H., 1955, 'Certain aspects of Chinese customary law in the light of Japanese scholarship', *Bulletin of School of Oriental and African Studies*, 17, pp. 535–47.

Macciocchi, M. A., 1972, *Daily Life in Revolutionary China*, New York, Monthly Review Press.

McCreery, J. L., 1976, 'Women's property rights and dowry in China', *Ethnology*, vol. xv, pp. 163–74.

Mace, D. and V., 1960, *Marriage East and West*, London, MacGibbon and Kee.

Mair, L., 1969, *African Marriage and Social Change*, London, Frank Cass.

Malinowski, B., 1963, *Sex Culture and Myth*, London, Rupert Hart-Davis.

Marsh, R. M. and O'Hara, A. R., 1961, 'Attitudes toward marriage and the family in Taiwan', *American Journal of Sociology*, vol. LXVII, pp. 1–8.

Marshall, G. A., 1968, 'Marriage: comparative analysis', *Encyclopaedia of Social Sciences*, ed. Sills, D. L. New York, The Macmillan Co. and the Free Press, pp. 8–18.

Meijer, M. J., 1971, *Marriage Law and Policy in the Chinese People's Republic*, Hong Kong University Press.

Mitchell, J. C. 1966, 'Theoretical orientations in African urban studies', in Barton, M. (ed.), *The Social Anthropology of Complex Societies*, ASA monograph no. 4, London, Tavistock Publications.

Myers, R., 1970, *The Chinese Peasant Economy*, Cambridge, Massachusetts, Harvard University Press.

Myrdal, J., 1967, *Report from a Chinese Village*, Harmondsworth, Penguin Books Ltd.

Myrdal, J. and Kessle, G., 1973, *China: The Revolution Continued*, Harmondsworth, Penguin Books Ltd.

Nathan, A. J., 1976, 'Policy oscillations in the People's Republic of China: a critique', *China Quarterly*, December, pp. 720–34.

New China News Agency (NCNA)

  10 January 1951, 'Marriages in China are no longer based on economic considerations'.

  27 October 1951, 'East China launches extensive propaganda campaign on Marriage Law'.

29 October 1951, 'Preparations made in northwest for investigation into conditions implementing Marriage Law'.

31 January 1953, 'Implementation of Marriage Law in different parts of country is very uneven'.

9 February 1953, 'Feudal marriage system and malpractices still found in most parts of China'.

25 February 1953, 'Outline of propaganda on the thorough implementation of the Marriage Law'.

4 March 1953, 'What the new Marriage Law campaign means to me'.

5 March 1953, 'Marriage disputes'.

5 March 1955, 'Present conditions relating to implementation of Marriage Law stated by Committee for its Implementation'.

1 June 1955, Ministry of Internal Affairs promulgates regulations for registration of Marriages'.

12 August 1955, 'Ministry of Internal Affairs answers certain questions on registration of marriage'.

2 July 1957, Hunan Nongmin Bao, 'How to tackle the problem of love'.

29 August 1957, Report of National Women's Federation on Third National Congress.

8 March 1961, 'Wedding in village near Peking'.

7 March 1975, 'Chinese women criticise Confucian–Mencian concept of male supremacy'.

North China Herald (NCH), *9 August 1907*, 'The new women of China'.

O'Hara, A. R., 1962, 'Changing attitudes towards marriage and the family in free China', *Journal of the China Society*, vol. 2, pp. 57–67.

Oksenberg, M., 1969, 'Sources and methodological problems in the study of contemporary China', in Barnett, A. Doak (ed.), *Chinese Communist Politics in Action*, Seattle, University of Washington Press.

Osgood, C., 1963, *Village Life in Old China: A Community Study of Kao Yao Yunnan*, New York, Ronald Press.

Parish, W. L., 1975, 'Socialism and the Chinese peasant family', *Journal of Asian Studies*, vol. XXIV, no. 3, May, pp. 613–30.

Parsons, Talcott, 1959, Foreword in Yang, C. K., *Communist Society: the Family and the Village*, Massachusetts, MIT Press.

Pasternak, B., 1972, *Kinship and Community in Two Chinese Villages*, California, Stanford University Press.

Peking Review (PR)

18 November 1958, Yang Kan-ling, 'Family life: the new way'.

8 March 1960, Fan Jo-yu, 'Why we have abolished the feudal patriarchal family system'.

13 March 1964, Yang Liu, 'Reform of marriage and family system in China'.

11 February 1972, Soong Ching-ling, 'Women's liberation in China'.

Bibliography

People's China (PC)

  16 June 1949, Ku Yu, 'New way of doing new things'.

  1 March 1951, Yang Yu, 'Freed from unhappiness'.

  1 June 1951, Ling Meili, 'The growth of a new outlook on marriage'.

  1 December 1951, Ma Feng, 'The wedding day'.

  1 March 1952, 'Little son-in-law'.

  1 June 1952, The Marriage Law of the People's Republic of China.

  1 March 1952, 'The women of Wu village'.

  1 December 1952, Teng Ying-chao, 'China's women advance'.

  1 March 1953, Yang Yu, 'Three conditions: a story of how the Marriage Law rights wrongs in new China'.

  1 March 1953, Teng Ying-chao, 'Breaking the yoke of the feudal marriage system'.

  16 November 1957, Tso Sung-fen, 'New marriages, new families'.

Perkins, D., 1969, *Agricultural Development in China 1368–1968*, Edinburgh University Press.

Potter, J., 1968, *Capitalism and the Chinese Peasant: Social and Economic Change in a Hong Kong Village*, Berkeley, University of California Press.

Radcliffe-Brown, A. R., 1948, *The Andaman Islanders*, Glencoe, Illinois, Free Press.

  1950, *African Systems of Kinship and Marriage*, Oxford University Press.

  1951, 'The comparative method in social anthropology', *Journal of the Royal Anthropological Institute*, vol. 81, pp. 15–22.

Rivière, P. G., 1971, 'Marriage, a reassessment', in Needham, R. (ed.), *Rethinking Kinship and Marriage*, ASA Monograph no. 11, London, Tavistock Publications.

Rossi, P. H. and Bauer, R. A., 1952–3, 'Some patterns of Soviet communications behaviour', Public Opinion Quarterly, vol. xvi, Winter, pp. 653–70.

Sahlins, M., 1974, *Stone Age Economics*, London, Tavistock Publications.

Salaff, J. W., 1971, 'The urban communes and anti-city experiment in Communist China', in Lewis, J. W., *The City in Communist China*, California, Stanford University Press.

Schak, D. C., 1973, *The Evolution of Dating and Free Courtship in Modern China as Manifested in Taipei, Taiwan*, Berkeley, University of California Press.

Schapera, I., 1966, *Married Life in an African Tribe*, London, Faber.

Schran, P., 1969, *The Development of Chinese Agriculture 1950–59*, Illinois, University of Chicago Press.

Scott, J. F., 1968, 'Sororities and the husband game', in Winch, R. F. and Goodman, L. W. (eds.), *Selected Studies in Marriage and the Family*, New York, Holt, Rinehart and Winston.

Sheridan, M., 1968, 'The emulation of heroes', *China Quarterly*, no. 33, January–March, pp. 47–72.

Sidel, R., 1972, *Women and Child Care in China*, New York, Hill and Wang.

Siu, B., 1975, *Fifty Years of Struggle: the Development of the Women's Movements in China (1900–1949)*, Hong Kong, Revomen Publications.

Skinner, G. W., 1958, *Leadership and Power in the Chinese Community of Thailand*, Ithaca, New York, Cornell University Press.

  1964, 'What the study of China can do for social science', *Journal of Asian Studies*, vol. 23, pp. 517–22.

  1964–5, 'Marketing and social structure in rural China', *Journal of Asian Studies*, vol. 24, pp. 3–43, 195–228, 363–99.

Skinner, G. W. and Winckler, E. A., 1969, 'Compliance succession in rural Communist China: a cyclical theory', in Etzioni, A. (ed.), *Complex Organisations, A Sociological Reader*, New York, Holt, Rinehart and Winston.

Smelser, N. J., 1966, 'The modernisation of social relations', in Weiner, M. (ed.), *Modernisation: The Dynamics of Growth*, New York, Basic Books.

Smith, A. H., 1902, *Proverbs and Common Sayings from the Chinese*, Shanghai.

Snow, E., 1972, *The Long Revolution*, New York, Random House.

Stouffer, S. A., 1940, 'Intervening opportunities: a theory relating to mobility and distance', *American Sociological Review*, December, pp. 845–67.

Survey of World Broadcasts (SWB)

  21 March 1953, 'Campaign for the implementation of the Marriage Law, no. 237, pp. 16–21.

  14 February 1974, 'Rusticated young people marry peasants', Far East (FE) 4526/B11/1.

  21 March 1974, 'A girl's refusal to accept a pre-arranged marriage in Hebei', FE 4556/B11/17.

  28 November 1974, 'Kiangsi conference on planned parenthood', FE 4767/B11/25.

  30 Janary 1975, 'Shandong county – planned parenthood', FBIS/CHI/75–21.

  11 February 1975, 'Hebei county launches effective birth control campaign', FBIS/CHI/75–29.

Taeuber, I. B., 1970, 'The families of Chinese farmers', in Freedman, M. (ed.), *Family and Kinship in Chinese Society*, California, Stanford University Press, pp. 63–86:

Tang, M., 1973, *Life and Family Structure in a Chinese City: Taipei, Taiwan*, New York, Columbia University Press.

Teng Ying-chao, 1950, 'On the Marriage Law of the People's Republic of China', in *The Marriage Law of the People's Republic of China and Other Essays*, Peking, Foreign Languages Press.

Thrupp, S., 1948, *The Merchant Class of Medieval London*, Illinois, University of Chicago Press.

T'ien Ju-k'ang, 1944, 'Female labor in a cotton mill', in Shih Kuo Heng (ed.), *China Enters the Machine Age*, Cambridge, Massachusetts, Harvard University Press.

Bibliography

Treudley, M. B., 1971, *Men and Women in Chang Ho Ch'ang*, Taipei, Asian Folklore Social Life Monograph, no. 14, Orient Cultural Service.

Turner, V. W., 1957, *Schism and Continuity in an African Society*, Manchester University Press.

Tyau, M. T. Z., 1922, *China Awakened*, London, Macmillan Co.

Vogel, E. F., 1965, 'From friendship to comradeship: the change in personal relations in Communist China', *China Quarterly*, no. 21, January–March, pp. 46–60.

 1969, *Canton under Communism: programs and politics in a provincial capital, 1949–1968*, Cambridge, Massachusetts, Harvard University Press.

Waln, N., 1933, *The House of Exile*, London, The Cresset Press.

Wang Hsueh-Wen, 1971, 'A study of the rustification of youth on the Chinese mainland', *Issues & Studies*, January, pp. 84–95.

Ward, B. E., 1965, 'Varieties of the conscious model: the fishermen of South China', in Benton, M. (ed.), *The Relevance of Models for Social Anthropology*, ASA monography no. 1, London, Tavistock Publications.

 1967, 'Chinese fishermen in Hong Kong: their post-peasant economy', in Freedman, M. (ed.), *Social Organisation: Essays Presented to Raymond Firth*, London, Frank Cass.

Watson, J. L., 1975, *Emigration and the Chinese Lineage. The Mans in Hong Kong and London*, Berkeley, University of California Press.

Weber, M., 1951, *The Religion of China*, Glencoe, Illinois, Free Press.

Wei Tao-Ming, 1943, *My Revolutionary Years*, New York, Charles Scribner's and Sons.

White, D. G., 1974, 'The politics of hsia-hsiang youths', *China Quarterly*, vol. 59, July–September, pp. 491–517.

Whyte, M. K., 1974, *Small Groups and Political Rituals in China*, Berkeley, University of California Press.

Winch, R. F., 1971, *The Modern Family*, New York, Holt, Rinehart and Winston.

Winckler, E. A., 1976, 'Policy oscillations in the People's Republic of China: a reply', *China Quarterly*, December, pp. 734–50.

Witke, R., 1967, 'Mao Tse-tung, women and suicide in the May Fourth Era', *China Quarterly*, no. 31, pp. 128–47.

Wolf, A., 1968, 'Adopt a daughter-in-law, marry a sister: a Chinese solution to the problem of the incest taboo', *American Anthropologist*, vol. 70, pp. 864–74.

Wolf, M., 1972, *Women and the Family in Rural Taiwan*, California, Stanford University Press.

Wolff, E., 1966, 'Kinship, friendship and patron–client relations in complex societies', in Benton, M., (ed.), *The Social Anthropology of Complex Societies*, ASA Monograph No. 4, London, Tavistock Publications.

Women of China (WC)

   1 May 1950, Interview with Shiliang.

   1 October 1951, 'Judicial cadres must correctly and promptly dispose of cases involving marriage disputes'.

   1 June 1953, Mi Chun, 'Tang Yu-ying's marriage'.

   1 March 1962, Yang Chih-hao, 'Choosing a bridegroom'.

   1 April 1964, Huang Chang-lu, 'A happy inter-tribal marriage'.

   1 February 1966, Nieh Wen-chi, 'Choosing a son-in-law'.

Wong Su-Ling and Cressy, E. H., 1953, *Daughter of Confucius*, London, Gollancz.

Wu Chih-Hui, 1908, 'A critique of Mr Chü-p'u's "theory of men and women mixing freely"' *New Century Magazine*, no. 42, 21 April, Paris.

Yang, C. K., 1959, *Communist Society: The Family and the Village*, Massachusetts, MIT Press.

Yang, M. C., 1945, *A Chinese Village: Taitou, Shantung Province*, New York, Columbia University Press.

   1962, 'Changes in family life in rural Taiwan', *Journal of the China Society*, vol. 2, pp. 68–79.

Zhang Chang, 1966, 'New wind in border village, nationalities solidarity', February, pp. 30–1, translated in *Chinese Sociology and Anthropology*, vol. 1, no. 1, 1968, pp. 65–9.

INDEX

age of marriage, x, 22, 60–79, 127, 158, 168; arguments for late marriage, 62–4; pressures for early marriage, 71–6, 158; recommended, 65; Republican China, 66
alliance theory, 3–4
ancestors, 34, 119
anthropology of marriage, 9–17
anti-Confucian campaign, 22, 64, 143
arranged marriage, x, 1, 3, 18, 19, 24, 25, 31–6, 39, 188; Taiwan, 135
auspicious days, 109, 118

betrothal, 19, 22, 41, 43–8, 50–5, 59, 76, 127–8, 157
birth control, 60, 63–4, 77, 158
bridal sedan chair, 110–12, 168

ceremonies of marriage, x, 22, 108–26, 168; see also pre-marital rituals; rituals of marriage
Chen, J., 15, 188
childbirth, 63
child care, 155–6
Chin Ai-li, S., 132
cities, 20, 50, 181–3
class categories, 88–92
Cohen, A., 6, 8
collectivisation, 7, 8, 144, 152; see also production units
Communist Party, 27, 39, 87–91, 97, 106, 166–7, 170–4
courtship, 22, 42–3, 47–50, 54–9, 127–8
cross-cousin marriage, 80–1, 84
Cultural Revolution, 11, 21, 106
cyclical patterns, 21

dating, see courtship
descent groups, 3–4
divorce, 24

domestic economy, 144, 152–9, 184; see also household
domestic group, 142–64; see also family; household
domestic labour, 154–5, 157
dowry, 109, 113–16, 169

early marriage, 61, 71–6
economic policy, 7, 9, 21; see also collectivisation; industrialisation; production
education for marriage, 6, 8, 9, 78, 83, 185–7; Republican China, 131–2; Taiwan, 136–7
endogamy, 97–8
Engels, F., 5, 82

factory workers, 20, 38, 48, 67, 71, 74, 77
family 2, 3, 6, 23, 39, 134, 139–41, 143, 163–4; see also household
Family Law (1931), 60, 80, 131, 137
family planning, see birth control
feasts in marriage, 109, 121–6, 169
feudal marriage, see arranged marriage
fieldwork, 10, 15–16
filial piety, 34, 35
free-choice marriage, x, 1, 27–32, 36, 39, 184–8; Republican China, 19–20, 131; Taiwan, 135–6
Freedman, M., 7, 9–10, 113
friendship, 55

Gallin, B., 138–9
Geddes, W., 123
Great Leap Forward, 21, 155
Greenblatt, S., 7, 14

heterogamy, 98–106, 126–7
Hinton, W., 48

homogamy, 5, 97–8, 106, 127
household: budget, 159–61; division, 141, 161–3; economy, 144, 163–4; estate, 150–1; labour resources, 152–6; recruitment of labour, 156–9; size, 145–50, 163–4; *see also* family
housing, 161–3

ideology, 8–9, 12, 17, 20, 24, 41–3, 60–4, 82, 106, 108, 185–8
industrialisation, 138–47, 164, 183, 185; Republican China, 130–5; Taiwan, 137–8
inheritance, 4, 150–1, 161
intra-familial relations, 28–40, 111–12, 129; Republican China, 132–4; Taiwan, 137

Jiang village, 16, 17, 68, 78, 84–5, 114–15, 123, 145–9, 154, 159, 161–3, 175–8

kinship, 2–4, 6, 23, 39, 80–1, 165–70, 176–183, 186–7

land reform, 7, 89, 151
Lang, O., 20, 148
Lethbridge, H., 167
letters to the press, 13, 14
Lévi-Strauss, C., 3, 17
Levy, M., 133–4, 148
life-histories, 11, 12
lineage, *see* kinship

marriage: campaigns, 8, 21, 171–3; ceremonies, x, 22, 108–26, 168; choice of spouse in, 4, 5, 22, 73–6, 82–107, 127–8; definition of, 2, 3, 142, 174; feast, 109, 121–6, 169; gifts, 123–4; registration, 109, 112; rituals, 109, 111–12, 121
Marriage Law (1980), x, 1, 17, 20, 22, 24, 32, 39, 41, 60, 80, 108, 165, 171–3
Marx, K., 5
matchmaker, 18, 25–7, 37, 44
mate selection, 4, 5, 22, 73–6, 82–107, 127–8; Republican China, 131
matrilocality, 143
Meijer, M., 9
migration, 175–6, 180

modernisation, 127–41; *see also* industrialisation
Myrdal, J., 15, 51, 156

negotiation of marriage, 24–40, 127–8
neighbourhoods, 23, 166–74, 179, 181–3, 186–7; *see also* kinship; primary groups

open-marriage system, 4, 80

patrilocality, 90, 143
peasants, 90, 101–3, 112; *see also* villages
physiological development, 62–4
political associations, 165, 170–4; *see also* Communist Party, women's organisations; Youth League
political consciousness, 83, 86
political status, 86–93
post-marital residence, 142–3, 150
preferential mates, 75, 83, 95–6, 105–6
pre-marital rituals, 22, 41–59, 127–8
primary groups, 23–4, 39, 71–3, 140, 158, 166–70, 174–87; Republican China, 133–4; Taiwan, 137–8; *see also* kinship; neighbourhoods
private plots, 154–5
production, 8, 144, 151, 154
production units, 175–9, 185

registration of marriage, 109, 112
Republican reform in marriage, 19, 130–5
research methodology, 9–18
residential propinquity, 85–6, 103
retirement, 156
rituals of marriage, 109, 111–12, 117–21; *see also* ceremonies of marriage
romantic love, 56–7; *see also* courtship

semi-arranged marriage, 26, 30
sexual segregation, 36–8, 167–8, 180–1
Skinner, W., 7, 10
social change, 6–9, 11, 23, 138–9, 183–8
social engineering, 6, 7, 9, 129–30; *see also* industrialisation
social status, 4, 93–6
social stratification, 4–6, 80–101
students, 57, 64, 67, 75
surname exogamy, 36, 80–1, 84

Taiwan, 23, 135–9
teasing of the bride, 120
traditional marriage, *see* arranged
  marriage

uxorilocal marriage, 143

villages, 10, 15, 19, 30, 36–8, 48–9, 68,
  85, 94, 101, 133, 155, 167–70, 174–6,
  180–1, 185, 188; *see also* Jiang village
virilocal marriage, 143
Vogel, E., 167

Ward, B., 17–18
wedding guests, 123–4

Wolf, M., 33
women's organisations, 27, 139, 166–7,
  170–4; *see also* political associations

xiaxiang youth, 103–5, 166

Yang, C. K., 9, 19, 134, 139, 167
Youth League, 27, 37–9, 87–91, 97, 106,
  166–7, 170–4; *see also* political
  associations

Zhongguo Funu (Women of China), 11,
  13, 22
Zhongguo Qingnian (Youth of China), 11,
  13, 22